This book examines Aristotle's metaphysics and his account of nature, stressing the ways in which his desire to explain observed natural processes shaped his philosophical thought. It departs radically from a tradition of interpretation in which Aristotle is understood to have approached problems with a set of abstract principles in hand – principles derived from critical reflection on the views of his predecessors.

A central example in the book interprets Aristotle's essentialism as deriving from an examination of the kinds of unity that various sorts of things have, and from his account of elemental motion, alteration, transformation, and the growth of organisms. An important conclusion of this argument is that a substance may, under certain circumstances, lack some of its essential attributes.

The book goes on to develop a notion of incomplete substance and explores the connection between Aristotle's concept of nature and its role in scientific explanation. In this way Cohen breaks down the sharp division that many interpreters have chosen to see between Aristotle's natural science and his philosophy.

Aristotle on Nature
and Incomplete Substance

Aristotle on Nature
and Incomplete Substance

SHELDON M. COHEN
University of Tennessee

CAMBRIDGE
UNIVERSITY PRESS

PUBLISHED BY THE PRESS SYNDICATE OF THE UNIVERSITY OF CAMBRIDGE
The Pitt Building, Trumpington Street, Cambridge, United Kingdom

CAMBRIDGE UNIVERSITY PRESS
The Edinburgh Building, Cambridge CB2 2RU, UK
40 West 20th Street, New York NY 10011–4211, USA
477 Williamstown Road, Port Melbourne, VIC 3207, Australia
Ruiz de Alarcón 13, 28014 Madrid, Spain
Dock House, The Waterfront, Cape Town 8001, South Africa

http://www.cambridge.org

First published 1996
First paperback edition 2002

A catalogue record for this book is available from the British Library

Library of Congress Cataloguing-in-Publication Data
Cohen, Sheldon M.
Aristotle on nature and incomplete substance / Sheldon M. Cohen.
p.   cm.
Includes bibliographical references and index.
ISBN 0 521 56081 0 hardback
1. Aristotle – Contributions in metaphysics. 2. Metaphysics.
3. Philosophy of nature. 4. Substance (Philosophy) I. Title.
B491.M4C64   1996
110'.92 – dc20   95-51036
CIP

ISBN 0 521 56081 0 hardback
ISBN 0 521 53313 9 paperback

Portions of this book are based on articles that previously appeared in *Ancient
Philosophy, New Scholasticism, The Philosophical Review,* and *Phronesis.*

On the fiftieth anniversary of the end of the Second World War in Europe:

- to Joseph P. Rivers, for the care with which he supervises the American military cemetery at St. Laurent-sur-Mer, portal of freedom
- to Robert Elmer, Salerno beachmaster, who also served in North Africa, Noumea, at Utah Beach, and in Operation Anvil, and who landed Darby's Rangers at Gella
- to Jacques Vico, president of the Union des combattants volontaires de la Résistance du Calvados
- to my uncles, Irving Schiller, 741st U.S. Tank Battalion, wounded in action, September 1944, in the liberation of Brest, and Maurice Basem, 702d U.S. Tank Destroyer Battalion, wounded in action early June 1944, at an unknown location in Normandy; August 1, 1944, in the liberation of Tessy-sur-Vire; and near Puffendorf, Germany, in the spring of 1945
- and to their comrades in arms who rest in honor and glory in England, France, Belgium, and Luxembourg.

Contents

Acknowledgments

I would like to thank the University of Tennessee Department of Philosophy for giving me a semester off to finish this book, and my colleagues George Brenkert and Richard Aquila for their particular support and encouragement.

It is not my custom to ask other philosophers for comments on works in progress, so I have no one to thank on that score – much to everyone's relief, no doubt. I have nonetheless benefited a great deal from other people's efforts. Mary Louise Gill is perhaps the person I cite most often – usually in opposition, but that is a measure of my respect for her work. Sarah Waterlow Broadie's work has also been of immense value to me, as has been that of William Charlton, Frank Lewis, Dorothea Frede, Gary Matthews, Myles Burnyeat, Jonathan Barnes, and the comments of two anonymous Cambridge University Press readers – to name just a few. I mention these people because of particular points they have made that have helped me along my own way, but I owe at least an equal debt to many others who have labored in these same fields.

And I must grudgingly acknowledge one person who works in a different field: William R. Carter, who has gravely and graciously warned me about some of my more dangerous ideas.

S.M.C.

Introduction

I know twenty or thirty people who, given the chance, could come up with a vastly improved Aristotle. I count myself among this group, and if we had ever formed a committee to do the job, I know the assignment I would have wanted: inserting texts in which Aristotle says that as a given thing can survive without a certain characteristic, the characteristic is not essential to the thing.

Aristotle does, from time to time, invoke the survivability criterion, or what amounts to the same thing – most typically, in claiming that living things and their parts are essentially animate. And in the *Metaphysics* VII, 15, he criticizes those who would define the sun as "going round the earth": "they err . . . by adding attributes after whose removal the sun would still exist." On their view, if the sun were to stand still, it would no longer be the sun – a strange consequence, "for 'the sun' means a certain substance" [1040a28–33]. Outside of a biological context this sort of statement is rare, and at crucial junctures where a quick invocation of the survivability criterion would seem appropriate, Aristotle refrains.

In *Metaphysics* VII, 4, he addresses the question of whether an essence corresponds to "pale man" by asking whether "pale man" involves one thing's being said of another. How much easier it would have been to point out that, if the pale man spends some time in the sun, he will tan: that paleness is an attribute loss of which people survive each summer.

In *Metaphysics* X, 10, he mentions that "the same man can be, though not at the same time, pale and dark." But two paragraphs earlier, in chapter 9, arguing that there is no difference in species "between the pale man and the dark man, not even if each of them be denoted by one word," he does not say that this is clear, as the same man can be, though not at the same time, pale and dark. Instead he gives us the following:

For man plays the part of matter, and matter does not create a difference; for it does not make individual men species of man, though the flesh and the bones of which this man and that man consists are other. The compound thing is other, but not other in species, because in the formula there is contrariety, and man is the ultimate indivisible kind. Callias is formula together with matter; pale man, then, is so also, because Callias is pale; man, then, is pale only incidentally. Nor do a brazen and wooden circle differ in species; and if a brazen triangle and a wooden circle differ in species, it is not because of the matter, but because there is a contrariety in the formula. [1058b5–15]

In this case my editing job would have been quite easy: to eliminate all the intervening text. The new, improved text would have read, "There is no difference in species between the pale man and the dark man, not even if each of them be denoted by one word . . . because the same man can be, though not at the same time, pale and dark."

Alas, our committee has not yet duly formed itself. So I reluctantly decided, for the time being at least, to leave the texts as they stand, retaining the obscure passage quoted above and many others that occur where an appeal to the survivability criterion would simplify matters (including all of *Metaphysics* VII, 12). This, I knew, would please the purists.

It then occurred to me that Aristotle's reluctance to invoke the survivability criterion might be attributable to something more than mere oversight. Perhaps he did not trust it. Briefly, the idea is that Aristotle was developing a new account of nature, and one of the consequences of this account was that he could get only limited mileage out of the survivability criterion. That it needs to be wielded with caution can be seen in the dialogues of Aristotle's teacher, Plato.[1] Toward the end of the *Phaedo,* in a well-known passage, Plato holds that snow in the face of heat must withdraw or perish – it cannot admit the hot. In the *Timaeus,* however, he hypothesizes that snow is water mixed with a little fire – just enough fire to keep it from becoming ice.[2] So not only can snow tolerate a certain amount of heat, it requires a certain amount of heat. Stating the survivability criterion is simple; applying it to the real world is tricky.

Furthermore, Aristotle's concept of nature made him a *qualified* essentialist: in his aristocratic world, some plebeian things come into existence and pass out of it without ever having an essence. So before we can wield the survivability criterion, we need an independent way of deciding whether a thing has been essentially blessed, for even if a thing has no essence, there still will be conditions it must meet to persist. We might, for example, be able to lay out the conditions under which my estate continues to exist – i.e., retains net value – but it does not follow that anything is essential to it. (Although my estate might have components – e.g., cattle and gold that do have essential natures, this is not the same as

1 See Chapter 2; "Elemental Change and Substances That Lack Some of Their Essential Characteristics," "The Paradox."
2 At 59D.

the pale-man case, because being a man *is* essential to him.) My example might seem adventurous, but the basic point is clear. For example, in *Metaphysics* VII, Aristotle invents the real/nominal essence distinction: even if "cloak" means "pale man," it does not follow that pale man as such has an essence; here we might have only the meaning of a word. Understanding the conditions under which an *F* ceases to exist need not, then, tell us what is essential to an *F*, for the *F* need not be essentially an *F*. (This will be so if one imagines that the pale man ceases to exist when he acquires a tan.)

We can see a problem even with Aristotle's example of the sun. On his view, celestial objects by their very nature possess a uniform circular motion. They cannot cease this motion, nor can anything else stop it. If, given what they are, this motion is necessary to them, how can Aristotle suggest that as "'the sun' means a certain substance" it would still be the sun even if it stopped moving? Wouldn't that mean that it had become a different substance (e.g., no longer composed of ether)?

The difficulty arising here has an even greater range in the mundane realm. For example, on the received interpretation Aristotle holds that clay by its nature has a downward motion. Yet when the potter lifts some clay from the floor to her wheel, it has an upward motion, and as she shapes it on the wheel it has a rotational motion. If what belongs to something in virtue of its nature belongs to it essentially, it would seem that clay can lack a characteristic essential to it (downward motion), and even possess characteristics contrary to its essential nature. Aristotle addresses this difficulty by distinguishing natural as opposed to forced motions, though, as we shall see, there is a great deal more to this story. But even if there were not, our example suggests that the survivability criterion has to be used with discretion: we cannot say without qualification that if being *F* is natural or essential to a thing, that thing cannot exist without being *F*. At a minimum we have to ask whether something external is hindering the thing from being *F* or whether it is by force that it lacks *F*. This will require an empirical investigation and, for some values of *F*, may require, say, a general theory of motion as well.

That is at a minimum. More realistically, we will have to say a good deal more. For how can something be so determined to exist that it will not give up the ghost even though it has been shorn of essential characteristics, so long as the shearing was by force or due to external causes? Whether I am murdered or die of natural causes, my song has ended.

II

Most Greek philosophers tried to explain the world by appealing to basic substances. For two centuries they did this by postulating material elements: basic forms of matter out of which the nonelemental things arose.

Then Plato struck out in a new direction. The abiding basic natures were not elemental forms of matter but immaterial substances – Plato's Forms.

To Aristotle the most attractive options had been presented by Plato and Empedocles, but he could not wholeheartedly embrace either. Plato's Forms were too detached from the physical world for Aristotle's taste, and though he was attracted to Empedocles' view that the elementary physical substances are earth, air, fire, and water, he could not accept his claim that these elements are eternal and unchanging: it was obvious to Aristotle that they come into existence and perish – we *see* this happen, he protests.

This partial embrace of Plato and Empedocles sets the stage for Aristotle's own thought. He accepts Empedocles' elements, but they are not imperishable; he accepts Forms, but they are not separate from the physical world. But perishable elements and incarnate Forms are almost oxymoronic in the Greek tradition, and Aristotle will not have an easy time readying these notions for the philosophical marketplace.

To take one example of the pressures generated by his approach, once Aristotle declares that the most basic forms of matter are not eternal, a primary source of intellectual comfort and explanatory force in pre-Socratic accounts of nature has been jettisoned. The things we see around us in his model cannot be regarded as various permutations of unchanging building blocks. If the building blocks themselves are in flux, how does stability arise? From the Forms, as in Plato? But if forms are not segregated from the growth and decay of the material world – a material world in which, at that, the elements themselves are prone to decay – how can they be sources of stability? Greek metaphysics had, up until Aristotle, anchored itself in material elements or separate Forms. Aristotle cuts himself loose from both of these anchors and is in danger of being adrift.

In this study I argue that Aristotle dealt with this situation by forging a new concept of nature, based on the ideas that: (1) nature is an internal source of change and stasis in substances, (2) a thing's right to be called a substance is a function of the type and degree of unity it possesses;[3] and (3) a thing can exist without possessing all the properties that belong to it by nature.

Working out this new concept of nature proved to be an extremely difficult task. At almost every turn, Aristotle found that as soon as he answered one question, others arose, leading him into new and uncharted territory. The study that follows traces his progress. I begin by examining one of the roots of the problem in the *Categories* and go on to show how Aristotle attempts, in various ways, to deal with the problem. In

---

3 One of the effects of this new approach is to downgrade the status of the elements. They will not, in his system, be quite the principles they used to be; their role becomes more local.

doing so I roughly follow the generally accepted order for his writings, such as it is, but chronology plays little or no role in my story. My thesis is that Aristotle undertook several distinct marches on his problem, each of which helped somewhat, but none of which proved totally satisfactory. (This is not a sign of a poor philosopher; Aristotle was a great philosopher, honestly wrestling with difficult issues.) I have little to say about the order in which he explored these ideas; he most likely explored several of them simultaneously. These approaches to his problem are connected in some ways, but they are basically independent: each is a fresh start – a new way of addressing the same issues. They are, to twist Aristotle's phrase, *pros hen* lines of inquiry.

One approach, following a Platonic innovation, was to introduce the notion of essence. This, however, does not tell us what sorts of things have essences, and it seems clear that Aristotle held that some things, at least in some sense of "things," do not have essences. A second advance comes in the *Physics*, where Aristotle introduces nature as an internal principle of change or stasis. He embarks on a third approach under the general rubric of "the problem of the unity of definition." This culminates in the *Metaphysics* Z doctrine of proper differentiae. A fourth approach can be seen in his attempts to distinguish different types of unity. A fifth depends on the notion of complete and incomplete substances, an outgrowth of commitments he accumulated in the course of the other approaches. At this point he has a fairly consistent doctrine, and one far more coherent and articulated than he began with, though in some respects it is still troubled. (Again, this is not a criticism of Aristotle – life is troubled.)

My Aristotle stands in stark contrast to, say, the view presented by Daniel C. Graham in *Aristotle's Two Systems*. As Graham sees it, we have two more or less monolithic Aristotles, each with his own system (S_1 and S_2), each system being fairly consistent. I see a far messier Aristotle. Mine begins working in one room and moves on to others as the limitations of each room press in on him. In each new room he improves on the work he did in previous rooms, yet he keeps going back to the old rooms to check his notes. He is making progress, but he does not always see how to reconcile every conclusion he arrives at in a new room with the sheaf of notes he has brought with him from earlier rooms. Convinced that those earlier investigations were not totally misguided, but equally convinced that his more recent investigations are an improvement upon them, he enters each new room clutching notes from the earlier rooms, and he does the best he can, often presenting both the old and the new, even if they seem to conflict. He thinks that in the end he can work it all out, and perhaps he can, but he is so busy that he never really finds the time to do so.

This is not a man with two neat positions but one simultaneously pursuing different lines of investigation, uncertain whether they will all take him in the same direction – and even whether they all deal with the same problems – and constantly modifying his own position. (I have attributed five rooms to him, but if I had more time I could claim ten or twenty-seven.) He has a few principles that, he is convinced, cannot be very wrong, but he is not sure how they fit together, and he expends more effort in exploring new avenues of investigation than he does in trying to reconcile everything to which he has become, in the course of his investigations, committed. He never formulates a completely consistent system – something is always nibbling at the edges.

Nonetheless, though he never reconciles everything, he does end up with a mature doctrine which, on my interpretation, has a surprising feature. It is a characteristically Platonic doctrine that at least some particulars are imperfect instances of forms. On my account, Aristotle ends up holding the same view, for he maintains that particulars sometimes incompletely possess their essential properties. I will argue that he claims this both for his most elemental substances – the elements themselves – and for some of his least elemental substances – people. Unlike Plato (on one reading), Aristotle holds that this is not an inherent defect of particulars, but is due to the fact that nature's work, which is to perfect particulars, is not always finished. But this too, may be thought of as a Platonic doctrine in that, for Aristotle as for Plato, the existence of imperfect particulars is the price we pay for the existence of the realm of becoming, or at least of Aristotle's analogue to Plato's realm of becoming – the sublunar realm.

Two Terminological Notes

1. At the heart of Aristotle's metaphysics and philosophy of nature is his inquiry into *ousia*, usually rendered as "substance." If we mean to be speaking current English, this is a dreadful choice, for "substance" in English has come to be a general mass-term, roughly synonymous with "stuff": cocaine is a substance; a dog is not. "Substance" is therefore now closer in meaning to Aristotle's "matter" than it is to his *ousia:* in current English the only "substance" we are dealing with when we deal with a bronze statue is bronze.

If we focus, on the other hand, on the etymological connotation of "substance" as that which stands under or supports, Aristotle already has a word for that: *hypokeimenon*, generally translated as "subject." As *ousia* is a participle from the verb "to be," this might make the Latin translation, *ens* ("being"), seem the best choice, but then we lose the important nuances that derive from the frequent opposition of *ousia* to characteristic, property, or accident, and the occasional opposition of *ousia* to matter. It seems to me that in English this is best captured by playing things off against both characteristics and the stuff things are made of, so in discussion I sometimes use "thing" where Aristotle would use *ousia*. For direct translations of Greek passages, however, I have retained the hallowed "substance."

Unfortunately, "substance" has another meaning: "the substance of his remarks" is, roughly, the essence of his remarks. This is a translator's convenience when Aristotle is asking about the *ousia* of a thing, and in this case "the thing of his remarks," let alone "the thing of a thing," would be quite senseless.

No one word can happily handle all these contexts. I have accordingly felt free to translate *ousia* in a variety of ways, though at the price of occasionally holding it up for display in brackets. In general, however, I have translated it as "substance" or "thing."

2. Another warning is in order for "change" and "motion." The Greek, *kinêsis*, once corresponded to the Latinate "motion." Motion then covered various sorts of change, of which change of place – locomotion – was only one. In current English, however, "locomotion" has come to be redundant: "motion" has come to mean "locomotion." We do not speak of a leaf's motion from green to orange, nor of a man's changing down the road. Both the man's progress and the leaf's change of color are, however, instances of *kinêsis*. Kinêsis must therefore sometimes be translated as "change," sometimes as "motion," and sometimes as "process." Where the distinction is important, Aristotle may specify that he is talking about a *kinêsis* of place, or an alteration, or all types of *kinêsis*, but in general the reader must beware, for a passage in which Aristotle seems to be talking about motion may be a passage in which he is talking about change in general, and vice versa.

A Final Admonition

Many of the concepts that we take for granted were not available to Aristotle, and some of them were to a large extent developed by him.[4] In this latter case, what we obtain as a birthright he had to wring laboriously from his own philosophical inheritance. To do so, he did not hesitate to do some violence to common usages.[5] One of the notions he thus recast is the concept of nature. "Nature" became, for Aristotle, a technical term: what he finally means by "nature" is not what any of his predecessors meant by it, and it is not what we mean by it today. If we want to understand his account of nature, we must recapture that meaning. Fortunately, he has given us a proof-text.

4 For example, the concept of matter or the distinction between chemistry and biology.
5 Despite the fact that he is often said to be, with some justification, a defender of commonsense views.

In my first chapter I examine that text and sketch out an interpretation of what Aristotle means there by "nature." This turns out to involve several strands, each with its own textual and philosophical burdens, and each raising questions about its compatibility with other strands and texts. Most of this book is an exploration of these problems, but to keep the exegetical sprawl within tolerable limits, in this first chapter I turned a deaf ear to their cries. My intention here was to get an initial account out into the open. The obstacles are tackled in subsequent chapters.

The Aristotle quotations are generally from the revised Oxford translation by Jonathan Barnes, *The Complete Works of Aristotle* (Princeton University Press, 1984), although with a reduced number of semicolons. Where I have used a different translation, that is indicated in a footnote; where I have chosen to modify the Barnes translation, I have included the relevant transliterated Greek in brackets.

1

Nature and Things

To the delight of scholars, Aristotle's surviving writings are both extensive and obscure. One of the sources of this obscurity is familiar to us from scholastic philosophy: the arguments often seem to meander through a nearly featureless theoretical countryside. In this barren realm we find few familiar landmarks, so that even with the road map provided by the arguments, we are often unable to tell where we are headed or why we have taken a turn.

The first part of this chapter briefly sketches out some important features of the theoretical road map as it is presented in Aristotle's earlier, logical works, the *Organon*. This is not intended as a primary study of those features. Those seeking that can find other, far more detailed, discussions. My purpose is to introduce some key notions and to point out their limitations.

In the second I turn to the *Physics* and to questions about the geography and population of the landscape there. Some of these features are quite basic to Aristotle's philosophical concerns yet are never explicitly discussed by him; others he touches upon only tangentially or in unexpected contexts; still others he discusses over and over again. None of them is in any way esoteric: they are all homely features of the world that have been noted by ten year olds throughout history – things like spiderwebs, earth, houses, sheep, and ponds. To understand Aristotle's system, we need to see how these things fit into it. That is the job of later chapters. For the moment my purpose is simply to introduce a few of these things and show how questions about their status created options for Aristotle. Some previous thinkers had treated these mundane objects as worthy of philosophical investigation, but the gravity and methodological sophistication with which Aristotle approaches them, quite apart from the answers he gives to the questions they raise, was perhaps the most distinguishing characteristic of his philosophical stance; never before had a thinker so seriously addressed them. Aristotle's system of the world thus made everything that came before it look simplistic and was at the same time bound to be more complex and unwieldy than anything that had hitherto been offered. The handyman's shop is always cluttered with unfinished projects.

I. Before the *Physics*

A. *Freestanding Subjects*

In the *Categories*, generally thought to be one of his earliest surviving works, Aristotle tells us that some things are *present in* other things and some things are *said of* other things. Knowledge, for example, is present in the soul, and said of grammar. "Present in" is a technical term here. By "present in the soul" he means that (1) it is in the soul, but (2) not as a part, and (3) it cannot exist apart from the soul [1ª24–25].

What sorts of things are, in this technical sense, present in you? There is a disagreement among scholars about the answer to this question. On the view I am inclined to accept, your weight is an example of the sort of thing he has in mind. It is in some sense there in your body; it is not a part of your body (as your heart is); and it cannot float around apart from your body. Someone else might be the same weight, but that person's weight is that person's weight, and your weight is your weight, even if each of you weighs 160 pounds. On this view Aristotle holds to property-particulars: your weight is numerically diverse from mine even if we are the same weight, just as you and I are numerically diverse even if we are both human beings.

On the alternative view, Aristotle does not accept property-particulars.[1] This Aristotle would say that if I get a tan, my original complexion can continue to exist in other people and thus *can* exist apart from me. On this view the properties Aristotle is talking about are universals, and he holds only that my complexion cannot exist apart from bodies, not that my complexion cannot exist apart from me. Whichever of these interpretations we adopt, Aristotle is saying that it is characteristics or properties that are present in other things. On the first interpretation, these properties are particulars, peculiar to their bearers; on the second, they are not.

"Said of" is a technical term, too, in the *Categories*, for Aristotle explains that by it he does not just mean cases in which one term is predicated of another: he stipulates that if *F* is said of *a*, all things said of *F* are said of *a* as well, hence the definition of *F* must be predicable of *a* [1ᵇ10–15]. So, although we can say, "Socrates is white," in his technical sense white is *not* said of Socrates, for the definition of "white" would be, in part, that white is a color, but though Socrates is white, Socrates is not a color [2ª19–34], so the definition of "white" cannot be predicated of Socrates.

1 See, e.g., Michael Frede (1987).

Man, on the other hand, *is* said of Socrates, for Socrates is a man, and man is an animal, and Socrates is an animal. Aristotle's intention seems to be that it will be species, genera, and differentiae that are "said of" things, and he calls the first two "secondary substances."

If we set aside species, genera, and properties as the things that are present in or said of other things, we are left with the things that are neither said of nor present in other things, and these Aristotle calls "primary substances." The examples he gives are this man or this horse – particular substances. And since everything else is either said of or present in primary substances, primary substances are the bedrock on which reality is grounded: "If the primary substances did not exist, it would be impossible for any of the other things to exist" [2ᵇ5–6].

In sorting things out this way, Aristotle is deliberately opposing the Platonic doctrine of the primacy of abstract forms. Plato held that without the Forms nothing else could exist, while the existence of the Forms is unaffected by the existence or nonexistence of non-Forms. In other words, even if there are no individual men, Man Itself still is what it is. In Plato the Forms are the primary substances. The closest analogues to Plato's Forms in the *Categories* are species, genera, and properties, and Aristotle turns their relation to concrete individuals around. Socrates, not man or justice, is the primary substance:

animal is predicated of man, and therefore also of the individual man; for if it were predicated of none of the individual men it would not be predicated of man at all. Again, color is in body and therefore also in an individual body; for were it not in some individual body it would not be in body at all. . . . So if the primary substances did not exist it would be impossible for any of the other things to exist. [2ᵃ36–2ᵇ6]

The examples Aristotle gives of primary substances in the *Categories* are all common, concrete particulars – e.g., your neighbor and his dog – not specimens from a philosopher's private collection of exotics. The basic layout of the *Categories*, then, seems designed to underline the contrast between Aristotle's scheme and Plato's, and can be thought of as a philosophical declaration of independence.

B. Essence

Aristotle's account, however, contains a number of loose ends and nascent problems. First, there is the problem of what he will subsequently call "the unity of definition." No substance, primary or secondary, is present in a subject. The individual man is not in a subject, but neither is man (the species) in the individual man, though it is said of the individual man; similarly, animal (the genus) is said of the individual man, but is not in the individual man [3ᵃ7–15]. For while it is possible for the *name* of what is in a subject to be predicated of the subject – he has in mind statements like "Socrates is pale" – it is impossible for the definition of what is in a subject to be said of the subject in his technical sense. And since the definition of a secondary substance can always be predicated of that of which the secondary substance is said, no secondary substance can be in a subject. This, he continues, is not peculiar to substance: "since the differentia also is not in a subject. For footed and two-footed are said of man as a subject but are not in a subject; neither two-footed nor footed is *in* man."

That species and genera are not present in the individuals that fall under them has generally been explained through (3) above: species and genera can exist apart from the individual; Socrates perishes, but his species and genus persist. But this justification is not open for Aristotle's claim that the differentia is not in the species, because he has already told us in chapter 3 that "the differentiae of genera which are different and not subordinate one to the other are themselves different in kind" [1ᵇ16ff.].[2] In the sense of *d* in which *d* is a differentia of the genus *G*, *d* cannot be a differentia of a nonsubaltern genus. If sharpness is a differentia of musical notes, it cannot in that same sense be a differentia of knives; if legged is a differentia of animals, it cannot in the same sense be a differentia of furniture.

Thus it seems false that the differentia of a species can exist apart from that species, and hence it cannot be (3) that Aristotle has in mind in saying that the differentia of man is not in man.[3] His actual reason is quite explicit – the differentia is not present in the species, not because it fails (3), but because it fails (1): "For footed and two-footed are said of man as a subject but are not in a subject: neither two-footed nor footed is *in* man." This is just the same reason he in fact gave for the species not being in the individual: "man is said of the individual man as subject but is not in a subject: man is not *in* the individual man." The clause following the colon in both sentences is not a redundancy: Aristotle is giving us the reason differentiae and species are not present in subjects – namely, because they are not in subjects at all.[4]

For Aristotle, what is in another is, though dependent upon that other, nonetheless different from that other: colors cannot exist apart from bodies, but colors are not bodies. The problem he is beginning to wrestle with here is: if the species, genus, or differentia that specify the sort of thing I am, are different from me, then I am distinct from the sort of thing I am; but if I am distinct from the sort of thing I am, how can I be a thing of that sort? It is a grudge Aristotle has with Plato that Plato makes

2 See also *Topics*, 107ᵇ19–32, 144ᵇ11–31.
3 I say "the differentia," though in the later biological works he seems to allow multiple differentiae for a species.
4 See Sheldon M. Cohen (1973).

the essences of things to be things different from the things whose essences they are.[5] How can that be, Aristotle wonders? If my essence is something different from me, something I am just related to in a certain way, then it cannot really be my essence, for I must already be something if I can enter into relations with other things. So it becomes a tenet of Aristotle that in some way a thing and its essence must be one. Aristotle's denial in the *Categories* that the species is in its members and that the differentia is in the species is his first step in this direction: the relation of Socrates to his weight is different from the relation of Socrates to his humanity, for man is not in Socrates as one thing in another.

Second, there is the problem of essence itself. White, Aristotle says, signifies simply a certain qualification, whereas secondary substances signify "the qualification of substance – they signify substance of a certain qualification" [3ᵇ13–21]. To be told that something is white is to be told that it has a certain quality; to be told that something is human is to be told that the substance it is, is qualified in a certain way. He wants to say that it is a certain sort of substance, but he does not have the tool that would enable him to drive this point home (or, if he has it, it stays in his toolbox): the distinction between what is essential and what is accidental. He is close, for he has formulated a distinction between secondary substances and that which is present in a subject, and he is clear that the definitions of secondary subjects can be said of the individuals they are said of, whereas this is not the case for things present in other things. But he has yet to say that individuals cannot survive change in regard to the qualification of their substance, though he has said that they can take on contraries. He does not even suggest this. It is compatible with the *Categories*, for example, that a persisting thing's substance is qualified as tadpole at one time and as frog at another, and that these are different species – i.e., that a thing can start its career belonging to one species and switch species in midstream. "Tadpole," "frog," and "child" are phase sortals, as applying to a thing during a limited part of its life history in virtue of the thing's being in a specific chronological phase. Other sortals, e.g., "pedestrian," might be called "sporadics"; still others, e.g., "physician," "durables." Aristotle needs to exclude all of these from counting as species. I do not think he had it in mind to allow them to count as species as he wrote the *Categories*, but there is nothing in the explication of the "said of" relation that excludes it. At 12ᵇ37–41 and 13ᵃ20–21, heat belongs by nature to fire, and whiteness by nature to snow, and it is not possible for snow to be black or fire to be cold, so some things possess necessary properties. But this is compatible with holding that a thing might belong to different species, and so possess different natures, at various stages during its career – people do say that children are by nature ram-

5 See *Metaphysics* VII, 6.

bunctious but eventually outgrow it, and at 10ª27–10ᵇ11 the runner and the boxer are so-called by virtue of their respective natural capacities – or even to different species at the same time.

He has told us that the individual man and the individual horse are primary substances, for they are neither in a subject nor said of a subject. Does he realize that the individual stonecutter, philosopher, child, and Greek meet these same criteria? And that whatever can be said of stone-cutter can be said of the individual stonecutter – if Socrates is a stonecut-ter, the definition of stonecutter can be said of Socrates – so stonecutter, just as much as man, seems to meet his criterion for being said of a subject? Why not say, then, that stonecutter is a secondary substance, indicating "substance of a certain qualification," and that the individual stonecutter is a primary substance?

Aristotle may have known what sort of things he was willing to counte-nance as species and genera, and may not have noticed that stonecutter is said with combination. Alternatively, in chapter 4 he tells us that "of things said *without any combination,* each signifies either substance or quantity or qualification." The whole discussion of the *Categories* may be on the assumption that stonecutter is not said without any combination, though if that is the case, we were entitled to more of a warning: the distinction is explicated as a distinction between terms and propositions rather than between different sorts of terms. But it could be extended to cover the latter: if "man runs" is said with combination, and "man" and "runs" without combination, it could also be that sprinter or stonecutter are said with combination – sprinting man or stonecutting man.[6] What it seems Aristotle needs to do initially is to explicate "said with combina-tion" so that what is said with combination always involves one thing's being present in another, to explain why it is that what is said of a thing is never present in that thing, and to do so in such a way, as "colt" and "stonecutter" show, that whether we use a noun or an adjective plus a noun (e.g., "rational animal") to point out our candidate will not be crucial. To do this may very well be to argue that sometimes "*x* is *F*" introduces one thing, and sometimes two things.

In any case, the issue never comes to the fore in the *Categories*. In chapter 5 Aristotle elaborates by listing some characteristics of substance that we might not have expected simply from the formal criteria of being neither said of nor present in. We are told that:

---

6 This may not really be different from the problem of the unity of definition, which is the problem of how some combinations (e.g., rational man) form essential unities, while others (e.g., pale man) do not. But if this problem is lurking in the combined/ uncombined distinction of *Categories* 2 and 4, it is only in an inchoate form. I am not oblivious to the use-mention confusions here: Aristotle means to be talking about non-linguistic entities, but quotation marks are still helpful aids. With the reader's in-dulgence, I take the marks to distinguish *things said,* not words.

1. Every substance seems to signify a certain "this." As regards the primary substances, it is indisputably true that each of them signifies a certain "this"; for the thing revealed is individual and numerically one.
2. There is no contrary to substances: nothing is contrary to an individual man or to man.
3. One pale thing may be more pale than another, but no man is more a man than another.
4. It seems most distinctive of substance that what is numerically one and the same is able to receive contraries. In no other case could one bring forward anything, numerically one, which is able to receive contraries.

But each of these propositions, with the possible exception of (3), seems equally applicable to the colt. Of course, as the colt is a substance (though a "phase substance"), and not a quality, quantity, etc. Gareth B. Matthews has talked about "kooky entities" in Aristotle, entities like the sitting man, who perishes when the man rises.[7] When I leave my car, I become a pedestrian, and the pedestrian I become seems to meet points 1 through 4, and the formal criteria as well. The more durable boxer, runner, and stonecutter seem to meet them as well. The only ground on which the *Categories* may be poised to exclude all these is that they are said with combination, but as yet we have been told too little to know how to bring charges along these lines. In *Metaphysics* VII Aristotle will tell us more.[8]

The concepts Aristotle needs in order to address these problems are introduced, bit by bit, in other treatises in the *Organon: On Interpretation, Posterior Analytics,* and *Topics.* In the *Posterior Analytics* II, 2, Aristotle says that, to understand what something is (*ti esti*) and why it is (the cause or reason) are the same. "The what it is" (*to ti esti*) is a standard formula, often and unobjectionably rendered as "essence," and the remainder of Book II is a discussion of definition, since "definition seems to be of the what it is" [90^{b}4]. But his major example makes it clear that he is not thinking of the what-it-is question as in particular a question directed toward substances: a lunar eclipse is a privation of light on the moon by the earth's blocking the sunlight, and it is caused by the absence of light due to that blocking, so to know what a lunar eclipse is, is to know what causes a lunar eclipse. Because a lunar eclipse is not a substance – technically, I suppose it is a passion – the what-it-is question is not linked in any special way to substances as opposed to items that fall under the other categories. Since we can ask "What is it?" of an eclipse or of a quality, as well as of a substance, the question does not seem to be a guide to substance.

7 Matthews (1982).
8 See Chapter 4, sec. I, "The Unity of Definition."

Yet in *Posterior Analytics* II, 3, Aristotle says that definition is of the what-it-is *and of substance* [90ᵇ30]. We are thus pointed in two directions: we can ask what it is of a passion, a quantity, quality, etc., and in so doing we are somehow inquiring into substance. This link between essence and substance is also evident in *Topics* I, 9, where the list of categories from *Categories* 4 is presented again, but now with *ti esti* replacing substance as the first category. Still, Aristotle makes it clear that substance is not gone from the first category: if we say that what Socrates is is a man, we say what he is and signify a substance, and if we say that what white is is a color, we say what it is and signify a quality.

As in the *Posterior Analytics,* we can ask what the essence is for an item in any of the categories, so the essence question does not single out substances: that a man is a substance while a color is not does not follow from the one's having an essence while the other lacks an essence – each has an essence. We might even say, taking our lead from the equation of essence and substance in the *Posterior Analytics* passage mentioned above, that in asking what the essence of white is we are asking what its substance is. On what grounds, then, is saying what Socrates is signifying a substance, whereas saying what white is is signifying a quality? Something is missing.

What is missing is the subject criterion ("present in") that in the *Categories* is used to distinguish substances from items in other categories. Perhaps Aristotle thinks it unnecessary: if you know what Socrates is, and what color is, you know that Socrates is the subject of color, because to know what Socrates is is to know that he is a substance, and to know what color is is to know that it is a quality. The essence itself reveals the subject and the substance. This may help us distinguish between the status of people and colors, but it does not help us distinguish between the status of people and stonecutters or children. Stonecutters and children are not properties; they are bearers of properties. We still want to know which bearers of properties are primary substances – or are they all equally primary substances?

The *Topics* adds a useful terminology, but the terminology by itself will not settle the substantive question. *Topics* I, 5 tells us that an *accident* is something that may belong or not belong to the same thing: the same thing may be white at one time, not white at another, or sitting at one time, not sitting at another [102ᵇ3–10; see also 120ᵇ30–35]. This notion, though, need not lead to men as primary substances: one can argue that the same thing can be a man at one time and a corpse at another – i.e., one can argue that being a man is accidental to the things that are men. And one can argue that youthfulness is an essential property of colts and children. (In fact, it will take an argument to show that the addition of an accident cannot create a new substance. Puerto Rico may be a U.S. protectorate one year and independent the next. In becoming independent, it may become a new entity, something that had not previously existed, even while persisting.)[9]

Properties, in Aristotle's technical sense, by contrast, are proper to their subjects and convertible with them: if a thing is capable of learning grammar, it is a man, and if it is a man, it is capable of learning grammar. This, too, requires supplementation, for one might argue that a detailed knowledge of quantum mechanics is an essential property of nuclear physicists. A *definition* "is a phrase signifying a thing's essence" [101^{b}35], but this will not help unless we know that the stonecutter as such does not have an essence.

The what-is-it question cannot handle all of Aristotle's problems – not unless it is heavily supported by ancillary devices. It may enable us to distinguish things designated by substantives – count nouns and mass nouns – from things designated by adjectivals,[10] but it cannot by itself distinguish between count nouns and mass nouns, let alone give priority to either of these two, or to a subset of one of them. Yet, as Aristotle's thought unfolds, this is just what he wants to do. In this connection, it is interesting to note that in the *Categories* he mentions honey at 9^{a}33–35 as the subject of sweetness, snow and fire at 12^{b}38–41, and wheat and wine at 15^{b}25, but he never discusses whether this stuff meets his criteria for primary substances, although in chapter 5 what is most distinctive of primary substance is its ability to take on contrary properties while remaining numerically one, and it seems plausible to say that the honey in the jar, while remaining numerically identical, can at different times be hot or cold, light or dark, or more or less viscous.[11]

C. The Unity of Definition

Chapter 11 of *On Interpretation* raises the issue of compound things: "man is perhaps an animal and two-footed and tame, yet these do make up some one thing; whereas pale and man and walking do not make up one thing."[12] They do not make up one thing even if there is one name for pale walking men, in which case to call someone by that name would still be to make more than one affirmation, while to call a man a tame, two-footed animal is (on the hypothesis that this is a definition) to make one affirmation, "for two-footed and animal are contained in man" [21^{a}18]. Aristotle does not explain what he means by this, but clearly he does *not* mean that "man" means "two-footed animal": even if there were one

---

9 This is one way of understanding the scholastic doctrine of a plurality of substantial forms.

10 This is grammatically simplified.

11 Although olive oil and wine, he will later say, have the same substratum, and olive oil and peanut oil may belong in the same genus. See Chapter 4, sec. II, "Unity."

12 I prefer "pale" to "white" because Aristotle says that the same man can be *leukos* at one time, *melas* at another. *Categories*, 4^{a}19–20; *Metaphysics*, 1058^{b}33–35.

name – say, "cloak" – for pale, walking men, to call someone a cloak would be to make more than one affirmation. The differentia and the genus somehow make up one thing in a way in which a substance and two nonsubstances cannot.

Aristotle justifies this by introducing the notion of *accidental* predication: "Even if it is true to say that the pale man is musical, 'musical pale' will still not be one thing; for it is accidentally that the musical is pale." By contrast, "two-footed and animal are contained in man." But he gives us no reason for believing that two-footedness is contained in man in a way in which musicality is not, and the absurdities that he introduces to support this claim are question-begging. He says that if pale and man can be predicated as one, then pale can be predicated of the compound, so that we will have a pale pale man. Here he seems to be thinking that if pale man is predicated as one, the pale man is a substance, of which paleness can (again) be predicated. But it is not clear why the same alleged absurdity does not arise in the other case, as the two-footed animal substance is two-footed.

The theme is picked up again in *Posterior Analytics* II, 5–6. In chapter 5, criticizing the method of division, Aristotle points out that when its practitioner asks whether man is terrestrial or aquatic and replies terrestrial, it does follow that man is terrestrial by necessity, and it does not follow from what has been said that man is the whole – that is, both terrestrial and animal – by necessity: "For what prevents the whole from being true of man, without clarifying the what it is or the essence?" [91ᵇ25ff.]. The method of division, like induction, will lead us to say that man is a terrestrial animal, but this gives us no warrant for believing that this is the essence of man.

In chapter 6 Aristotle puts this a different way:

And in both cases – if you prove in virtue of a division and if you produce a deduction in this way – there is the same puzzle: why will man be a two-footed terrestrial animal and not animal and terrestrial? For from the assumption there is no necessity for what is predicated to become a unity, but it might be as if the same man were musical and literate. [92ᵃ27–32]

D. Persistence through Change

A related theme can be found in *Posterior Analytics* I, 22:

One can say truly that the white thing is walking, and that that large thing is a log, and again that the log is large and that the man is walking. Well, speaking in the latter and in the former ways are different. For when I say that the white thing is a log, then I say that that which is accidentally white is a log; and not that the white thing is the underlying subject for the log; for it is not the case that, being white or just what is some white, it came to be a log, so that it is not a log except accidentally. But when I say that the log is white, I do not say that something else is white and that that is accidentally a log, as when I say that the musical thing is white (for then I say that the man, who is accidentally musical, is white); but the log is the underlying subject which *did* come to be white without being something other than just what is a log, or a particular log. [83ª1–14]

Something that just was a white thing, but not a log, did not come to be a log, so that its being a log is accidental to it, but rather, something that was a log came to be white (while remaining a log). The log's claim to be the underlying subject rests on its having been a log before it was white and its coming to be white while remaining a log, as opposed to the impossibility of something's just being a white thing and then coming to be, accidentally, a (white) log. Thus it is the log's ability to persist through change that entitles it to be the underlying subject, while it is in the nature of white not to indicate a persisting underlying subject.

II. *Physics* I

A. Physics *I, 7: Matter, Subjects, and Change*

In the *Physics* I, 7, Aristotle introduces the notion of matter. Greek did not have a term for matter, so he takes the term for wood, *hyle,* and says we must understand it by analogy, that as bronze is to the statue and wood to the bed, so is *hyle* and "the formless before receiving form to anything which has form" [191ª10]. Since matter is introduced as the correlate of form, in introducing matter Aristotle is also recasting the notion of form. The subject (*to hupokeimenon*) is now taken to be complex: one in number, but two in form [190ᵇ24], for when a man becomes cultured, there is the man (here taken to be the material factor) and there is the form, the culture he acquired.

Because the form the man acquired – culture – would, in the *Categories,* be an accident, it might look as though, in the *Physics,* the substance is the material factor ("the man, the gold – in general the countable matter" [190ᵇ25]), so that the primary substances of the *Categories* are here identified with matter, the underlying nature. But this is not quite what Aristotle is saying. First, when he explains how we are to understand the underlying nature by analogy (as bronze is to the statue or wood to the bed), he says "so is the underlying nature to substance – the this and the existent" [191ª11]. The underlying nature is not identified with substance but is related to it as bronze is to the statue.[13]

13 That matter is meant to survive substantial change is clear from chapter 9: "For my definition of matter is just this – the primary substratum of each thing, from which it comes to be, and which persists in the result, not accidentally." But this does not really tell us what Aristotle has in mind, for we might take him to mean simply that matter cannot be created nor destroyed – that in any change, the original matter is preserved. The original matter (e.g., hay) might be transformed into a different type of matter, so

Second, *Physics* I, 7 concludes with the observation, "Whether the form or what underlies is the substance is not yet clear."[14] (In *Metaphysics* VII, Aristotle finally answers the question and form emerges as the winner.)

Third, *Physics* I, 7 seems quite tentative on substantial change. Aristotle raises the issue by saying that when nonsubstances come to be, it is quite clear that there must be some underlying subject:

Now in all cases other than substance it is plain that there must be something underlying, namely, that which becomes. For when a thing comes to be of such a quantity or quality or in such a relation, time, or place, a subject is always presupposed, since substance alone is not predicated of another subject, but everything else of substance. [190a33ff.]

The coming-to-be of the Cheshire cat's smile presupposes that there is a Cheshire cat, as everything but substance is predicated of or present in substance. But substances, too, come to be from some underlying subject: "For we find in every case something that underlies from which proceeds that which comes to be; for instance, animals and plants from seed." The underlying subject in this case, the seed, is not something that persists through the change: when we have an oak tree, we no longer have an acorn. (A few lines earlier he has said that when we say that something comes to be out of [*eks*] something, we generally have in mind cases in which that out of which the change proceeds does not survive the change.) So Aristotle's point cannot be that when a substance (the oak tree) comes to be, it comes to be in a subject (the acorn), as the smile in the cat: if the seed were a subject of which the oak is predicated, the oak tree would not be a substance. His point is that the coming-to-be of a substance presupposes the prior existence of subjects. He has been arguing that whereas his predecessors attempted to explain change through contraries, an adequate account must also include the underlying subject. This is obvious, he thinks, for accidental changes, but equally true for substantial changes: substances come to be from already existing subjects. The point is that if there were no subjects, substances could not come to be, not that the coming-to-be of a substance is a modification of an underlying subject that persists through the change.

Or is it? The passage continues:

Things which come to be without qualification, come to be in different ways: by change of shape, as a statue; by addition, as things which grow; by taking away, as the Hermes from the stone; by putting together, as a house; by alteration, as things which turn in respect of their matter. It is plain that these are all cases of coming to be from some underlying thing.

that although at the end of the process one still has matter (e.g., milk), it is not the same matter one had originally. Though I have not had time to study it thoroughly, this may be the view in Scaltsas (1994b), pp. 22–25.

14 At II, 1, 193b6, he adds that the form, rather than the matter, is nature.

The list is unsettling. A clay statue comes into existence through a change of shape, and the persisting clay is the underlying subject. A city comes into existence by growth, but the village from which it grows does not persist, and the same is true for the tree and the seedling. The Hermes is carved from stone, some of which persists in the Hermes. The building materials survive in the house, but unless "underlying subject" is considered a synonym for "matter," it is not clear in what sense the building materials are the underlying subject of the house. Finally, "by alteration, as things which turn in respect of their matter" is enigmatic. Elsewhere Aristotle suggests that in substantial change the matter itself undergoes a transformation; perhaps this is what he has in mind here. He ought not to have in mind mere alteration, for that is not the coming-to-be of a substance, though one can treat it as falling under this rubric: the man, as matter for the change, becomes musical, and so the matter has turned musical. But then the coming-to-be of a musical man is the coming-to-be of a substance, whereas one would have thought that the coming-to-be of a musical man was a case of qualified coming-to-be (a man comes to be so-and-so), not of unqualified coming-to-be.

In fact, the entire discussion of unqualified coming-to-be in *Physics* I, 7 seems hesitant. Aristotle begins it by distinguishing unqualified coming-to-be from coming-to-be so-and-so [190ª32], saying that only substances are said to come to be without qualification. Yet a few lines later [190ᵇ1] he introduces the passage we have been discussing by saying, "that substances, too, *and anything that can be said to be without qualification,* come to be from some underlying thing, will appear on examination." This allows that some nonsubstances might be said to be without qualification.

One may attempt to reconcile these passages by arguing that what can be said to be without qualification need not have come to be without qualification.[15] Yet the passage may merely reflect Aristotle's uncertainty over how to identify substances. In our passage statues and houses are given as examples of substances, coming to be through changes of shape or through assembly. In later works Aristotle expresses doubt about such cases.

B. The Broad and Narrow Characterizations

In *Metaphysics* VI, 1, Aristotle distinguishes physics (in his sense, not the current sense) or the study of nature from mathematics and first philosophy or theology. First philosophy studies things that are separable and changeless. Mathematics treats its objects as though they are separable from matter and motion, which in thought at least they are, even if in

---

15 See, e.g., Williams (1989), pp. 54–55.

reality they are not.[16] It studies concavity, which is "independent of perceptible matter," as opposed to snubness, which is concavity in a nose, and hence in formula inseparable from matter.

Physics, on the other hand, theorizes about "such being as admits of being moved, and only about that kind of substance which in respect of its formula is for the most part not separable [from matter]" [1025b26–28].[17] This is Aristotle's *broad characterization* of the study of nature: physics studies things that are moveable and whose formulae involve matter. He lists the following as examples, at 1026a1: "nose, eye, face, flesh, bone, and, in general, animal; leaf, root, bark, and, in general, plant (for none of these can be defined without reference to movement – they always have matter)."

Yet a few lines earlier he had said that physics studies "that sort of substance which has the principle of its movement and rest present in itself."[18] I shall call this the Internal Principle (of change or stasis) Principle (IPP). This is the *narrow characterization*. On the broad characterization, physics studies things that admit of being moved – that is, the material universe. On the narrow characterization, physics studies a subset of the material universe: among the things that admit of being moved, it studies only those that have an internal principle of motion and rest. Because, as we shall see, Aristotle believes that there are things that admit of being moved but lack an internal principle of motion or rest, the subset selected by the narrow characterization is a proper subset.

We can reconcile the broad and narrow characterizations in at least two ways. First, we can take the broad characterization to be informal: physics studies the things that have an internal principle of motion or rest, and as whatever has an internal principle of motion or rest is moveable, it follows that physics studies things that are moveable. (On this reading Aristotle is not claiming that physics studies *everything* that is moveable.) Second, Aristotle says that physics studies the *substances* that have an internal principle of motion or rest, and *things* or *beings* that admit of motion; we might be able to reconcile the two characterizations on the ground that for Aristotle substances are a proper subset of things or beings. Either way, the two characterizations can be reconciled. My interest here is not in identifying an inconsistency, but rather in exploring the significance of the narrow characterization.

Even if Aristotle does not really mean that physics or the study of nature treats of everything that is material or moveable (these two are

16 For this claim see *Physics* II, 2, 193b31–34, *On the Soul* III, 7, 431b12–16, and *Metaphysics* XI, 3, 1061a29–35.
17 There are textual problems with Aristotle's discussion: see Kirwan (1993), p. 187.
18 Commentators frequently, though somewhat unaccountably, leave out "and rest" when they explicate the principle; see, e.g., Lang (1992), p. 27: "for Aristotle nature possesses an innate impulse to change."

extensionally the same for him), this claim seems initially plausible. The study of nature, we might think, is the study of the entire visible universe, not of a select group of privileged objects within it.

Once having said that, though, we might begin to have doubts. Does the study of nature include the study of 1957 Chevrolets, automobiles being visible things? Does it include the study of books? Perhaps it includes the study of books if they are considered in certain ways (as composed of such and such kinds of matter, for example), but not if they are considered in other ways (on the basis of their literary merit, subject matter, or the national languages in which they are written). But should even this count as the study of books, or is it the study of matter (paper), rather than of books, though books are material objects? If the latter, then we might conclude that the study of nature is not the study of everything in the visible universe, as it does not include the study of books, and books are visible.

As Aristotle sees the history of thought up to his own time, these sorts of questions, central to his own philosophical enterprise, were inadequately dealt with in earlier accounts of nature, and perhaps nothing on his agenda is more important to him than reworking the concept of nature so that these questions will be reflected in it. As he sees it, the earlier students of nature, the *physiologoi*, identified nature with matter, and that was a mistake.

C. The Lists

There is a third way Aristotle has of characterizing the things the study of nature treats: by enumeration. I have just quoted a passage in which he gives us a list: "nose, eye, face, flesh, bone, and, in general, animal; leaf, root, bark, and, in general, plant." This list is consistent with those he gives in other places of things that exist by nature or consist of natural substances. *Physics* II begins: "Of things that exist, some exist by nature, some from other causes. By nature the animals and their parts exist, and the plants, and the simple bodies (earth, fire, air, water) – for we say that these and the like exist by nature." At the start of *On the Heavens* III we find a similar list: "By '[natural] substances' I am talking about the simple bodies – fire, earth, and the other terms of the series – and all things composed of them, for example, the heaven as a whole and its parts, and again animals and plants and their parts." In the *Metaphysics* VII, 2 [1028ᵇ7], where Aristotle is talking about substance *simpliciter*, and not natural substances as such, we are again given the same list:

Substance is thought to belong most obviously to bodies; and so we say that both animals and plants and their parts are substances, and so are natural bodies such as fire and water and earth and everything of that sort, and all things that are parts of these or composed of these (either of parts or of the whole bodies), e.g., the heaven and its parts, stars and moon and sun.

These lists are noteworthy for their brevity: (*a*) animals, plants, and their parts, and (*b*) the elements or simple bodies and things composed of them. If we were reading "element" from our own century's point of view, they would also be noteworthy for their redundancy: as we take animals and plants and their parts to be composed of the elements, animals, plants, and their parts would be brought in under both (*a*) and (*b*). If this were what Aristotle had in mind, he need not have mentioned (*a*) at all; he could just have said that natural substances are the elements and things composed of the elements. Plants and animals would still count as natural substances on the ground that they are composed of the elements.

Had he done this, however, automobiles and books would also seem to be natural substances, as presumably they are composed of the elements, and this would commit him to the broad characterization. If he is going to hold that all material things are composed of the elements, and that whatever is composed of the elements is a natural substance, then the study of nature, if it is the study of natural substances, is the study of all material things, not of some proper subset of them. If the mention of (a) is not a redundancy, then, Aristotle must think that animals and plants are not composed of the simple bodies.[19]

To be reconciled with these lists the narrow characterization requires that not every material object count as either a simple body or a thing composed of simple bodies. If every material object did so count, every material object would be a thing existing by nature, and so possess an internal principle of change or stasis, and the narrow characterization would select the same objects selected by the broad characterization. A desk, if it is composed of simple bodies, would be an object that exists by nature, and so have an Internal Principle (IP). Since, as we shall see, Aristotle holds that artifacts do not have an IP, it would seem that he is committed to holding that they are not composed of simple bodies. This is problematic, for it seems easy enough to imagine artifacts composed of simple bodies: mudpies, sand castles, or marble statuary, for example.[20] We can even conceive of artifacts composed of a single simple body: ice scupltures, for example, and perhaps the flame rising from a candle's wick. To deal with this problem and with others that will arise along the way, Aristotle must avail himself of a few distinctions and a few metaphysi-

---

19 Shields (1988) says that "if material elements do not even constitute forms [as opposed to being identical with them], then forms are not material (in the sense of having essentially material parts)." On my view, material elements do not constitute plants, yet plants have essentially material parts: roots, leaves, etc.

20 Although perhaps these are not composed of Aristotelian simple bodies, but of Aristotelian homogeneous stuffs.

cal claims. But before we enter this tangled field, we must take a closer look at the IPP itself.

D. Nature and Matter

Of things that exist by nature, Aristotle says, in Book II of the *Physics:*

each of them has within itself a principle of change and of stasis (in respect of place, or of growth and diminution, or by way of alteration). On the other hand, a bed and a coat and anything else of that sort, qua receiving these designations – i.e., in so far as they are products of art – have no innate impulse to change. But insofar as they happen to be composed of stone or of earth or of a mixture of the two, they do have such an impulse, and just to that extent. [192b13–21]

This is nature as the realm of things that have within themselves a principle of change and of stasis. A coat is subject to various sorts of change. You may hang it up in the closet, put it on and go to the store, dye it another color, have a tailor alter it, or toss it into the fireplace. In all of these cases the coat itself is not the source of the changes it undergoes – you are. The coat, *as such,* has no internal source of change.

It does, however, have a source of internal change of sorts: if, for example, it is cotton, it will decay over the years. But this is a change the coat undergoes not because it is a coat, but because it is made of cotton. The change is due to the nature of the material out of which the coat is made, not to the fact that the material is in the form of a coat. The cloth would decay even if the tailor had not made a coat out of it.[21] This points us toward a distinction between a *thing* and the *matter* out of which it is made: the coat as opposed to the material.[22] The coat *as such* (qua coat) may not have an internal principle of change, yet as being made of cotton it does. There are, of course, characteristics the coat has precisely because it is a coat, and not in virtue of its material. If that were not so, cotton coats would not differ from cotton vests or trousers. But Aristotle thinks that these characteristics do not involve a principle of change.

The passage also points to a distinction between artifacts and things that exist by nature: the bed is an artifact; the wood out of which it is made is not. Aristotle's examples might seem to suggest a connection between this distinction and the thing/matter distinction: the matter of the bed and coat – wood and cotton – is natural, whereas the bed and the coat made out of them are artifacts. So we might suspect that in general it is the matter out of which things are made that is natural, and the finished products that are the artifacts. But this congruence, Aristotle thinks, will not hold in every case. Identifying nature with the matter out of which things are made is a move Aristotle takes some of his pre-

---

21 On closer inspection, it is not even the cloth that has an internal source of change but rather the cotton out of which the cloth is woven.
22 This distinction was explicated and revived in Wiggins (1967).

decessors to have made, but that he himself opposes. He argues that some things – trees, for example – and not just their matter, exist by nature.

Of course, those predecessors did not believe that the matter out of which things are made is natural and the things themselves artifacts. They would have put their point, somewhat strangely, by saying that the matter exists by nature and the things by convention (*nomos*). They would have meant by this that somehow the matter of things is what we are really dealing with when we deal with things, and the things themselves are nothing more than arrangements of matter. To the Greek atomists we are a swarm of atoms that happens to be deployed in a humanoid cloud; to Empedocles, if our vision were more acute we would see that we are juxtapositions of more enduring forms of matter. The forms of matter that exist at the elementary level are, to these thinkers, what reality is composed of. The compositions named by us (e.g., Aunt Alice) are merely groupings of these exotic elementary beings; hence they exist by *nomos*, not by *physis*. We give names to certain configurations, much as we designate an area defined by certain borders as "Tennessee." But Tennessee exists by law, then, not by nature.

Aristotle, on the other hand, is struck by the ability of some of these compositions to endure and to replicate themselves, so that individuals persist, grow, and flourish, and though individual people come and go, the human form persists. The tenaciousness of these compositions indicates to him that they obey their own laws: they are not merely by-products of elementary interactions obeying elementary laws, but rather, they are using elementary interactions and laws to further their own ends. They are active players in the cosmos, not mere configurations of elementary matter. They exist by *physis*, not by *nomos*, and it is one of Aristotle's central aims to formulate an account of nature that will re-install them in what he takes to be their rightful place. This account requires that we a give preeminent place to matter's correlate: form.

Aristotle's instincts express themselves in his discussion of generation and corruption, where he sees himself as walking a middle road between Plato and the pre-Socratics.[23] Plato's *eidos*,[24] he tells us [*On Generation and Corruption*, 335ᵇ18–20], cannot account for generation and corruption, for if the *eide* are causes, "why do they not continually generate, but only now and then, since they and the things that participate in them always exist?" It is not health itself, but the physician, who makes the patient healthy.

To point to matter as the cause of generation and corruption is more in accordance with the study of nature (*physikôteron*) [335ᵇ25]; yet matter

---

23 See, e.g., *On Generation and Corruption* II, ix (335ᵇ8–336ᵃ14).
24 *Eidos* is usually translated "form," but here, where Aristotle is about to play off form (*morphe*) against *eidos*, that rendering would make the passage incoherent.

is not the most proper (*kuriôteran*) cause of generation and corruption. For things that come to be by nature and by art, matter is what is acted upon, not the productive cause: "Water will not produce an animal out of itself, nor does wood produce a bed, but art does," which implies that nature itself, not matter, produces animals [335^{b}31–33]. These thinkers omit [335^{b}35–336^{a}1] the "most proper cause: . . . the essence and the form." Moreover, those who do away with the formal cause attribute powers to matter that are inadequate to produce the observed effects:

For since, as they assert, it is the nature of the hot to separate and of the cold to bring together and of each of the other qualities the one to act and the other to be acted upon, it is out of these and by means of these, so they say, that all the other things come to be and perish. But it is evident that fire itself is moved and is acted upon; moreover, they are doing much the same thing as if one were to ascribe to the saw or to any other tool the causation of objects which are brought into being; for division must take place when a man saws and smoothing when he uses a plane, and a similar effect must be produced by the use of other tools. Hence, however much fire is active and causes motion, yet they fail to observe how it moves things, namely, in a manner inferior to that in which the tools act. [336^{a}3–13]

Neither matter nor Platonic forms can account for generation and corruption.

If objects (as opposed to their matter) can exist by nature, perhaps, conversely, matter need not always exist by nature. Consider the widely used example of the bronze statue. In the ancient world statues were not cast out of preexisting bronze. Bronze, an alloy of tin and copper, was produced in the mold as the statue was cast. The bronze, as much as the statue, was a product of the manufacturing process. Why not say that the bronze, as much as the statue, exists by art, not by nature? The jewelry box is made of silver, and the saw of iron; but though silver and iron ore are dug out of the ground, the metals silver and iron are produced at the refiner's shop and so might be held to be products of art. Aristotle in fact does *not* hold refined metals and alloys to be products of art, and this raises the question of what he means by "products of art" and shows that "products of art" is a term of art in Aristotle.

E. The IPP

In our passage Aristotle gives us a reason why things that exist by art do not exist by nature, besides the obvious reason that they are artifacts: "a bed and a coat and anything else of that sort, *qua* receiving these designations – i.e., insofar as they are products of art – have no innate impulse to change." Because things that exist by nature do have an innate impulse to change, it follows that products of art do not exist by nature.

But of course in one sense products of art do *not* exist by nature, they are products of art. We need not accept any novel philosophical principles to grant that beds do not exist by nature, we need only visit a furniture factory. We distinguish things that exist by nature from things that do not, and put statues and beds and washing machines in the latter category because people make them. If this were all Aristotle had in mind, he could have just said (trivially) that products of art do not exist by nature.

Instead he reaches for another explanation: products of art, *because they lack an IP*, do not exist by nature. Does he mean that all and only things produced by art lack an IP, and all and only things arising through natural causes have an IP?

On a narrow interpretation of our passage we might take Aristotle to be implying no more than this, so that it is only insofar as things are artifacts that they have no IP. The class of things that lack an IP will then be coextensive with the class of artifacts, and the class of things that have an IP will be coextensive with the class of things that occur naturally. But there is no need to read him in this way. He might mean only that typical products of art lack an IP, which does not entail that whatever comes about through natural causes has an IP. Once he has said that artifacts do not exist by nature *because* they lack an IP, the possibility opens that some things which come about through natural processes might lack an IP, and that a few artifacts might possess an IP, and so in a technical sense exist by nature.

The "insofar as they are products of art" distinguishes the bed, which has no innate impulse to change, from its matter, which does. *In this case* the thing that per se has no innate impulse to change is an artifact, but this does not exclude the possibility that some things which occur in nature may lack a per se IP (even if their matter does not).[25] Conversely, the cases of bronze, Rhode Island Red roosters, and genetically engineered tomatoes suggest that we cannot assume that merely because something does not occur naturally, but is a product of human art or industry, it does not "exist by nature." Some products of art may possess an IP.

On this broad interpretation, some things that have no IP may occur naturally, and some things that have an IP may not occur naturally. The IPP, then, can allow Aristotle to decouple the notion of a thing's existing by nature from the notion of a thing's coming into existence by natural

---

25 Sarah Waterlow (now Sarah Waterlow Broadie) takes Aristotle in our passage to be distinguishing things brought about through nature from things brought about through skill or coincidence (Waterlow 1982, pp. 2–3), and it is not clear to me that spider webs and polar ice caps would fit into either of these categories. Despite this, I believe that my account of Aristotle's intent in the passage is in keeping with her central lines of interpretation.

processes. Whether something has an IP will be determined by watching how it behaves, to see whether it has by nature a per se internal principle of change or stasis.[26] (A neonate and a stillborn child are produced in the same way, but the one might have and the other lack a *per se* IP.)

On the narrow reading, the only consequence of the IPP would be that artifacts do not exist by nature. This is a sensible claim, but Aristotle would not get much out of it. On the broad interpretation, the IPP creates a number of difficulties, but it also creates opportunities. It makes it possible for us to go on a long (and no doubt trying) philosophical journey, precisely because we have no reason initially to think that all and only artifacts lack an IP. This allows Aristotle to argue that among the things which occur *naturally*, some are privileged (in possessing an IP), and this is central to his purposes.

Natural Artifacts. I have tentatively cited bronze as an example of something that does not occur naturally yet that Aristotle might want to count as having an IP. I want to suggest some candidates for the opposite category: things that might lack an IP even though they occur naturally.

Consider the spider's web and the swallow's nest. Aristotle provides a sense in which they are natural: what by nature behaves in a certain way cannot be trained to behave in another way [*Metaphysics* II, 1103ª19–25]. The web- and nest-building activities of spiders and swallows are natural in this sense, as opposed to being due to habit, convention, art, or deliberation [*Physics* II, 199ª20–21]. If we extend Aristotle's remarks to cover not just the activities of web or nest building but the products of these activities, the web and nest are natural in being the outcomes of activities that occur by nature. But though they arise by nature in this sense, why should they thereby possess an IP anymore than a bed should?[27]

Consider cases in which the very same sort of thing is produced both by art and by nature. We can certainly discover that things we know only as products of art are also produced by nature (in the pertinent sense). Perhaps we routinely create ponds by building dams of mud and saplings and then one day discover that beavers build just the same sort of dams. We can imagine that the principles of construction and the materials used are so similar that we cannot determine by inspection whether a given dam has been constructed by people or beavers. This would seem to be a case in which the same results were the outcomes of both art and natural activities. And if the result is the same in both cases, then if our

26 I say "by nature a per se internal principle" to rule out the bed, which has by nature an internal principle qua wooden, but not qua bed.
27 Lewis (1994, p. 264), says that, for Aristotle, since blood's heat is essential to it but is supplied by the heart as opposed to deriving from an IP, "blood is more like an artifact than a natural object." It is not clear, however, that blood's heat is essential to it (see Chapter 5, I [B], "Flesh and Blood").

dam lacks an IP, so must the beavers', and if the beaver's dam has an IP, so must ours. "If the ship-building art were in the wood," Aristotle says, "it would produce the same results by nature" [*Physics* II, viii, 199ᵇ28]. If the result in either case is the same, then if the man-made ship lacks an IP, so must the ripe ship picked off the boat bush.

Or we can imagine art imitating nature. A kindhearted ornithologist might help out an injured swallow by building a nest for her. He collects the same sorts of materials that she would and puts them together the same way she would. The result is a nest that neither a swallow nor an ornithologist could tell is not swallow-built; it is indistinguishable from a swallow-built nest (though, of course, if you had watched the ornithologist building it, you would know that it was not swallow-built). Because this nest is exactly the same as a swallow's nest, it cannot lack an IP if a swallow's nest has one; for if I build a nest exactly the same as a swallow's nest, I have built a swallow's nest.

Or imagine that I disassemble a swallow's nest and then reassemble it exactly as it was. Would the nest thereby lose its IP? An intrinsic impulse to change must be an intrinsic property of the thing that has it, not a genetic property,[28] even if as a matter of fact only things that arise in certain ways possess intrinsic impulses to change. If bacteria possess an IP, and you create a bacterium, you have created something with an IP. If I, after deliberating, make something that lacks an IP, and a swallow makes the very same sort of thing without deliberating, the swallow's creation will lack an IP too.

We are not ready to give an account of what an IP is. But whatever it is, it does not seem plausible that the spider's web can have one if the birder's snare cannot.

Terrain. Spider webs, ant nests, beaver dams, and bird nests are natural in the sense of being the outcomes of activities that occur by nature (as opposed, for example, to cottages) yet they are artifacts as being products of labor. Let us call them "natural artifacts." Although they come into existence through natural processes, if they lack an IP they will not be, in Aristotle's sense, "things that exist by nature." (This is hypothetical, as I have not yet given any reasons for believing that they lack an IP, other than suggesting that in the relevant ways nests are not different from beds.)

There are other things that are the outcomes of natural processes but that we are not inclined to call "artifacts" at all: forests, for example, or lakes, or tadpoles. I shall argue that, in general, natural artifacts do not,

---

28 By a "genetic property" I mean a property like having-been-manufactured-in-Korea or having-been-born-in-Chicago.

on Aristotle's view, possess an IP any more than human artifacts do. But I shall also argue that there are things that are not artifacts even in the sense in which the bird's nest is an artifact – not artifacts in any sense at all – which nonetheless may not have an IP in Aristotle's scheme. That argument will come later; for now I merely make an observation.

The beaver makes a dam, and the dam creates a lake, but a mudslide might block the stream to just the same extent and at the same point at which the dam does, creating a lake just like the lake created by the beaver's dam. If the lakes are indistinguishable, then if either lake has no IP, neither should the other, and if either has an IP, so should the other. This says nothing, of course, about whether Beaver Lake and Mudslide Lake have an IP.

Now consider two distinct lakes: Arizona's Lake Meade, which is man-made, and Lake Michigan, which is natural. Can Lake Michigan have an IP, and so be a thing existing by nature, while Lake Mead lacks an IP, and so is not a thing existing by nature? Do the Rocky Mountains, the polar ice caps, and the Straits of Gibraltar have an IP? The wildebeest is a gregarious animal and so by nature is found in herds. But though wildebeest herds are natural, the herd may not be something that Aristotle would count as having an IP, not because it is artificial in any sense – it is not – but because, like lakes, mountains, ice caps, and straits, a herd might not be the right sort of thing in the first place.

F. Per Se Beings

In Book II of the *Physics*, Aristotle says that some people think that the substance or nature of a thing is its matter. Antiphon, he says, pointed out that "if you planted a bed and the rotting wood acquired the power of sending up a shoot, it would not be a bed that would come up, but wood, which shows that the arrangement in accordance with the rules of the art is merely an accidental attribute, whereas the substance is the other [i.e., the matter out of which the bed is made]" [193ª12–15]. Aristotle will eventually take this to show, not that the substance of a thing is its matter, but rather that the substance of a thing is its form, and will conclude that the bed possesses its form in a degenerate manner – accidentally.

Things that are artifacts possess their forms accidentally, at least in some sense, but at this point it is still an open question whether *all* things that possess their forms accidentally are artifacts, and whether some artifacts that are not things but rather substances in the current, mass sense of "substance" – e.g., bronze and honey – possess their forms essentially.

By way of anticipation, we shall see that the question of whether a given thing possesses its form essentially or accidentally is tied to an account Aristotle gives of the different sorts of unity things have.[29] For a heap of laundry to exist is for soiled clothes to be piled up. Until those clothes are tossed into a pile, there are dirty clothes but no pile of laundry. For a village or a forest to exist is for houses or trees to be in close proximity. If the houses and trees are sufficiently remote from others of their kind, there is no village or forest. A house exists because various boards, bricks, and panels have been assembled in a certain way. Until that takes place, there are building materials but no house, and after a tornado there may again be building materials but no house. A fasces exists because a bundle of wheat has been tied together so that the wheat stalks can be moved as a single unit. Before the stalks were tied together, and after the cord is cut, there is no fasces, there are just wheat stalks. The existence of the house and the fasces consists in their respective parts being joined in a certain way: nailed and glued in the one case; tied together in the other. Houses and bundles of sticks are assemblages. Their unity is due to each part's being contiguous with some other part; this is what makes a bundle of sticks one bundle, or a house one house.[30]

A tree's unity, on the other hand, does not consist in its various parts (its leaves, trunk, roots, and branches) being contiguous. Each part might be touching some other part, and yet there might not be a tree. This is true even if the parts are assembled in the correct order: the leaves taped to the branches, the branches nailed to the trunk, and the trunk cemented to the roots. There must be functional bonds between these parts – active interconnections that allow for the parts to enter into certain sorts of transactions with each other.

None of Aristotle's "things that exist by nature" possess the relatively weak unity of mere contiguity or proximity of parts. They may possess the unity of the tree; at the very least they possess the unity of a substance whose substratum does not differ in kind (*Metaphysics* V, 1016a18–23). Water has this latter kind of unity: a sample taken from the water in the pan is the same sort of substance as what is in the pan (i.e., water), whereas a sample taken from the pan is not the same sort of thing as the pan (i.e., is not itself a pan). A sample taken from a tin pan is the same mass-substance as the pan, for the sample will itself be tin. But it will not be the same *thing* as the pan, as a chunk of the pan is not a pan.

These are the basic problems and considerations that Aristotle faced as he sculpted his account of nature. The remainder of this book is an examination of his progress. I begin with his account of matter in its least informed state.

---

29 And by way of anticipation of the discussion of unity in Chapter 4, does it not seem odd to treat honey and milk, on the one hand, and spiders' webs and birds' nests, on the other, as on a par with one another on the ground that they are natural products?
30 See *Metaphysics* IV, 1003b23–33.

2

Elemental Motion and Alteration

In Chapter 1 we saw Aristotle introduce the Internal Principle of Change Principle (IPCP), but it remained rather abstract and we did not see how Aristotle applies it to actual cases. In this chapter I discuss his use of the principle in his accounts of elemental motion and alteration. This develops the notion of an Internal Principle of Change (IPC) and, I argue, leads him to the view that things need not always possess all their essential properties, though they must by nature be disposed toward possessing them. We can think of this as a principle of essentialist generosity, balancing his tendency to a restricted and elitist essentialism mentioned in the Introduction. (On the one hand, some plebeian things do not have essences; on the other, things that have essences get credit for trying, even if they fail.) In Chapter 5 I return to this theme.

I. Aristotle's Elements

In *On the Heavens* III, 3, Aristotle gives the following definition: "An element . . . is a body into which other bodies may be analyzed, present in them potentially or actually . . . and not itself divisible into bodies different in form" [302ª16–18]. He then goes on to say that fire and earth are potentially present in flesh and wood, for they can be drawn out of flesh and wood, but that flesh and wood are neither potentially nor or actually present in fire, for they cannot be drawn out of fire.[1]

In *Metaphysics* V, 3, an element is:

the primary component immanent in a thing, and indivisible in kind into other kinds, e.g., the elements of speech are the parts of which speech consists and into which it is ultimately divided, while they are no longer divided into other forms of speech different in kind from them. If they are divided, their parts are of the same kind, as a part of water is water (while a part of the syllable is not a syllable).

---

1 I say "drawn out" rather than the more common "separated out" because the latter seems to me to imply that the elements are actually present in the substance, whereas Aristotle leaves open the possibility that they are there only potentially.

33

Thus we should talk about the elements of F, rather than elements *simpliciter*. The elements of speech will not be the elements of material objects or bodies.

Why should we think that there are elements of bodies? In *Physics* I, 4, Aristotle argues that change is explicable through contraries, and he approves of his predecessors' having made basic contraries fundamental principles of nature, on the grounds that basic contraries meet a condition for fundamental principles: they "must not be derived from one another nor from anything else." This leaves open the question of which contraries are basic, but Aristotle's tendency is to accept the contraries favored by association with the traditional Greek elements: earth, air, fire, and water.

He has two distinct ways of justifying this. One, in *On Generation and Corruption* II, 2, is through his claim that the elements, being the principles of perceptible bodies, must differ perceptibly, and tangibility being the most primitive of perceptible characteristics, must differ according to tangible contraries: "That is why neither whiteness and blackness, nor sweetness and bitterness . . . constitutes an element." Perhaps he is thinking that perception involves a physical interaction between perceived and perceiver, and that therefore the most fundamental characteristics of perceptible bodies must pertain to them qua tangible.

He then argues that all tangible contraries are derived from two particular pairs: the hot and the cold, and the solid and the fluid. These two pairs of contraries constitute the elements: fire (hot and solid), air (hot and fluid), water (cold and fluid), and earth (cold and solid). Other tangible contraries, like viscous–brittle and coarse–fine, are derivative. The primary contraries must explain the active and passive powers of the elements, and Aristotle claims that heat–cold and solid–fluid do this. Heat and cold are active powers, heat associating similar substances, and cold associating both similar and dissimilar substances; and the fluid is that whose shape is determined by other things, while the solid is that which is "not readily adaptable in shape."

In settling on hot/cold and fluid/solid as defining the elements Aristotle explicitly excluded lightness and heaviness as contrary principles of perceptible bodies:

We must segregate the tangible differences and contrarieties, and distinguish which amongst them are primary. . . . Of these heavy and light are neither active nor susceptible. Things are not called heavy and light because they act upon, or suffer action from, other things. But the elements must be reciprocally active and susceptible, since they combine and are transformed into one another. [329a18–24]

Nevertheless, his second way of arriving at the elements is through a consideration of motion (which allows him to introduce the fifth, celestial, element). In *On the Heavens* IV, 4–5, he argues that there are four terrestrial elements through a consideration of natural motion, on the grounds that there must be absolutely heavy and absolutely light bodies, and relatively heavy and relatively light bodies. The Atomists explained the fact that small objects (e.g., iron balls) can be heavier than large objects (e.g., sponges) by saying that although all matter has an intrinsic downward tendency – that is, weight – some things are composed of densely packed atoms, while other things are composed of loosely packed atoms with a good deal of empty space between them. Matter, then, is inherently heavy, but whether a particular thing is heavy or not depends not simply on how much matter it incorporates, but on how diluted that matter is by voids between the atoms – depends, in other words, on its density. If an object of a given volume contains as much matter as an object of a smaller volume, the smaller object will be heavier.[2] (Meaning, I take it, that per unit of volume the smaller object is heavier.) This allows only relative heaviness, in that every body would have a downward tendency, and the difference between bodies would be only in how heavy they are. But Aristotle takes it to be an obvious truth that fire does not merely sink more slowly than earth, it actually rises. This could not happen if fire were a very dilute heavy substance; in that case it should fall, though slowly. That it rises shows that is by nature light, and not a dilute solution of heavy stuff. The atomist account allows only for relative lightness and heaviness; it allows that one body may weigh less than another, but it does not allow that a body might be absolutely light. It does not allow, in other words, that a body might have an actual upward tendency, rather than having a downward tendency that might seem like an upward tendency compared with other swifter downward tendencies. So Aristotle takes it as incompatible with the fact that some objects do not just sink more slowly than others but move in the opposite direction.

What shows this to be so is the fact that the earth is spherical and objects fall toward its center: the atomist account assumes that the earth is flat, and that there is no downward limit to an object's descent. In fact, the earth's crust is the limit, and fire really does rise from it – away from the center.[3] Aristotle has both theoretical and empirical observations for the earth's sphericity (*On the Heavens* II, 14). Empirically, the earth's shadow in lunar eclipses, and the fact that stars that set at temperate latitudes are circumpolar at more northerly latitudes, and, more generally, that travel north or south alters the altitude of observed stars, show that the earth is a sphere. (Aristotle's generation was the first for whom this was the dominant view.)

So earth is absolutely heavy and fire absolutely light. But there must

2 *On the Heavens*, 308ᵇ30–309ᵃ18, discussed in Cherniss (1935), pp. 210–211.
3 See Furley (1987), pp. 196–200.

also be elemental substances that are relatively heavy or light, intermediary between earth and fire, as there are substances that are lighter than earth but heavier than fire (*On the Heavens* IV, 5). The alternative would be for these substances to be mixtures of the absolutely light and heavy elements. Water, for example, might be 75% earth and 25% fire, and air 75% fire and 25% earth. But in that case a large quantity of water could contain more fire than a small quantity of air would (313ª11ff.).

Aristotle seems to view this as a decisive objection and says that he has often pointed this out, but it is difficult to see why this would refute the alternative view: even if a large amount of water contained more fire than a small amount of air, earth would still predominate in the water, so the water would still be heavier than the air. Aristotle seems to be assuming that either heaviness or lightness is a privation of the contrary characteristic rather than an opposing tendency. In explaining the alternative view, he supposes that the two forms of matter are void and plenum. Perhaps he is conceiving of plenum as having weight, and void as lacking weight, so that the more plenum an object has, the heavier it is, and void does not neutralize weight. In that case a large air bubble would be heavier than a drop of water, and we should occasionally see water droplets rising through air, "But such a thing has never been observed anywhere." This consideration might refute certain views of elemental motion, but why should it be telling if fire is conceived, as Aristotle conceives it, to have an actual upward tendency that could cancel out earth's downward tendency? The answer lies in his account of intermediate bodies.

Explicating intermediate bodies he says: "In its own place every body endowed with both weight and lightness has weight – whereas earth has weight everywhere – but they only have lightness among bodies to whose surface they rise" [312ᵇ2]. Air is light in water, but in its own place it is not light, and it sinks until it reaches water or until it is supported by underlying air. (That air has weight is shown "in the fact that a bladder when inflated weighs more than when empty" [311ᵇ9].) So a body that is heavy in one place can be light in another: "In air, for example, a talent's weight of wood is heavier than a mina of lead, but in water the wood is the lighter" [311ᵇ2].[4] Imagine a pallet of lumber heavier than a cannonball; but in water the cannonball is heavier than the lumber: the lumber floats, the cannonball sinks.

Now suppose we try to explain this on the assumption that the lumber is a mixture of Aristotle's earth and fire – 75% earth – while the cannonball is 100% earth. A mina being a sixtieth of a talent, the lumber has fifteen parts of fire that are offset by fifteen parts of earth, and a remainder of thirty parts of earth that give it its weight. The cannonball has one part of earth that gives it *its* weight. But this will be true whether the

---

4 Greek coins were based on weights of silver.

lumber and the cannonball are on land or are dropped into a lake, so we cannot *ex hypothesi* explain why the lumber floats in water while the cannonball sinks. There must be at least one elemental substance that is intermediate in weight between earth and fire. And since some things are heavy in air but light in water, these must both be such intermediary substances.

So there are four terrestrial elements – fire, hot and solid; air, hot and liquid; water, cold and liquid; and earth, cold and solid – with heat associated with lightness, cold associated with heaviness, and fluidity marking the intermediaries.

II. Elemental Motion[5]

A. The Elements Not Self-Movers

In *Physics* VIII, 4, Aristotle is trying to demonstrate that whatever is in motion is moved by something. This is obvious for unnatural motions: the man who throws a rock causes its upward motion [254b25]. It is less obvious in the case of the natural motions of self-movers, but even here we can be led to see, Aristotle thinks, that when an animal moves itself, one part is the mover and another the moved, and the animal as a whole moves itself only insofar as the mover moves the moved.

However, when we turn to the natural motions of inanimate substances, a difficulty arises. Aristotle, in talking about their "unnatural" motions, has implied that they also have natural motions: the light naturally rises; the heavy naturally falls. What is the mover in these cases? When a rock rolls downhill there is no obvious external mover, but rocks cannot be self-movers either: "It is impossible to say that they move themselves, for this is proper to animals and living things" [255a5–7].[6] Disregarding why he holds that only living things move themselves, let us examine the consequences of the belief.

Although the terrestrial elements have natural motions, because they are inanimate these motions must be due to external movers. But even if we took the terrestrial elements to be animate, there would still be the problem of explaining how they could effect their natural motion. In *On the Heavens*, Aristotle argues that spheres are by nature suited for rotation, but not for locomotion:

There is . . . the absurdity that nature has bestowed upon them no organ for such movement. For nature makes nothing by chance, and would not, while caring for animals, overlook things so precious. Indeed, nature seems deliberately to have stripped them of everything which makes self-originated progression possible, and to have removed them as far as possible from things which have organs of

5 This section has appeared in *Phronesis* (1994).
6 See also *Movement of Animals*, 700b6: "all inanimate things are moved by another."

movement. . . . For while of shapes the sphere is the most suitable for movement in the same place . . . for forward movement it is the most unsuitable, least of all resembling shapes which are self-moved, in that it has no discontinuous or projecting part, as a rectilinear figure has, and is in fact as far as possible removed in shape from ambulatory bodies. [290ª29–290ᵇ8]

Things that can move themselves along from place to place require organs that effect that motion, and spheres lack this: they have no wings, fins, or legs. (They can rotate, but that is "movement in the same place.") As they have no organs that could effect such a motion, they would seem to be incapable of initiating it.

Fires, rocks, clumps of earth, and quantities of air or water similarly lack organs. They are homogeneous rather than organic substances – uniform, rather than composed of functionally diverse parts. Their matter is internally undifferentiated – continuous in formula. At *Physics*, 255ª10–15, Aristotle, trying to explain the natural motions of the light and the heavy, asks:

How can anything continuous and naturally unified move itself? Insofar as a thing is one and continuous not merely in virtue of contact, it is impassive: it is only insofar as a thing is divided that one part is by nature active and another passive. Therefore none of these things move themselves (for they are naturally unified), nor does anything else that is continuous: in each case the mover must be separate from the moved. . . .

Only insofar as something is divided or internally differentiated can one part be active and another passive, which is required if the whole is to move itself from place to place: internal differentiation is necessary for progression, and the elements lack this.

Aristotle, then, has at least two reasons for maintaining that his simple terrestrial bodies are incapable of moving themselves: they are inanimate, and only animate things are self-movers, and in any case they do not possess the means for moving themselves. His main task now is to explain how, given that they are not self-movers, they can have natural motions. As a secondary task, he might also want to tell us what the mover is in the case of elemental motion. As the elements are not self-movers, there must be some external mover for them. What could this be? If he cannot do this he will either be unable to mark off the inanimate from the animate – rocks, in virtue of their natural motion, will turn out to be animate – or he will have to abandon the claim that self-movers are animate.[7]

---

7 This latter move would allow him to hold that the heavens are inanimate, though they are self-movers. His claim that self-movers are animate involves special problems when it is extended to the celestial realm. At 254ᵇ33–255ª21, Aristotle says that if the elements are self-movers they ought to be able to stop themselves (things that can make themselves walk can cease walking). So, he continues, if fire can move itself upward, it should also be

B. Nature and Internal Principles of Motion

There is a another way of framing the problem. Aristotelian natural motions fall into two kinds: (1) natural motions due to an internal mover, so the thing that is moving is, as a whole, self-moving (these are living things); and (2) natural motions due to an external mover. Cases of type (2) must be distinguished from violent motions, which also have external causes. Aristotle does not deny that the rock's fall is a natural motion – he insists on it. What he denies is that the rock is causing its own fall. Both the rock's violent and natural motions originate in another.

Since every motion must be either violent or natural, it follows that none of the rock's motions originate within it. This might seem to conflict with Aristotle's claim that the elements are "things that exist by nature," for as we saw in Chapter 1, he states in Book II of the *Physics* that, for things that exist by nature:

each of them has within itself a principle of change and of stasis (in respect of place, or of growth and diminution, or by way of alteration). On the other hand, a bed and a coat and anything else of that sort, *qua* receiving these designations – i.e., insofar as they are products of art – have no innate impulse to change. But insofar as they happen to be composed of stone or of earth or of a mixture of the two, they do have such an impulse, and just to that extent. . . . [192^{b}13–21]

If the natural motions of the elements are caused by another, rather than having an internal source in their natures, it might seem that they do not proceed from an internal principle, and so ought not to be counted as *natural* motions in the first place. I said earlier that Aristotle's main task is to explain how elemental motions can be natural, granted that they have an external cause. But the problem is not only to come up with an answer to this question, but to come up with an answer that is compatible with the account of nature in *Physics* II, which seems to require an internal principle for natural motions: how can a motion be natural to a body if that motion is due to an external cause?

C. Some Interpretations

In recent years several scholars have grappled with these problems, and there is general agreement on one portion of Aristotle's answer: Aristotle

able to move itself downward. (He gives no reason for this.) But if this were correct, he would have to give up his doctrine of celestial motion: the motion of the spheres and stars (a usage that includes the sun, moon, and planets) is eternal and unchanging – they cannot stop or reverse direction. Granted his view on celestial motion, the most, then, that could be said about the terrestrial elements on these grounds is that they are not the sort of self-movers that animals are, not that they are not self-movers at all.

Aristotle might nonetheless want to argue that his remarks are valid for the terrestrial realm. His claim of animacy for the heavens is, in any case, a difficult one for him, and conflicts with the account of life he gives in *On the Soul* II, 1; see Bolton (1978).

identifies the external cause of the motion as that which generated the element or that which removed the impediment to its natural motion. But this agreement about what Aristotle says is usually accompanied by some apprehension about the merits of his answer.

Sarah Waterlow Broadie argues that in giving this answer Aristotle abandons a principle he laid down in *Physics* III, 2: the changer determines the motion while it is happening:

> the remover of hindrances not only does not determine the form of the change, but might rather be said to gain its character *as* remover of hindrance from the very change of which it is supposed to be the agent. For what constitutes a hindrance, and what (therefore) the removal of one, depends on the direction of the tendency pre-existing in the simple body.[8]

I take her to mean that the person who, by pushing a rock off a ledge, removes the impediment to a rock's fall, does not make the rock fall; rather, the ledge is a hindrance only because the rock already has an intrinsic tendency to fall. (If the rock had an intrinsic tendency to rise, the ledge would have been no impediment to the rock's motion.) We can imagine a rock wedged in a horizontal crevice, unable to move up or down. The person who frees the rock by pushing it out of the crevice makes it possible for the rock to fall or to rise. Which path the rock will take is determined not by the pusher but by the rock.

Helen S. Lang points out that the generator and the impediment-remover are only accidental causes of the motion [255b27], not essential causes.[9] The essential cause of the motion, she says, is the rock's natural place, which causes the rock's natural motion.[10]

Mary Louise Gill points to another aspect of Aristotle's answer to the problem – his statement that although the elements have a principle of change, it is not a principle of changing something but of undergoing change [255b30–31] – a passive principle, and comments: "Aristotle's conclusion seems strangely unsatisfactory. What justification does he have for denying to the elements, which are responsible for their own motions, an internal active cause?"[11] But she concludes that Aristotle does have a justification. She sees Aristotle as believing that the elements would need an internal active principle only if they behaved in conflicting ways, and she takes him to hold that they do not do this:

> The elements move automatically upward or downward according to their natures, but they stop moving only because they are compelled to stop. Fire is not programmed to stop at the periphery; if there were no boundary contained by the fifth element, fire would continue its upward progression. Similarly, the down-

8 Waterlow (1982), pp. 167–168.
9 Lang (1984), pp. 69–106).
10 Ibid., p. 92.
11 Gill (1989), p. 238.

ward progress of earth is limited when it reaches the center because it can proceed downward no further.[12]

On this view, "The simple elements . . . which are constantly active, would move upward or downward indefinitely, except for the fact that their motion is externally limited."[13]

D. Another Interpretation

On Gill's view, the terrestrial elements have a "proper activity" of moving upward or downward according to their natures. This motion stems from their natures: it is intrinsic to them, and their motions cease only if something prevents them from moving farther. Their natural places, then, are the places where they can no longer continue to engage in their natural motions, either because they come up against another element or because they cannot continue downward once they have reached the center. On Lang's interpretation, "the proper activity of each element is to go to its proper place" – an activity that is actualized by the element's proper place.[14]

These accounts both accept an interpretation adopted by Friedrich Solmsen: "To be fire is to have a certain movement."[15] On Gill's interpretation, that movement is upward; on Lang's it is intrinsically to fire's natural place, but in either case to be fire is to have a certain natural motion.

The problem with this is that if the rock has its natural motion as its proper activity, then once the rock has arrived at its natural place it can no longer perform its proper activity – no longer actualize the pertinent potentiality. At that point the motion is no longer possible, and if the motion is no longer possible, the rock no longer has the potentiality for that motion.[16]

In explaining elemental motion Aristotle invokes his principle that potentiality is said in many ways [255a32]: the student of geometry and the scholar of geometry are potentially contemplators of geometrical

12 Ibid., p. 239
13 Ibid., p. 238. Gill takes elemental motion to be limited by the superior, confining, adjacent element, which therefore is the limit, and so in a sense the form of the inferior element [310b14–15]. Although the superior element is, in fact, the limit of the immediately inferior element, it does not follow that it limits or stops the inferior element. (Since earth's tendency is downward, water is not actively limited by water.) On my reading, air would remain in its natural place even if there were no circumscribing fire.
14 Lang, (1984), p. 85.
15 Solmsen (1960), p. 254; see also p. 269.
16 Lang's interpretation has the additional burden of explaining in what way places can act as causes. Lang cites Aristotle as saying that places have powers, but these could be passive powers, and at Physics IV, 1, 209a18–22, Aristotle, arguing against the claim that place is a body, asks, "of what in things is place the cause," for not one of the four types of cause can be ascribed to it?

truths in different ways. Water is potentially light in the way in which the student is potentially a contemplator: if the student studies, he will one day be able straightaway to contemplate geometrical theorems; and if water is transformed into air, it will be able straightaway to rise (lacking an impediment). Both the student and the water must change before they can acquire the pertinent disposition, but once the disposition is acquired it can generally be exercised without any further ado.

Once the rock is in its natural place, though, it can no longer exercise a disposition to move downward. It has become like the student, not the scholar, and must now undergo a change of place in order to reacquire its disposition downward. If someone throws it upward from the center, as it rises it reacquires the disposition. But if the disposition in question were intrinsic to the rock, then when the rock was at the center the rock possessed the disposition only *en dunamei,* just as water only possesses the disposition to rise *en dunamei.* And if the disposition is intrinsic or proper to rocks, it would follow (according to a well-known Aristotelian principle) that, at the center of the cosmos, rocks are rocks in name only – that is, that rocks can exist only away from their natural place.

We can avoid this difficulty by rejecting the premise that led to it: that is, by denying that Aristotle holds that fire, by its nature, has a natural motion. The potentiality for natural elemental motion, and thus the motion which is the actualization of that potentiality, is accidental to the elements. That a potentiality for *natural* motion could be accidental to its subject may sound paradoxical, but it is not. What is natural is the direction in which the substance, under certain conditions, will move, but the motion is not the actualization of an intrinsic disposition for that movement.

An intrinsic principle, according to Aristotle, need not be a principle of motion or change; it can be a principle of rest or stasis. Being inanimate, earth does not have an internal principle of motion: all its motions have an external principle. But it will nonetheless be "a thing that exists by nature" if it has an internal principle of rest or stasis. It is by invoking such a principle that Aristotle seeks to account for earth's natural motion. In the case of something with an internal principle of rest or stasis, all its motions, violent or natural, must have an external source. Its violent motions will be those that move it from its natural condition of stasis; its natural motions those that carry it toward its natural condition of stasis:

Rest, also, must either be violent or natural, violent in a place to which movement was violent, natural in a place to which movement was natural. Now manifestly there is a body which is at rest at the centre. If then this rest is natural to it, clearly motion to this place is natural to it. . . .

The moving thing must stop somewhere, and there rest not by constraint but naturally. But a natural rest proves a natural movement to the place of rest. [*On the Heavens,* 300ᵃ28–31, 300ᵇ6–8]

The change that restores it to its natural condition of stasis is natural in following from an intrinsic principle of rest. As we shall see, if we managed to turn something that is naturally hot cold, our cooling it would be a violent change and its subsequent change back to being hot once our meddling stopped would be a natural change. But the change back to its original condition would not take place because the thing has an intrinsic principle for *becoming* hot, but because it has an intrinsic principle for *being* hot. This principle is fully actualized once the object is hot; its actualization does not require that the object continue becoming hotter. Similarly, when the elements reach their natural places, their motions cease naturally. They do not need to be brought to a halt by external causes, though they do need to be brought into action by external causes. We can think of this as analogous to the tendency of sponges and springs under compression to revert to their normal forms. Once the compressive force is removed, they expand, not because they possess a natural tendency to expand, but because they possess a tendency to return to their natural condition of stasis. (And so it is the piston that compressed the spring which ultimately caused the spring's subsequent expansion, though the more direct cause is the force that withdrew the piston.) If they possessed a natural tendency to expand, the expansion would continue until it was brought to a halt by an external hindrance.

Aristotle holds, in other words, that although the rock has a natural motion downward, that is not because it has an intrinsic potentiality for downward motion. There is no intrinsic potentiality for downward motion, nor for any kind of motion, in rocks or earth. Indeed, for Aristotle an intrinsic potentiality for a natural rectilinear motion is impossible in a finite cosmos, for the continued actualization of such a natural principle would be inconsistent with the finitude of the cosmos. Eventually the object whose nature possessed the principle would reach either the outer boundary of the terrestrial universe or its center, at which point it would have a natural intrinsic principle that could not continue to be actualized, and Aristotle sees nature as a system that is structured by the actualization of natural potentialities, not by the thwarting of them.

What is natural to earth is not motion, but rest: to be, to stay, to remain in a certain place – i.e., down – not movement toward that place. The actuality of the heavy is not to move toward the center, but to be at the center, and once the impediment is removed that has been keeping a rock from being there, the rock's potentiality to be in that place is immediately actualized – or at least it would be were it not for the resistance of the medium.[17] The rock's natural potentiality to be in that place is

---

17 Aristotle denies the existence of a void on the grounds that since it is the resistance of the medium that slows things down, in a void speed would be infinite (Lloyd 1970, p. 114). Lloyd does not cite a passage in support of this claim; perhaps he had *Physics*, 215ᵇ12–23, in mind. On p. 115, Lloyd says that "the paradigm of Newtonian dynamics is one that we never observe except under artificial conditions, namely frictionless move-

straightaway actualized, just as the perceiver's capacity to see is straight-away actualized by the perceptible, but this actualization is not a motion: "the activity [*energeia*] of lightness consists in the light thing's being in a certain place, namely high up" [*Physics* VIII, 4, 255ᵇ11]. The actualization of the rock's intrinsic potentiality does not consist in its admittedly natural motion toward its natural place, but in the absence of motion when the rock is in that place, and perhaps in the rock's resistance to being moved from that place.

Of course, if the rock is away from that place this requires motion, but it is the rock's arrival in that place, not its motion toward that place, that is the actualization of the rock's nature as heavy: *the nature of the heavy is not to move toward some place, or in a certain direction, but to be in that place, and it actualizes that nature not by falling, but by being where fallen things end up.* So the motion is not caused by any intrinsic principle for motion in the rock, which as an inanimate object has no natural impulse to move. It is caused by whatever it is that is responsible for the rock's not being in its natural place. This might be something that brought the rock into existence away from its natural place, or something that moved it away from its natural place. Once this has happened, if there is no impediment, there will be a *kath' hauto* motion, for the motion is due to the rock's nature as heavy, though the rock has no intrinsic potentiality for the motion. Thus we may say either that the essential cause of the rock's natural motion is its nature, though not as a motive principle, or, in view of this qualification, that there is no essential cause for the rock's motion – there are only accidental causes.[18] No essential cause is needed, for the motions of the terrestrial elements, whether natural or violent, are accidental to them. (The case is quite different with the fifth element, but then the fifth element possesses an eternal motion.) This is why, following Sarah Water-low Broadie's remarks, the (accidental) cause does not determine the motion while it is happening.[19] (And note that motion toward some place and in a certain direction are not the same: water's natural motion is always toward its natural place, but whether this is a motion upward or downward depends on whether the water is generated in the earth or in the sky, and is itself in that way accidental.) Perhaps this is the point of

ment through a void." If we look up at night we observe such motions under natural conditions.

18 This may require a broader notion of accidental causation than is allowed for by Cynthia A. Freeland (1991), pp. 53–54 and 69. On Freeland's view, accidental causation "always depends upon two things: a proper or intrinsic causal relation, and an accidental unity." The accidental unity might obtain between, e.g., a professional philosopher and, as we say in Tennessee, a "shade-tree" mechanic – i.e., someone who is not a mechanic by profession but does his own car repairs. Such an accidental unity *may* be involved in the motions I am discussing, but it is not clear to me that it is.

19 Cf. the scholastic distinction between essentially and accidentally ordered series of causes. Only with an essentially ordered series of causes does the persistence of the effect require the persistence of the cause.

Aristotle's closing assertion, at 256ª4, that rocks fall not because they move themselves but because they have a principle, not of causing motion, but of undergoing it. The rock suffers natural motion due to an external cause, and moves only that it may rest in peace.[20]

I do not mean by this to suggest that Aristotle's elements have no active natural potentialities. Fire's heat is an active natural potentiality, but it is a principle of change in others, not in the fire: fire's heat does not cause any changes in fire, but it can melt snow. The light and the heavy do not in this way act on other things. See *On Generation and Corruption* II, 1 329ᵇ21–22: "heavy and light are neither active nor passive: for neither because they act on others nor are acted upon by others are things called heavy or light." In saying that things which exist by nature have an internal principle of change or stasis, Aristotle means that they have an internal principle for change or stasis in themselves. He does not mean that they possess internal principles for producing change or stasis in others. If he did, curbs would be things that exist by nature because they have an intrinsic capacity to arrest the motion of carts.

III. Elemental Change and Substances That Lack Some of Their Essential Characteristics

We are inclined to think (1) that if a thing cannot exist without a certain characteristic, that characteristic is essential to the thing, and conversely, (2) that if a characteristic is essential to a thing, that thing cannot exist without that characteristic.[21] But as I said in the Introduction, outside of the biological works Aristotle is reluctant to use the survivability criterion. In Chapter 4 we shall look at reasons for this having to do with his accounts of unity and the unity of definition. I will argue, for example, that there are reasons for taking Aristotle to deny that heaps have essences, and by this I do not mean that a heap *as such* has no essence: I mean that heaps have no essence *at all*. If this is so, he cannot argue that if a thing cannot survive without a certain characteristic, that characteristic is essential to the thing. For even if my woodpile has no essence, we nonetheless can describe circumstances (e.g., post-tornado) under which it will have ceased to exist. In other words, the fact that x can only persist if it has characteristic C does not entail that C is essential to x. If x has no essence, nothing is essential to it, but we can still describe the conditions under which it will have perished. This gives us a reason why Aristotle might have been reluctant to argue that (1) if x cannot exist without C, C is essential to x. A similar case might be made for artifacts in Aristotle, for it is possible that he held that although they do not have

---

20 This view seems to be accepted by Wedin (1994), pp. 95–96.
21 Though White (1972) pointed out that "the modal notions of necessity and possibility . . . play no explicit role in Aristotle's cogitations concerning sensible particulars."

essences, they can be defined in a sense:[22] we can explain what a house is and in so doing set forth conditions under which houses come into and pass out of existence. So it is not clear that Aristotle is committed to (1). A completely different line of inquiry gives us a reason why Aristotle might have been reluctant to accept (2) – the principle that if C is essential to x, x cannot exist without C – and this is the subject of the current section.

Aristotle's account of the elements differs from those of some of his predecessors in that he allows the elements to be transformed into one another, and not only to move about but also to undergo alteration. The way in which he does this raises some problems. We say that a characteristic is *essential* to something if that thing cannot exist without it. But, I will argue, although this *may* be Aristotle's usage in the logical works, it is not his usage in his later works. There he holds that things can exist while lacking essential characteristics. I will derive this conclusion from a consideration of Aristotle's account of elemental alteration but then immediately argue that it is also implicit in his account of elemental motion.

A. The Paradox

We have seen that Aristotle distinguishes the terrestrial elements by means of a pair of primary contraries: hot and cold, solid and fluid. Fire is hot and solid, air hot and fluid, water cold and fluid, and earth cold and solid (see, e.g., *On Generation and Corruption*, 330[b]1–5). But if air is essentially hot, why do we bundle up when we go outdoors in the winter? And Aristotle knows that water can boil[23] and freeze:

We see the same body liquid at one time and solid at another, without losing its continuity. . . . It has passed from the liquid to the solid state without any reordering or transposition in its nature. Nor are there contained within it those hard (i.e., congealed) particles indivisible in their bulk; on the contrary, it is liquid – and again, solid and congealed – uniformly all through. [327[a]16–23]

Plato, using a similar example, came up with a different account: "snow will never . . . admit the hot and still be what it was, namely snow, and also hot; but at the advance of the hot it will either get out of the way or perish" [*Phaedo*, 103D].[24] On Plato's view, snow and ice are essentially cold, and if they admit the hot, they perish. On Aristotle's view, they do not perish when they melt; they merely undergo an alteration, becoming liquid water.[25]

But how can water boil or freeze in the first place, "without any reordering or transposition in its nature," if water is essentially cold and

---

22 See, e.g., *Metaphysics* VII, 4, 1030[a]6–17.
23 In fact, he says that boiling water "is more scalding than flame" (*Parts of Animals*, 648[b]26).
24 I use the Gallop translation in the Clarendon Plato Series.
25 See also *Posterior Analytics*, 95[a]16–20, and *Metaphysics* VIII, 1043[a]9–10.

liquid? How can something that is *essentially* cold and liquid possess the contrary characteristics? Yet Aristotle acknowledges that this happens: "Ice, for example, or any other solidified fluid, is spoken of as being actually and accidentally solid, while potentially and essentially it is liquid [*Parts of Animals*, 649ᵇ11–13]." Ice, being water, is essentially fluid, though being frozen water it is actually solid. Hence, because a characteristic is essential to a thing does not mean that the thing will actually have it. It may have it only potentially, and it may accidentally have the contrary characteristic.

This problem does not just arise for elemental alteration. It also arises for Aristotle's other way of distinguishing the terrestrial elements – i.e., according to their natural motions or places – and here too the equivalent paradox arises. We just saw in Section II ("Elemental Motion") that on the received interpretation of his doctrine of elemental motion, he thinks motion toward a certain place is essential to terrestrial elements: earth, for example, has an innate tendency to move downward; fire, an innate tendency to move upward.[26] According to my interpretation, what is essential to the elements is not an inherent tendency to move toward some place, but rather to be at rest in that place: what is essential to earth, pace Aristotle, is not motion toward the center of the universe, but to be at rest in the center. (Of course, this requires motion if the rock is up on a ledge.) But on either interpretation, one of these will be true: it is an essential characteristic of the rock on the ledge to be at the center of the universe, or it is an essential characteristic of the rock on the ledge to be falling toward the center. Yet, on either interpretation, the rock does not have the property in question. It is sitting on a ledge on a mountainside. It is neither resting at the center nor moving toward the center. One can say, as Aristotle does, that the rock is where it is, and is stationary, owing to an external impediment. But in any case there is something that seems to be essential to the rock that it lacks. It is immobile, high up, yet its nature is either to be heading toward the center or to be at rest at the center.

We are inclined to think that if a characteristic is essential to a thing, the thing cannot exist without the characteristic. Aristotle thinks that a thing can be essentially cold, yet hot; essentially fluid, yet solid; essentially falling, yet stationary; essentially there, yet here.

In the paragraph of the *Parts of Animals* that follows the one I have cited, Aristotle says that blood

is spoken of as boiling water would be if it were denoted by a single term. But the substratum of blood, that which it is while it is blood, is not hot. Blood, then, in a

26 This will not quite work for Aristotle's two intermediate elements, air and water, for whether they have an inherent tendency to move upward or downward will depend on where they are: air in a submerged balloon moves upward, while air in the fiery realm sinks; water that forms in the sky moves downward, but subterranean water rises.

certain sense is essentially hot, and in another sense is not so. For heat is included in the definition of blood, just as paleness is included in the definition of a pale man, but so far as blood becomes hot from some external influence, it is not hot essentially.

Fire is essentially hot. Blood, on the other hand, is heated by the heart, and once it leaves the body it cools. The necessity whereby blood is hot is, in the medieval terminology, *de dicto:* it is just as though, he says, we had a single term for boiling water. Boiling water is *de dicto* necessarily hot, since it is boiling, but it can cool off while remaining water.

His claim, then, is that something that is essentially cold or liquid can survive becoming hot or solid if it has become hot or solid due to some external cause. The water in the kettle boils, but is still water; the water in the ice-cube container freezes, but is still water. An essential characteristic lost through external cause or impediment remains essential to the subject, though *per accidens* the subject no longer possesses it. The subject survives so long as its list of essential characteristics is unchanged, but it need not actually possess all the characteristics on its list. So long as its shopping list is intact, it is intact.

B. Dispositional Essentialism

Aristotle was not oblivious to the paradoxical sound of these statements, and he has a way of addressing this problem. He does so by drawing a distinction between actual characteristics and natural tendencies.

I argued above that the rock's natural motion downward is due to an external cause, and that the rock's nature (and that of all other inanimate substances) is an internal principle of stasis, not of change: the rock's nature is not to move – if it moved by nature its motion would not require an external cause – but rather to rest at the center. We can similarly suppose that water, by its nature, is cold and liquid, and has no tendency to change. Under external influence, though, it may freeze or become hot. Withdraw that external influence and it is in a similar condition to the rock suspended in midair, and will revert to its natural condition. What is essential to a thing, then, is indicated, not by the characteristics it actually possesses, but by the characteristics its nature calls forth, whether or not reality complies.

The difference between ice and earth, then, is that while both are cold and solid, the solidity of earth is natural, whereas the solidity of ice is violent. (*Kinêsis* can cover changes that are not movements.) The freezing of water is due to external cold, whereas the melting of ice is a natural alteration: withdraw the external source of coldness and the ice reverts to the state dictated by its internal heat. Aristotle conceives water to have a natural heat that under normal conditions maintains it as a liquid, so "ice is an excess of cold" (*On Generation and Corruption*, 330^{b}26). Similarly, water's coming to a boil is a violent alteration due to external heat, its subsequent cooling a natural alteration dictated from within. The distinction between violent and natural motions in Aristotle is accompanied by a distinction between violent and natural alterations (though I do not recall his ever using this phrase).[27] As early as the *Topics* this notion is emerging: "every affection, if intensified, subverts the substance of the thing, while the differentia is not of that kind, for the differentia seems rather to preserve that which it differentiates" [145a4–6].

To deal with inhibited elemental motion he introduces a distinction. "Potentiality" is said in many ways. One who is learning geometry "knows potentially in a different way from one who while already possessing the knowledge is not actually exercising it" (*Physics* VIII, 4, 255a33–35). The President of France can speak French. American children (but not kittens) have the ability to speak French, too (after all, some of them will one day speak it, and French children can speak French, though they are no brighter than American children), but in a different sense: the American child must first learn French. To actualize the second sort of potentiality requires going through a process of change: the student must study, and this takes time. But once you actually possess the relevant capacity, it can be exercised straightaway, in the absence of any external impediment. Once you have sight you have only to look to see – unless someone has turned out the lights. Once water has formed in the atmosphere it will immediately fall – unless it formed in a cup. The actualization of the capacity to speak French rather than to learn French does not require any further changes.

Sometimes Aristotle pushes this to a third degree of potentiality. Every American child can grow up to be president, but first he has to grow up – there is a minimum-age requirement. The human fetus is potentially sentient, but not in the sense a sleeping child is: the fetus must go through a process of development in which sense organs form; the child need only awaken. Infants can speak French, but not while they are infants.

In *On the Soul* II, 1, Aristotle says the soul is a form and first act of a living thing, where by "first act" he means an actual capacity as opposed both to its exercise and to potential capacities. Invoking the same rubric, we can say that heaviness is a form and first act of the rock. What is really essential to the rock, then, is not motion toward or resting at the center, but rather the corresponding first act: the natural disposition or capacity of the rock to move toward or be at the center, the exercise of which "follows at once upon the possession of it unless something prevents it."[28]

---

27 Gill, in Gill and Lennox (1994), pp. 25–28, discusses "enforced changes" in Aristotle, drawing on examples that are not cases of locomotion.
28 *Physics*, 255b22–23, where Aristotle is talking about the exercise of knowledge.

The living thing is defined as having a certain set of capacities that it need not always be exercising; the rock similarly.

He makes the same appeal to the actuality–potentiality distinction when he addresses the corresponding problem with contrary qualities. In *Parts of Animals*, 649ᵇ10–13, he says that "solid" and "liquid" are said in different ways: "Sometimes, for instance, they denote things that are potentially, at other times things that are actually, solid or liquid. Ice, for example, or any other solidified fluid, is spoken of as being actually and accidentally solid while potentially and essentially it is liquid." An infant, perhaps, is essentially and potentially rational, though it cannot handle the simplest syllogism. Aristotle seems in general to take the same approach with all living things, which only intermittently engage in their essential activities: reproduction, self-nourishment, growth, perception, desire, etc. What is really essential to them, we might say, is that they are disposed toward these activities or have the capacity to engage in them, not that they actually do so. If I am right to invoke the infant, this includes cases in which the thing has *never* actually possessed the characteristic in question. Even if I am wrong to invoke the infant, the same claim may apply to hail, if Aristotle thought it can form in the atmosphere directly from vapors without first becoming liquid water. And even if I am wrong on both of these points, it remains true that Aristotle, at least when he was writing the *Parts of Animals*, thought that you do not have to possess a characteristic for it to be essential to you.

C. Generation and Corruption

In *On Generation and Corruption* II, 2, Aristotle defines fluid as "that which, being readily adaptable in shape, is not determinable by any limit of its own, while solid is that which is readily determinable by its own limit, but not readily adaptable in shape." Water adapts itself to the shape of the container; the rock does not. Aristotle, in the passage quoted above (649ᵇ10–14), means to be distinguishing solids from solidified liquids, and liquids from melted solids. The solidified liquid and the melted solid are accidentally in their current states, but this does not change their essential natures. The solidified liquid, we might say, is not *really* a solid. And we would seem then also to have to hold that boiling water is not *really* hot. It has merely been heated.

But there must be some conditions under which the change has a more lasting effect, and the water is transformed into earth, even if this requires some admixture of earth as a sort of catalyst. In *Meteorology* IV, 1, he describes the action of heat and cold in forming new substances:

Next we must describe the operations of the active qualities and the forms taken by the passive. First of all, unqualified becoming and natural change are the work of these powers and so is the corresponding natural destruction; and these are found in plants and animals and their parts. Unqualified natural becoming is a change introduced by these powers into the matter underlying a given natural thing when they are in a certain ratio; and matter is the passive qualities we have mentioned. When the hot and the cold are masters of the matter they generate a thing: if they are not, the object is imperfectly boiled or otherwise unconcocted. [378^{b}31–379^{a}2]

In some cases of concoction the end of the process is the nature of the thing – nature, that is, in the sense of form or essence. In other cases it leads to some latent form. [379^{b}25–27]

"Concoction," he says, "is a process in which the natural and proper heat of an object perfects the corresponding passive qualities [solidity and fluidity], which are the proper matter of any given object. For when concoction has taken place we say that a thing has been perfected and has come to be itself. It is the proper heat of a thing that sets up this perfecting, though external influences may contribute in some degree to its fulfillment" [379^{b}19–23]. We are to imagine that under the right but unspecified conditions, a liquid can be so transformed that its natural heat has become that of earth, and its natural heat then solidifies the substance. This new substance will not melt at room temperature.

Aristotelian natural substances possess an intrinsic heat. Extrinsic heat may make them hotter, but withdraw the source of extrinsic heat and they revert to the degree of warmth dictated by their intrinsic heat. (The situation might be compared to that of a house whose furnace is set to sixty-eight degrees on a day when the outside temperature reaches ninety degrees.) Sometimes, though, the hot and the cold "master the matter" and "generate a thing." In this case a new substance has formed, with a new intrinsic heat. The water boils and turns to steam, which heated further may be transformed into air. Now we have a new substance: air is not hot water, though it is hot and fluid, and boiling water is not air, though it is hot and fluid. Air, even cold air, is essentially hot, while boiling water is only accidentally hot. Aristotle accepts what might be called a "*dispositional essentialism*": though hot water and hot air are both hot, and though both can cool without perishing, the difference is that air is disposed toward being hot, and water disposed toward being cool – this makes them essentially different.

This may not have always been Aristotle's view. In the *Topics*, widely thought to have been written before he worked out the actuality-potentiality distinction, an accident is something that may belong or not belong to the same thing: the same thing may be white at one time, not white at another, sitting at one time, not sitting at another [102^{b}3–10; see also 120^{b}30–35]. Presumably an essential characteristic would be one that must belong to the same thing at all times.[29] In the *Physics, Politics,* and *Parts of Animals,* however, he holds that even an essential characteristic may or may not belong to the same thing: water may be liquid at one time and solid at another, yet remain essentially liquid; air may be hot at one time and cold at another, yet remain essentially hot. "Essentially F" must be read dispositionally: being essentially F does not entail being actually F. To say that a thing is essentially F means that it has a natural tendency to be F, and this can be so even if it is not F.[30] And since a natural tendency is a tendency resulting from an IP, only things with natures have essences.

Aristotle's usage allows that a thing may be essentially F even though it is not actually F. It will be essentially F if it is F by nature, even though it is not at the moment actually F. It follows that the fact that a characteristic is essential to you is not a guarantee that you will have it for as long as you live. Indeed, you may never have it, and never have had it.

Gill has pointed out the tendency of higher-level Aristotelian substances to be self-maintaining or self-preserving.[31] I see that same tendency even at the level of Aristotle's elements. His elements are disposed to be what they are – disposed to claim their essential birthright – but they live in a dangerously diverse world in which external forces can overwhelm the inherent power of air and fire to be hot, or of water and earth to be cold. The ultimate cause for their perilous condition is, I take it, the same as the cause for their generation: the movement of the sun along the ecliptic, generating the seasons by warming and cooling the terrestrial realm.[32]

D. Conclusion

We can treat this as a matter of mere usage. We can say that Aristotle, speaking loosely, says that water is essentially liquid, but that, speaking

---

29 Though the same warnings I voiced earlier still apply: how we interpret this depends on what counts as a thing; if a child is a thing, we are free to hold that it is essentially youthful. In fact, one of the motives for dispositional essentialism may be to allow ruling out children per se (and ice per se) as things.

30 In the *Timaeus,* Plato holds that water and metals mixed with fire are liquid [59D]; with the fire driven out they are solid. (Liquids, for Plato, are mixtures involving fire, but water, composed of smaller and less uniform particles than metals, requires less heat than metals do to be liquid – i.e., water is more disposed to fluidity.) This seems to imply that pure water and pure metals are solid, while liquid ice (water) is a mixture of ice and fire, and molten iron a mixture of iron and fire. By their natures, then, Platonic water and metals are solid, though fire may turn them into liquids.

31 Gill (1989), pp. 212–242; see also Matthews (1992), pp. 191–193.

32 *Generation and Corruption* II, 10. Aristotle, like many people today, gets the mechanism wrong, assuming that the seasons are due to changes in the distance between the sun and the earth (which plays a very minor role), rather than the angle at which the sun's rays strike an area.

strictly, he should say that water is essentially *disposed* toward being a liquid, which is compatible with actually being solid.

Even so, at the very least we need to read Aristotle more carefully. For whether he is speaking loosely or strictly when he says that *x* is essentially *F* must be determined from the context, and the context might not always give a clear verdict. Furthermore, treating this as a matter of mere usage may not give sufficient weight to the philosophical difficulties Aristotle's position engenders. At the two ends of his metaphysical inventory of the terrestrial realm – elements and people[33] – his essentialism is dispositional. It is possible that everything in the terrestrial realm fits this pattern. The celestial realm works differently. The motion of the celestial spheres is eternal and unceasing. Heavenly objects do not face external impediments, so the potential–actual distinction plays a smaller role there. Jupiter is potentially in Gemini but actually in Taurus; the Sun has just risen but is potentially on the meridian – that is all you get. In the celestial realm, motion is natural and unthwarted, and celestial objects continually engage in it. Their capacities are exercised without interruption.

The growth of a child, on the other hand, though natural, can be thwarted by an inadequate diet. The decently fed child, however, does not decide to grow; his growth, to a certain limit, is natural, though contingent on external circumstances. This is why Aristotle can identify the formal cause with the final cause for things that are not artifacts: the formal cause is the final cause because the child by nature, barring external impediments, will actualize his potentiality to possess the characteristics he is essentially disposed to possess. By contrast, the unassembled toy will not. The only thing it is disposed to do by nature is to fall to the ground and rust, and that is not because it is the toy it is, but because of its matter.

On the other hand, anyone who has hired a contractor knows that it is false that a carpenter's ability to build will be exercised if there is no external impediment. Sometimes you even have to cajole him. The distinction between the exercise of a capacity and other forms of change is no help here. What Aristotle needs to work out is the distinction between essential and accidental or acquired dispositions.[34] Can he do this without giving up something else? For example, I take it that he wants to hold that the descent of a rock, as the exercise of a first act, does not involve the rock's changing, and this makes some sense: the rock moves to a different place, so its location changes, but the rock *itself* is not undergoing an alteration as it moves – it looks just the same on arrival as it did at departure. But can he maintain that since the melting of ice is also the

33 For the account of people and other living things, see Chapter 5.
34 Note that the distinction between natural and acquired dispositions is not the same as that between natural and artificial potentiality in Whiting (1992), pp. 91–92.

exercise of a first act, ice as it melts is not altering? Or that, for the same reason, the coffee in my cup is not undergoing an alteration as it cools? Although one can make sense of the claim that a car can go from here to there without changing (at the end of the trip, assuming no accidents enroute, the car arrives in just the condition in which it left), cooling and melting are paradigmatic alterations.

I have quoted Aristotle as saying that even though blood is hot, "the substratum of blood, that which it is while it is blood, is not hot." I take it that he would then also say that the substratum of ice is liquid, and the substratum of boiling water is cold. As ice melts, then, its substratum is not changing. This will have important repercussions for his accounts of elemental transformation and of the difference between alteration, on the one hand, and generation and corruption, on the other – the topics of our next chapter.

It would seem unlikely that Aristotle will be able to provide a plausible sense in which melting and cooling are not changes, and therefore retain his account of the difference between change and the actualization of a capacity – at least, as I have explained the doctrine. The doctrine, however, was ill-fated from the start if it is taken to cover all dispositions: the cracked vase *has* changed. If we take it to cover only the exercise of natural active capacities, the chances look better. But how, then, do we account for the development of an embryo? Growth is a form of change. We shall turn to this problem in Chapter 5.

Chapter 5, however, deals with living things, and before we can explore Aristotle's account of them, we first have to discuss Aristotle on unity. So far we have dealt only with the elements, but Aristotle has a complex account of unity according to which the unity the elements possess is not highly developed, whereas his account of living things involves both the dispositional essentialism I have argued for in this chapter and his account of their unity. Thus Chapter 5 follows Chapter 4, which is an exploration of Aristotle's account of unity. His is an account of what he thinks makes a thing be one thing; but before we can understand this, we need to discuss the circumstances under which he thinks one thing ends and another begins. So the topic of the next chapter is generation, corruption, and persistence. We begin with the most elemental cases and work our way up, but we cannot work our way up very far without Chapter 4.

3

Elemental Transformation and the
Persistence of Matter

Aristotle's elements, we saw in Chapter 2, have a bipolar constitution: on
the one hand, each element has an Internal Principle of Change (IPC) in
virtue of which it is disposed to be what it is; on the other hand, each
element can be driven by external forces from what it is, lose its nature,
and perish. The first of these possibilities it owes to its form; the second
its owes somehow to its matter.

In the last chapter we were primarily concerned with elemental motion and alteration. In this we turn to the role of these two factors (form
and matter) in two basic processes: elemental transformation, which
Aristotle holds is the coming-to-be and perishing of elements; and the
creation of homogeneous compounds out of elements, which he holds
does not involve the coming-to-be and perishing of elements. I conclude
by showing how dispositional essentialism can help with some puzzles
regarding the difference between these two processes.

I. Change and Continuity

A. Prime Matter

For a quarter-century Aristotle's interpreters have disagreed over his
doctrine of prime matter.[1] One school contends that Aristotle is not
committed to prime matter;[2] the other, that he is committed to it.[3] The
issue has been put with admirable clarity by H. M. Robinson:

Aristotle argues that every change has something which underlies it (e.g.,
190ª31–b9). What underlies a change is the matter of that change (e.g., 1042b9–
11). This has traditionally been taken to mean that, in every change, there is

---

1 This section is a revised version of Cohen (1984).
2 See, e.g., King (1956); Charlton (1970 and 1983); Jones (1974); Furth (1988); Gill
   (1989); Scaltsas (1994b). Gill, p. 45, rejects the interpretation I advance here on grounds
   I address in sec. I (B) ("The Persistence of Matter") below. I am not convinced that when
   all the qualifications are factored in, her views and mine are all that different.
3 E.g., Solmsen (1958); Robinson (1974); Dancy (1978); Lewis (1991).

something which is first a part of the whole which precedes the change, and then a part of the whole which succeeds it; thus what underlies a change persists through it. When a substance alters in an accidental fashion the matter of the change is the substance itself, for that persists through the change. When the change involves the forming of a new substance from an old one, then the matter of the change is that which constitutes first the one substance then the other: thus if I turn an iron statue into cannonballs the iron is what underlies this change. Aristotle believes that the elements (air, fire, earth and water) can change into each other (e.g., 305ª14–35). As there is no identifiable matter more primitive than the elements (305ª14–35) there is a problem about what underlies such change. The traditional interpretation of Aristotle's treatment of this problem is that he posits a *prime matter,* a bare 'stuff,' lacking all positive determinations, which is the matter of the elements and which makes elemental change possible. This prime matter is nothing but a potentiality which can exist only as actualized in some determinate matter – i.e., in one of the elements – and which is what persists when one contrariety is replaced by another and the identity of an element changes.[4]

And then there is the novel interpretation. According to the new reading:

the elements are the most fundamental sort of matter. This alternative theory is the only one open to someone who rejects the traditional notion. It is agreed that Aristotle rejects the conceptions of a matter more basic than the elements which make it either a type of body in its own right, or separable from the elements or purely geometrical. . . . Therefore if there is some matter more basic than the elements it must not be a type of body in its own right, nor purely geometrical and it must be inseparable from the elements. These conditions describe prime matter as traditionally conceived. If this conception is to be rejected there can be no matter more basic than the elements.[5]

The one side, then, holds that Aristotle posits a common matter for the four elements and therefore is committed to prime matter. The other side holds that Aristotle does not posit a common matter for the four elements, and hence is not committed to prime matter. In the first section, "Common Matter and the Indeterminate," I shall argue that each side is half right and half wrong: Aristotle does posit a common matter for the four elements, but this does not commit him to prime matter. The common matter of the four elements is not prime – that is, it is not bare or characterless.

Not only are these interpretations wrong in taking Aristotle to be committed to a bare, indeterminate matter if he is committed to a common matter for the four elements; they are also wrong on the considerations that would lead Aristotle to infer a common matter for the four elements in the first place. Both the traditional and the revisionist inter-

4 Robinson (1974), p. 168.
5 Ibid., p. 169.

pretations hold that if Aristotle is committed to a common matter it will be because he thinks it a general truth that all change (and hence elemental transformation) requires a persisting substratum. But, I will argue in the second section "Elemental Transformation and the Persistence of Matter," Aristotle's case for a common material substrate for the four elements does not derive from a general claim about all change but from more local considerations: elemental transformation has a particular feature that indicates a persisting material substratum, but Aristotle denies that *every* change has this quality. He is not led to common matter because he holds a general doctrine of change that takes him there; if anything, I suspect that his general doctrine of change derives from his analyses of what seemed to him to be diverse types of change.[6]

When Aristotle turns to more complex substances and moves from physics to chemistry, and then to biology, he sees the principles of persistence shift. What was true for elemental transformation need not be true for growth or death. Form and final cause, which are obscure even if not absent at lower levels of organization (*Meteorology*, 389b28 ff.), come to the fore, and we are able to see that form has a greater claim than matter to be called "substratum." This suggests that to understand Aristotle we need to drive a wedge between the notions of a persisting matter and a persisting substratum to allow for cases in which form, not matter, is the more rightful substratum.

Common Matter and the Indeterminate. According to Robinson, the traditionalists hold that Aristotle believes that a persisting matter underlies every change. In elemental change,

as there is no identifiable matter more primitive than the elements . . . there is a problem about what underlies such change. The traditional interpretation of Aristotle's treatment of this problem is that he posits a *prime matter,* a bare "stuff," lacking all positive determinations, which is the matter of the elements and which makes elemental change possible. This prime matter is nothing but a potentiality. [Robinson (1974), p. 168]

Thus Dancy refers to "Aristotle's commitment to something characterless, which comes of applying the format for describing changes to elemental transformations."[7] The revisionists, on the other hand, hold that

---

6 Scaltsas (1994b), p. 15, n. 10, disagrees with me. His view is that "the numerical sameness of matter throughout transformation is a general requirement of Aristotle's theory of matter, deriving from the Physical Continuity Principle." On Scaltsas' view, Aristotle's general account of change requires physical continuity: "a seamless spatiotemporal material worm." I agree, but Scaltsas adds that this continuity involves the numerical identity through time of a material substratum: "The only requirement for the *numerical oneness* of the material substratum throughout the transformation process is that it remain material and physically continuous." I discuss this issue below, where I argue that Aristotle denies that continuity always involves numerical identity.

7 Dancy (1978), p. 391.

Aristotle acknowledges "no matter more basic than the elements." Both sides equate the claim that there is "a wholly indeterminate substratum" with the claim that there is a single matter for the four elements – a claim Charlton takes Aristotle to reject.[8]

This raises two questions. The first is whether Aristotle thought that there is a single matter for the four elements. As usual, Aristotle's answer is yes and no, and texts can be cited on both sides of the question. But in the main I think the answer is yes.

At *Generation and Corruption*, 332a3–18, Aristotle argues that fire cannot be hot air, for fire and air are distinguished by contrariety, fire being hot and air being cold, so that if fire were hot air the same thing would possess contrary properties: hot air would be both hot and cold. He concludes that "both fire and air, therefore, will be something else which is the same; i.e., there will be some other matter common to both."[9]

At 334a15–18 he says: "The theories that there is something common to all the elements, and that they are reciprocally transformed, are so related that those who accept either are bound to accept the other as well." Since everyone is agreed that Aristotle generates the elements out of one another, he seems here to be committing himself to something common to the elements, and at 23–25 he says, "Water can come to be out of fire, and fire out of water, for their substratum is something common to them both."

At 334a22 he talks about a difficulty that arises for those who generate the elements out of one another, and then at 334b2–3, where he seems to have his own view in mind, he talks about a difficulty arising for those who posit a single matter for the elements, apparently equating generating the elements out of one another with positing a single matter for the elements.

In *On The Heavens*, Aristotle gives us some details:

The same holds consequently of the matter itself of that which is heavy and light: as potentially possessing the one character, it is matter for the heavy, and as potentially possessing the other, for the light. It is the same matter, but its being is different, as that which is receptive of disease is the same as that which is receptive of health, though in being different from it, and therefore diseasedness is different from healthiness.

A thing then which has the one kind of matter is light and always moves upward, while a thing which has the opposite matter is heavy and always moves downward. . . . The kinds of matter, then, must be as numerous as these bodies – i.e. four – but though they are four there must be a common matter of all – particularly if they pass into one another – which in each is in being different. [312a17–33]

8 Charlton (1970), pp. 132–136.
9 But the passage that leads to this conclusion is conditional: if, as some hold, water and air and the like are the matter of the natural bodies. . . .

It is true that a few sentences later, at 312ᵇ20, he denies that there is one matter for all the elements. But this is in the context of, and is presented as an alternative to, his claim that we must posit as many differences in the matter as there are elements. If we take these differences to be differences in the being (*to einai*) of matter, the two passages are compatible. His point at 312ᵇ20 is that we get into trouble if we posit one matter "such as the void" – i.e., a matter incapable of supporting different specific forms.

I assume, then, Aristotle holds that the four elements have a common matter. But why should we assume that, if there is such a common matter, it must be the traditional prime matter: "a bare 'stuff,' lacking all positive determinations," "characterless," "a wholly indeterminate substratum?" Such a bare stuff – a stuff that is potentially anythingish but always actually nothingish, always on the verge but never over the threshold – gives many of us pause, and I do not think it unfair to say that some of the people who have argued that Aristotle does not accept a common matter for the elements have done so in the belief that they were acting as his friends, on the ground that common matter is objectionable because it is bare.

But Aristotle does not hold that it is bare. On the contrary, he insists that it cannot exist without perceptible contrariety [*Generation and Corruption*, 329ᵃ10–11], indeed, it is "always bound up with contrariety" (329ᵃ26). Why accuse Aristotle adhering to a bare stuff when he insists that the stuff is always clothed? I suppose that someone might object that this does not count, because characteristics are different from the matter that receives them, and the matter *in itself* is still characterless. But it is this objection, not the doctrine it is directed against, that is incoherent. It is like claiming that someone is naked because he is not wearing anything underneath his clothes. For matter to take on a characteristic is for the matter to become thusly characterized: the bronze that takes on the characteristic heat, becomes hot. The common matter of the four elements is at various times hot, cold, dry, and moist; it is never characterless.

Still, there might be a point to the claim that the common matter of the elements is *in itself* characterless. The claim would *not* be that common matter, apart from its characteristics, is characterless, for (1) Aristotle denies that common matter can be apart from characteristics, and (2) the same claim could be made about anything whatsoever: my dog, apart from the characteristics he has, does not have any. Apart from his characteristics, he is not even my dog. (Is he then a prime dog?)

Nor would the claim be that common matter, *considered* apart from its characteristics, is characterless, for (1) this claim, like the former, would if it were true be true of anything whatsoever, and (2) this claim is false. Common matter, considered apart from its characteristics, has as many characteristics as it has if it is considered with its characteristics, for thinking does not make it so. You, considered without your clothes, are not nude: you are only being considered to be nude, and nothing much will follow from that.[10]

The claim would be that common matter possesses no *kath' hauto* (per se essential) properties. The common matter of the heavy and the light is capable of being the matter of the heavy and of being the matter of the light, and when it is the matter of the heavy, it is actually heavy and potentially light, and when it is the matter of the light, it is actually light and potentially heavy, and the price it must pay for this freedom is that it is neither per se light nor per se heavy. Socrates is potentially healthy and potentially ill, so when he actually possesses one of these properties, he does so *per accidens*, not *per se*. But according to Aristotle, Socrates does possess essential attributes and an essential nature. With common matter the case might look different. If it is potentially the matter of all things, it might seem that it must be neutral in all regards – perfectly promiscuous – and therefore possess no essential properties; and some philosophers, though not all, would conclude that this makes the notion of common matter incoherent (this incoherence might be granted to be less shameful than the alleged incoherence I discussed in the previous paragraphs). David Wiggins has talked about dummy sortals: terms that seem to give us principles for counting things but really do not.[11] "Material object" seems to be such a term, for it is not clear how we are to enumerate things under that sortal: is my car one material object or many, and if many, how many? Perhaps if common matter is construed as having no essential properties, "common matter" is a dummy mass term, purporting to designate a type of stuff but failing to do so. And even if this is not incoherent, it may make one queasy.

However, I do not think we can lay even this charge at Aristotle's doorstep. The most that Aristotle would need by way of a substrate for elemental change would be a matter that is per se indeterminate vis-à-vis the four elements it underlies, and that would require a large degree of indeterminacy, not an absolute lack of essential characteristics. The common matter of the four elements would have to be per se neither hot nor cold, solid nor fluid, light nor heavy, but capable of becoming any of these, and never without some of them. This does not mean that common matter possesses no characteristics per se; in fact, that it is potentially light or heavy, and that any given time it will be light or heavy,[12] can itself be taken to specify a per se characteristic. And it would be a mistake to think that, even so, "common matter" will function as what I have called a "dummy mass term." Not in Aristotle's physical system. The common matter of the four elements is the matter of the light and the

10 On this point, see Stahl (1981), pp. 177–180.
11 Wiggins (1967), pp. 29, 32–33, 35.
12 Well, almost. Aristotle says that in their natural places the elements have no weight.

heavy, and there is, according to Aristotle, a fifth element, either, which is the matter of the stars, celestial spheres, sun, and moon [*On the Heavens* I, 2]. Aristotle denies that this fifth element can be generated from any of the four terrestrial elements, or that any of the terrestrial elements can be generated from it: the celestial element is ungenerated and indestructible. The matter of the fifth element does not possess a potentiality for natural rectilinear motion, which the light and the heavy require, and it is neither potentially hot nor potentially cold, whereas the matter of the terrestrial elements does not possess a potentiality for natural circular motion and is potentially hot and cold.[13] This establishes a per se difference between two sorts of matter in Aristotle's system, and it gives us observational criteria for distinguishing them – by vector analyses, for example.

The matter of the four elements is locked in the cycle of rise and fall, generation and decay, warmth and cold, growth and diminution. It is not per se earth, air, fire, or water, but neither is it totally indeterminate. It is decidedly terrestrial in a universe in which that distinguishes it from another material stuff.[14] So it is not the case that "applying the format for describing changes to elemental transformations" leads to a bare, indeterminate stuff, or even to a stuff that is per se bare and indeterminate, or even to a stuff that possesses only vacuous per se characteristics. Applying the format for describing changes to elemental transformations leads to the most fundamental distinction in Aristotle's physics: the distinction between terrestrial and celestial matter. (Other distinctions, e.g., form-matter, are more fundamental but belong to metaphysics rather than physics.) Thus, the common matter of the terrestrial elements is not absolutely indeterminate. It is not, in other words, prime matter. Given that the proponents of prime matter base their case on Aristotle's account of elemental transformation, and given that he forbids celestial-terrestrial transformation, prime matter as traditionally conceived is ruled out in Aristotle's physical system.

There is another way, independent of Aristotle's account, that one might try to introduce prime matter. In *Metaphysics* VII, 3, Aristotle imagines our stripping away all characteristics from a thing to arrive at an ultimate substratum, and nothing he says there precludes our starting

13 The apparent heat of the sun is due to friction between it and the impure medium through which it moves (*Meteorology*, 340^{b}7–19; 341^{a}13–36).

14 Happ (1971), p. 696, holds that prime matter is the substrate of the sublunar realm, that *Sternenmaterie* is the matter of the celestial realm, and that these two are "somewhat determinate" forms of a completely indeterminate *Hyleprinzip*. I believe that he bases the claim that prime matter is not the matter of the celestial realm at least partly on the claim that "two things between which no reciprocal action is possible have no common substratum" (p. 473). I argue below that, for two things to have a common substratum, mutual transformation must be possible. If I understand Happ's position, then on my view, but not on his, there is no common substratum for fire and flesh.

the process with the moon, Jupiter, or the Milky Way. The stripping-away experiment is independent of his account of change, and it can take celestial as well as terrestrial aim. Perhaps that is why, though his account of elemental transformation seems to lead him to a common matter for the terrestrial elements, the stripping-away experiment ends with his recoiling in horror. For radical stripping away does seem to lead to an absolutely indeterminate substratum.

By way of contrast, consider that even if Aristotle had held that terrestrial–celestial transformations were possible, or that there were no fifth element, he would not have been thereby committed to the absolutely indeterminate substratum of VII, 3. I say this for two reasons. First, because what led us to suppose that common matter might not have any per se characteristics (and that even if it did it might not be a distinct type of stuff) was the consideration that if common matter is potentially the matter of all things then it might seem to be neutral in all regards, and therefore to have no essential properties. But in the next section I will question the antecedent: an implication of my argument will be that common matter is not potentially the matter of all things, even in the terrestrial realm. It is potentially the matter of any of the terrestrial elements, but there is more to the universe than earth, air, fire, or water. There are also people and eyes, flesh and bones, milk and blood, houses and bricks, bronze and pitch, and many, many other things, and it is not clear that the common matter of the elements is ever the matter of any of these.

Second, because in designing a common matter along traditional lines we need only divest it of those per se properties that would prevent it from doing what we want it to do. If we want it to be the common matter of the terrestrial elements, it cannot be per se hot, cold, fluid, solid, light, or heavy, as it must be capable of becoming any of these.[15] If we want it to be the common matter of the stars as well (on Aristotle's astrophysics), we have to add that it cannot be determined to a natural rectilinear motion.[16] But we can still allow it to be essentially spatially extended and capable of motion and rest, for it will never be asked to become something that is not spatially extended or that is not capable either of moving or of being at rest. Richard Sorabji, in fact, has argued that prime matter as extension is a philosophically attractive reading of Aristotle.[17] In doing so he takes prime matter to be the matter of all five

15 Thus Scaltsas (1994b) p. 27, lists, as essential properties of "physical matter," "being thermal, being hydral, being spatial, and being a causal agent and/or patient. . . . " Scaltsas (1985) holds that though Aristotle may have accepted traditional prime matter, his arguments do not commit him to it.
16 Given Aristotle's premises, it would not really be this simple. Aristotle thinks that what has a natural circular motion cannot come to be or perish. Then, if the fifth element could be generated out of the other four, how could the stars move?
17 In Sorabji (1988), pp. 3–43.

elements.[18] So, even embracing the fifth element, it could at least have as much character as Descartes allowed to matter.[19] It is an oddity in the history of philosophy that Aristotle's concept of common matter, which is richer than Descartes's concept of matter, should have been thought to be more vapid. Aristotle at least allows that common matter can be warm, whereas on one reading Descartes allows this only in a Pickwickian sense.

Neither on the grounds that (*a*) Aristotle's common matter is characterless, nor (*b*) that is has no per se characteristics, nor (*c*) that even if it has per se characteristics it is not a distinct type of stuff can the doctrine be shown to be incoherent, if these are grounds for incoherence at all. But the doctrine as it was intended is certainly false, if only because the doctrine of the five elements is false. You can forget this if you work in this area long enough. You then tend to treat the Aristotelian problem of elemental transformation as a real philosophical problem. One may even believe, perhaps without giving it much thought, that there *must* be a real philosophical problem here. But that need not be so. It might be that what we have here is a coherent but false physical doctrine. It might be

18 Ibid., pp. 14–15.
19 Dancy (1978), pp. 389–390, cites a number of passages in support of the claim that common matter is not held by Aristotle to be a body, but I am not sure that Aristotle even claims that, as opposed to claiming that it is not another body in addition to the elements. If we ignore the passages cited to show that Aristotle held that common matter is per se imperceptible – something that in one sense I do not deny – we are left with the following:

On the Heavens, 306ᵇ16–22: This is cited as a passage in which Aristotle holds that the common matter is formless and shapeless. Here Aristotle, arguing against the Platonic claim that the elements are geometrical solids – pyramids, cubes, etc. – protests that the "shape" of water is determined by the container, and that if it were its shape that made it water, then when its shape changed it would no longer be water, "from which it is clear that shape does not define them [i.e., the elements]. . . . The substrate must be formless and shapeless." His point is not that the substrate is shapeless in the sense of being unextended, but that the shape is negotiable – no element has a particular essential shape. In *Physics* I, 7, he says that the bronze, before the statue has been cast, is shapeless. He does not mean that it has no shape at all.

Physics, 204ᵇ32–35: Aristotle, discussing the *apeiron*, says there is no perceptible body in addition to the elements. And in *On the Heavens*, 305ᵃ22–31, he says there is no body prior to the elements, so the elements could not have been generated from some other body: they must be generated from one another. This is compatible with my reading, for common matter is not "some other body": for the four elements to be generated out of one another is for them to be generated out of a common matter.

Generation and Corruption, 332ᵃ20, 26–27: Aristotle says that there is nothing perceptible prior to the four elements, and no one element from which the other four arise. (Common matter is not an element, but the matter of the elements.) 329ᵃ8–13: Those who postulate a single matter that is both bodily and separable are wrong. (Common matter is not separable from perceptible contraries.) 320ᵇ23: "there is also a matter of bodily substance, but of a body already of such-and-so a sort (for there is no such thing as a common body)." That there is no common body does not, I think, entail that a chunk of common matter is not a body.

To this list we can add *On the Heavens*, A, 1, where Aristotle says that body is extended in three directions and is the only magnitude defined by spatial extension. But from this it does not follow that common matter is not spatially extended.

that the doctrine is of philosophical interest only because of its alleged incoherence, and that if it turns out to be coherent it will then be of interest only to the historian of science. I am not claiming that this is the case. I am saying that if it is not the case, it should be determined why not.

But whether or not this doctrine is, if coherent, of philosophical interest, Aristotle's reasons for arriving at it are.

Elemental Transformation and the Persistence of Matter. I have argued that although Aristotle claims there is an underlying common matter for the terrestrial elements in the *On the Heavens* and *Generation and Corruption,* this common matter is not the traditionally construed prime matter. I now want to argue that the principle that every change requires a single persisting substratum, which must be distinguished from the weaker claim that at any moment there must be a substratum, does not give us Aristotle's reasons for positing this common matter.

The question of whether Aristotle holds to a persisting substratum for all changes has, to most current interpreters, seemed to depend primarily on whether we take *Physics* I, 7, 190a12-21, to advance a claim about any change whatsoever or only about alterations.[20] This is because Aristotle has been interpreted as claiming in this passage that, in every change the passage is intended to cover, there is a single substratum that under one description persists and under another does not: the man and the unmusical thing are identical, and that thing takes violin lessons, and under one description, "the man," survives, and under another description, "the unmusical," does not. So, if the passage is meant to cover all changes (as the introduction to it seems to imply), Aristotle is committed to a persisting substratum for all changes, but if it is intended to cover only alterations, he is not committed to a persisting substratum for all changes.

In neither case does the passage commit him to a persisting substratum for all changes. The appearance that it does is due to overly aggressive translations of line 15, Hardie's "this, though always one numerically, in form at least is not one," being the most extreme case. The *ei kai* in line 15 can be seen as concessionary rather than assertive. Denniston says that *ei kai* can have the force of "'even if' (representing the fulfillment of the condition as immaterial)," "often means 'if indeed,' 'if really' ('though I should be surprised if it were so')," and frequently cannot be distinguished from *kai ei* ("and if").[21] The passage says that there is always a substratum for change, and the substratum, "*even if* it is

---

20 See, e.g., Charlton (1970), p. 73; Jones (1974), pp. 478–479; and Dancy (1978), p. 385, n. 35.
21 J. D. Denniston, *The Greek Particles,* 2d ed. (Oxford University Press, 1966), pp. 301–305. For some cases in which a misunderstanding of *ei kai* has led people astray, see Verdenius and Waszink (1966), pp. 3–4.

one in number, is not one in form."[22] This does not commit Aristotle to a single substratum for each of the changes that are under consideration. The sense of the passage is that even if the substratum is one in number it is still two in form, and its being two in form explains how change is possible when there is only substratum: under one description the substratum does not persist. If the substratum is not one in number – if there is one substratum at the terminus a quo and another at the terminus ad quem, as seems to be the case at 190b1–5, where the seed is the substratum from which the plant grows – the problem does not arise. So the question is still open: does Aristotle posit a common matter for the four elements because he thinks that every change requires a persisting substratum?

He certainly does not put it that way when he introduces common matter (*On the Heavens*, 312a17–33, quoted above). He says that, as the elements arise *out of one another,* there must be a common matter for them. It is one of the more interesting properties of Aristotle's terrestrial elements that they come to be out of one another: any of the four can be transformed into any of the other three, and the resulting element can be transformed back into the original element. Air can be transformed directly into water, and water can be transformed back into air (or into fire, or earth, under the right circumstances). This generation out of one another (*eks allelon*), Aristotle says, requires a common matter. That does not commit him to a common matter for *every* generation out of another (*eks allou*).[23]

When Aristotle talks about elemental transformation, the cases he has in mind are all reciprocal: fire is potentially air, and air is potentially fire. But it is not always the case that if *A* is potentially *B*, *B* is potentially *A*. A tree is potentially ashes and smoke, but smoke and ashes are not potentially a tree – an acorn is potentially a tree. Fire exists potentially in flesh and wood, for one can burn flesh or wood, producing fire, but:

> neither in potentiality nor in actuality does fire contain flesh or wood, or it would exude them. Similarly, even if there were only one elementary body, it would not contain them. For though it will be [i.e., one day] either flesh or bone or something else, that does not at once show that it contained these in potentiality: the further question remains, in what manner it becomes them. [*On the Heavens*, 302a21–28]

Aristotle is not denying that you can start with fire and after some series of transformations end up with flesh. He is denying that it follows from this that fire is potentially flesh. He is denying that the statement "———— is potentially ————" introduces a transitive relation. You can make alu-

22 Lewis (1991), p. 194, seems not to agree.
23 This distinction also seems relevant to *Generation and Corruption*, 319a5–8.

minum out of bauxite, and you can make window frames out of aluminum, but you cannot make window frames out of bauxite – the stuff is too crumbly. *That very stuff* can be turned into aluminum, but not window frames. That very stuff possesses the dispositions that allow it to become aluminum, but it does not possess the dispositions that would allow it to be formed into window frames. It first has to become something else, which it can do, but that is its last gasp. The something else it becomes is potentially a window frame; it is not:

But we must distinguish when a thing is potentially and when it is not, for it is not at any and every time. E.g., is earth potentially a man? No – but rather when it has already become seed, and perhaps not even then, as not everything can be healed . . . but there is a certain kind of thing which is capable of it, and only this is potentially healthy. . . . The seed is not yet potentially a man, for it must further undergo a change in a foreign medium. But when through its own motive principle it has already got such and such attributes, in this state it is already potentially a man, while in the former state it needs another principle – just as earth is not yet potentially a statue, for it must change in order to become bronze [*Metaphysics*, 1048b37–1049a18]

We could try to "help" Aristotle here by taking him to mean only that fire, *under that description*, is not potentially flesh. So although smoke and ashes, under that description, are not potentially a tree, under another description – as so much earth, air, fire, and water – they are. But it is not clear that he would welcome this sort of help. In *On the Soul*, for example, where he says that the soul is the first act of a natural body potentially alive [412a27–28], does he want my jacket to count as such a body on the grounds that under one description – so much earth, air, fire, and water – my jacket is a natural body potentially alive? He might think that even under that description my jacket is not potentially alive. (Otherwise everything would be potentially alive.) He might think that there is no description under which my jacket is potentially alive. For flesh is not potentially in fire and: "Fire, air, water, earth, we assert, come to be from one another, and each of them exists potentially in each, as all things do that can be resolved into a common and ultimate substratum" [*Meteorology*, 339a36–339b2]. This passage, in conjunction with *On the Heavens*, 302a21–24 (quoted above), entails that there is no common substratum for fire and flesh. The same claim is behind a passage from *Generation and Corruption* that I partially quoted above, and that reads in full: "Water can come to be out of fire and fire out of water, for their substratum is something common to them both. But flesh, too, presumably, and marrow come to be out of them. How, then, do such things come to be?" Aristotle's point is that we can understand how fire can arise out of water and vice versa, because there is a common substratum for water and fire, but how can flesh and marrow come to be out of them, when there is no common substratum? And this claim may be behind 322b13–21:

And in this respect Diogenes is right when he argues that unless all things were derived from one, reciprocal action and passion could not occur. The hot thing, e.g., would not be cooled and the cold thing in turn be warmed; for heat and cold do not change reciprocally into one another, but what changes (it is clear) is the substratum. Hence whenever there is action and passion between things, that which underlies them [or, "the substrate nature"] must be a single something. No doubt, it is not true to say that all things are of this character, but it is true of all things between which there is reciprocal action and passion.

The common matter of the terrestrial elements is a common substratum for those elements, but there is no common substratum between fire and flesh: the common matter of the four elements is *not* the matter of all things. If we were to follow a series of changes that began with the four elements and ended with flesh, the substratum we would have at the end of the process would not, on Aristotle's view, be the substratum with which we had begun. (And if there were a common substratum for people and corpses, then corpses, not just embryos, would be potentially people.)

For nonreciprocal cases of generation Aristotle holds that there is (1) the subject/matter *out of which* that which arises arises – e.g., the oak tree from the acorn – for every substance comes to be from some subject (*Physics* I, 7, 190^{b}1–5), and "that out of which they come to be is what we call matter" (*Metaphysics* VII, 7, 1032^{a}17); and (2) the subject/matter *of* that which arises – for an oak, perhaps wood, bark, etc., or perhaps roots, leaves, branches, etc. Corresponding to (1) and (2), we say that (1) styrene is made out of petroleum, and (2) the chalice is made of silver. But (1) and (2) do not commit Aristotle to holding that the second matter, the constitutive matter of that which arises, is a persistence of the first matter, the matter from which that which arises, arises. The matter-from-which may itself have changed and ceased to exist.[24] By the time you have a seedling, the acorn is no more.

At *Generation and Corruption*, 317^{a}18–27, Aristotle says that some philosophers have mistakenly thought that when a change takes place in something that is continuous, the change is an alteration, whereas coming-to-be and passing-away are due to association and disassociation, as when atoms come together and form a larger whole, or go their separate ways. His own view, though, is that there is unqualified coming-to-be and passing-away when something as a whole changes from this to that, but others take this to be an alteration (perhaps on the grounds that even here there is something continuous).[25] These people do not see an important difference:

24 At *Physics*, 190^{b}8–9, and *Generation and Corruption*, 317^{a}23–26, Aristotle talks about changes that affect the matter itself.
25 Wiggins (1980), p. 52, approvingly quotes Leibnitz: "'By itself continuity no more constitutes substance than does multitude or number.'"

For in that which underlies the change there is a factor corresponding to the definition and there is a material factor. When, then, the change is in these factors, there will be a coming-to-be or passing away, but when it is in the thing's affections and accidental, there will be alteration.

At one extreme there are changes through which the matter seems clearly to survive: a sword is beaten into a plowshare. At the other extreme there are changes that seem to involve the complete loss of the stuff that was there at the start: water evaporates, flesh turns into dust, grass turns into milk. In this second sort of case the stuff itself seems, at least prima facie, to perish. But in some of these cases in which the original stuff seems to perish – the transforming of water into air, for example – there can be a transformation back into the original stuff that is as simply achieved as the original transformation. For these reciprocal cases of apparently perishing matter, Aristotle posits a common material substratum; for nonreciprocal cases he does not. In other words, he assimilates reciprocal cases of the second sort to cases of the first sort.

I can find little in Aristotle to explain why he does this. There is the enigmatic remark, quoted above, that even if there were only one element, and (eventually) flesh and bone arose out of it, it would not follow that flesh and bone were potentially in the element, but that "the further question remains, in what manner it becomes them." And there is the claim I just quoted: when something comes to be or passes away, the change is not (just?) in the thing's affections, but the thing as a whole, including the material substratum, changes. The rationale for this is, I suppose, that if a case of the first sort, in which it looks as though the stuff we have at the end is the stuff we had at the start, turned out not to be reciprocal, we could surmise that the matter itself had in fact changed.

Suppose that we beat the sword into a plowshare, and then found that we could not beat the plowshare back into a sword because the stuff had become brittle. Then the change from the sword-shape to the plowshare-shape was only a part of the whole change; the material itself had also undergone a change. This would be different from the change that takes place when water freezes, though in this case, too, the matter itself seems to change: ice is solid and brittle. But we freeze water by cooling it, and we can melt the ice by warming it: the change is completely reciprocative. In our hypothetical case we beat the sword into a plowshare but could not beat the plowshare back into a sword. It is brittle, and not in virtue of its new shape: any piece broken off the plowshare will be brittle as well. So the stuff itself has changed. Conversely, where the process is reciprocative, then even though the stuff is different, as water and ice are, we can postulate an underlying, abiding substance that, say, at low temperatures is solid and at higher temperatures is liquid; whereas if ice remained solid even when heated, we would have to look for some other explanation. (I am ignoring the problems raised by allotropes like coal and diamonds.)

The matter of the metals, Aristotle says, once was potentially the matter of water, but no longer is (*Meteorology*, 378ª33–34). Sometimes a change is just a change in a characteristic or two, as when the cold bronze sphere becomes a warm bronze cube. And sometimes the matter itself changes, and we are no longer dealing with bronze at all. The thing as a whole has changed – the definition and the matter. In this case there is still continuity, yet the change is not a mere alteration. It is the perishing of one substance and the birth of another.

This is just a beginning, for surely Aristotle does not want to say that *every time* the matter itself changes, there is a perishing – i.e., that there cannot be alterations in the matter itself: when a blacksmith heats, beats, and cools iron he changes its malleability, but iron's becoming more brittle is not the perishing of anything. Perhaps this is why Aristotle says that the change must be in the matter *and* in the definition.

Matter and the Substratum. Aristotle thought that as we move from the elements to more complex forms of matter (*Meteorology*, 389ᵇ23–390ª5), and even for the five elements themselves, that as we move from the center of the universe outward (*On the Heavens*, 312ª12), form and final cause play an increasingly prominent role. We can approach this claim in terms of the interpretation I presented in the last section, for the reciprocality that governs his terrestrial physics (i.e., his doctrine of the four elements), and that leads him to infer a common material substrate for the four elements, is, in his chemistry (his doctrine of homogeneous compounds), only one member of a ruling *junta*, and in his biology it is a mere civil servant. As Aristotle turns to more sophisticated and integrated substances, the directionality of the final cause – in the passage, say, from embryo to adult – replaces the dominance of reciprocality at lower levels, and form's hitherto obscure role is at last brought center-stage as the stuff provided by physics and chemistry is worked up into serious things like tigers and jewelry boxes. It is true that in many of Aristotle's discussions "matter" and "substratum" seem to be interchangeable, but when the issue comes to a head in *Metaphysics* VII they are not: there form, Aristotle says, has a greater right than matter to be taken to be the substratum – a claim that should give some pause to those who think Aristotle holds that every change requires a persisting substratum, and that that substratum is matter. And VII is not a bolt from the blue. In some of his works in which we find passages that seem to equate matter with the substratum, there are other passages that contest matter's exclusive rights in this area. In the *Physics*, for example, Aristotle says that the substratum comprises both matter and form [190ᵇ24–30], and we have seen him holding at *Generation and Corruption*, 317ª24 that both the matter and the definition are represented in the substratum.

I assume that the claim of the *Metaphysics* VII that form has priority over matter in the substratum is meant to imply, among other things, that in some way matter is what it is through the possession of form.[26] This latter claim seems to be implicit in the account of human beings in *On the Soul* II, 1: the form and matter of Socrates are his soul and his body; his body is composed of organs and potentially alive; and the body that is potentially alive has soul. This is understatement, for (1) Aristotle thinks that dead organs are not really organs at all, and so must hold that a body composed of organs is actually, and not merely potentially, alive, and (2) the body that has soul is actually, and not merely potentially, alive.[27] Aristotle is saying that the matter of Socrates is the ensouled body, the body vivified by substantial form, the body composed of functional organs, and not, say, a mere collection of atoms – Not low-level matter, but matter in its fullest flower and most extravagant bloom; matter in-formed by life. (So form is primary, for the matter is what it is through its possession of form, and a change in the *logos* will be a change in the matter as a whole: when Socrates dies, the nature of his body will change.) This informed body is the body that is the substratum and the matter [412ª18–19] of Socrates. But it does not follow that there are not other types of matter in Socrates.[28]

Aristotle contends that there are three or four levels of physical complexity [e.g., *Parts of Animals*, A; *Meteorology* IV, 12). First is the level of the elements. Second there are the homogeneous bodies composed of the elements. A homogeneous body is a compound (*mixis* as opposed to a mere mixture (*synthesis*). In a mere mixture the elements are actually present, as bricks and stones are present in a wall; this is the only sort of complexity Aristotle thought Empedocles allowed [*Generation and Corruption*, 334ª26–334ᵇ3]. In a compound, on the other hand, the elements are not actually but only potentially present, and "the compound must be uniform, any part of such a compound being the same as the whole, just as any part of water is water" [328ª11–12].[29] Because these compounds are homogeneous, the natural expressions for them are mass terms: "iron," "flesh," "bone," "milk," "glass," "pitch," etc.[30] A mixture of elements is formed into a compound by heat, so that compounds, like elements, possess a natural intrinsic heat, the loss of which causes the compound to revert to the elements out of which it was composed.[31]

In a living thing the homogeneous bodies, and collections of them, in

---

26 And to deny that, in that way, the converse is true – which will not be an easy task. I turn to this issue in Chapter 5.
27 The problem raised here has been the subject of extensive debate. See Chapter 5, n. 38.
28 There may, in other words, be nonproximate matter.
29 The interpretational problems raised by the merely potential existence of elements in a compound are discussed in sec. II ("Compounds"), pp. 88–100.
30 Although, of course, mixtures are also generally designated by mass terms – e.g., "minestrone."
31 See, e.g., *Meteorogy*, 379ª19–20; 389ᵇ7–8.

turn form the heterogeneous organs, such as livers and eyes. It is false that a part of heterogeneous bodies is representative of the nature of the whole: a piece of a hand is not an instance of a hand [*History of Animals,* 486ᵃ5–8]. And finally, the whole animal is composed of organs.

In an animal – Socrates, for example – death occurs when the heart (in nonsanguineous animals, that which is analogous to the heart) loses its ability to generate heat [*On Youth and Old Age,* 469ᵇ8–20]. At that moment Socrates is no more, and scattered throughout the Aristotelian corpus there is ample evidence for the claim that Aristotle thought that at that moment Socrates' organs are no more: the hands and eyes of a dead man are hands and eyes in name only. But what about the homogeneous substances that composed those organs? Do they perish at that moment or do they persist for a while? The texts point in two different directions.

At *Generation of Animals,* 734ᵇ24ff., for example, flesh is not flesh without soul, echoing the claim Aristotle frequently makes for the heterogeneous parts. On this line, when Socrates dies the flesh and bone perish and are subsequently flesh and bone in name only.

But elsewhere Aristotle adopts a different view. At *Metaphysics,* 1035ᵃ21–35, Callias is said to pass away into flesh and bones, which stand to Callias as bronze stands to the bronze sphere. In *Parts of Animals,* 649ᵃ14–17 and 649ᵇ20–35, we are told that it is due to extrinsic causes (primarily the warmth generated by the heart) that blood is hot and liquid, so that although blood can be defined as hot and liquid, it is as though we had a single word for hot water, or hot iron: "heat is included in the definition of blood just as paleness is included in the definition of a pale man, but so far as blood becomes hot from some external influence, it is not hot essentially." The implication is that though we may define blood as hot, hot blood is an *ens per accidens,* and the *ens per se* can survive the cooling that results from the perishing of the heart, or from blood's flowing out of the body.[32] This gives us the claim that cool blood really is blood, and not in name only, but the same stuff. And it opens up the possibility that the bones scattered in the field really are bones, and that the meat in the butcher shop is flesh.[33]

Aristotle is committed to this second view in the *Meteorology* as well. When a homogeneous body is losing its natural heat and, on Aristotle's view, is consequently drying out, it is decaying, and this is its perishing [379ᵃ3–4, 11–26]. The flesh rots; the bones crumble. The process can take years, and can be delayed by freezing (379ᵃ30). Loss of extrinsic heat, on the other hand, is not by itself the perishing of a homogeneous body.

32 See also *History of Animals,* 487ᵃ2–5; *Meteorology,* 389ᵇ9–18.
33 Blood is not an ideal example here, for me: I argue in Chapter 5 that Aristotle thinks blood is inanimate and not a part of animals (though it can be found in animals).

The difference between these two points of view surfaces elsewhere. In *Generation of Animals*, Aristotle, talking about flesh in particular, and in general about the homogeneous parts of which the organs are composed, states:

We may allow that hardness and softness, stickiness and brittleness, and whatever other qualities are found in the parts that have life and soul, may be caused by mere heat and cold, yet when we come to the principle in virtue of which flesh is flesh and bone is bone, that is no longer so. [734^{b}31–34]

But in the *Meteorology* he holds that what we would call "chemical" processes are sufficient to account for homogeneous substances:

Heat and cold and the motions set up as the bodies are solidified by the hot and cold are sufficient to form all such parts as are the homogeneous bodies: flesh, bone, hair, sinew, and the rest. For they are all of them differentiated by the various qualities enumerated above: tension, ductility, fragmentability, hardness, softness, and the rest of them, all of which are derived from the hot and the cold and the mixture of the elements. But no one would go so far as to consider them sufficient in the case of the non-homogeneous parts (like the head, the hand, or the foot) which these homogeneous parts go to make up. Cold and heat and their motion would be admitted to account for the formation of copper or silver, but not for that of a saw, a bowl, or a box. [390^{b}2–13]^{34}

In Chapter 5 we shall discuss the issue raised here. For now, though, let us take the Aristotle who holds the second view. He maintains that when Socrates dies, Socrates, and Socrates' organs, perish. But there on the slab where Socrates once was, there remain, at least for a while, the homogeneous parts out of which Socrates' organs were composed. This is the surviving matter. But it is not the matter of which Socrates was composed. For Socrates was composed of heterogeneous parts – "the material of animals is their parts: of the whole animal the nonhomogeneous parts, of these again the homogeneous, and of these last the so-called elements of bodies" [*Generation of Animals*, 715^{a}9–11]"^{35} – not of homogeneous parts, though his heterogeneous parts were in turn composed of homogeneous parts.^{36} Even if we held that the collection of homogeneous parts is composed of heterogeneous parts (calling, for example, whatever happens to be in certain spatial regions "parts"), *that* collection would not be identical with the collection of parts that constituted Socrates. So,

34 Aristotle is careless here, as elsewhere, when listing homogeneous parts: it should be *hair* and *sinew*, not *hairs* and *sinews*, as Aristotle says here. Barnes' translation is generous.

35 The relations between these are not the same: the elements are merely potentially present in compounds, whereas the homogeneous parts are actually present in the heterogeneous parts. (The heart is tissue formed into a certain shape.)

36 We must forgive Aristotle for saying that flesh and bone are the matter of animals, as we forgive him for using "man is a featherless biped" as an example of a definition. "It would be misleading to say that what we call the body Aristotle calls flesh and bones," Hartman (1977), p. 113.

on Aristotle's premises, it is false that this mass of flesh and bone, even in its better, more vibrant and organized days, ever was the substratum of that which promised Asclepius a cock. For that substratum was composed of organs, whereas this mass of flesh and bones is not, and to Aristotle neither "——— is the substratum of ———" nor "——— is the matter of ———" nor "——— is composed of ———" introduce transitive relations: for example, Socrates is composed of heterogeneous parts, heterogeneous parts are composed of homogeneous parts, but it does not follow that Socrates is composed of homogeneous parts. There is a matter in Socrates that may be the substratum of his organs, and that on this second view survives his death, but that matter was never the substratum of Socrates. So there is no persisting substratum for the substantial change, the death of Socrates. When Socrates dies, both his soul and that which was the matter of Socrates – his organic body – perish, and so whether his form, his matter, or the composite is his substratum, in any case the substratum does not persist. But there is matter that persists through this change: flesh and bone.[37]

Even if we go with the Aristotle who holds the first view – that flesh and bone perish when Socrates perishes – there is a general point that stands: part of Aristotle's answer to his predecessors is that the matter that is the substratum of Socrates is to be found at a higher level than Empedocles and the Atomists anticipated. What Aristotle takes to be their neglect of the formal (and final) cause has implications for the location of the material cause: if we eliminate the formal cause, the material cause drops to the next lowest level. But Socrates is not a configuration of atoms or of compounds or mixtures of the elements; as we shall see in Chapter 4, his unity is not the unity of a statue or a heap. He is a whole animal, composed of interrelated organs, and regardless of whether those organs are composed of atoms or mixtures or compounds of the elements, the persistence of atoms, mixtures, or homogeneous substances in that configuration need not be the persistence of the stonecutter's substratum. The stonecutter's substratum belongs to biology, not to chemistry or physics, and I will argue in Chapter 5 that the link between the acorn and the oak is not supposed to lie in the persistence of some numerically identical stuff, but in the persisting subjugation of stuff to a scheme of biological organization and development – to a specific nature, in the Aristotelian sense in which "specific" is the adjectival form of "species." In the same vein, a contemporary Aristotelian might want to argue that a cell is not a collection of molecules, that a giraffe is not a collection of

---

37 Cf. Bostock (1982), pp. 195–196, where "what underlies in the sense of what persists through change" need not be a substance but "might be . . . a mass." Another interpretation that accepts a version of prime matter while denying it the metaphysical laurel wreath – my agenda in this section – can be found in Lewis (1991), where on p. 299 prime matter is the primary subject but is not a substance.

cells, and that the persistence of matter when molecules survive the perishing of a cell, or when cells survive the perishing of a giraffe, does not imply the persistence of the original substratum.

I have argued that Aristotle accepts a common matter for the four terrestrial elements, but that this matter is not the matter of anything except the four elements. We now turn to a difficult question: does a common matter for the four elements mean that elemental transformation is a special kind of alteration?[38] Mary Louise Gill, for example, takes the view of matter that I have presented here to conflict with Aristotle's distinction between generation and alteration.[39] Indeed, this is a problem I have wondered about a good deal myself.

B. The Persistence of Matter

I have been dealing with the question of whether there is a persisting matter for elemental change, and I have answered with a hesitant yes, though the matter I see as underlying elemental transformation is not traditional prime matter. But we can press the question further, asking what it means to say that matter survives elemental transformation (or that there is a common matter for the terrestrial elements). Does it mean that there is a chunk of matter which a while ago was water and now survives as air, having persisted through the process, or does it merely mean that when there was water there was matter and now that there is air there is still matter, so that matter, like the poor, we shall always have with us, though the ranks constantly change?

At the beginning of *On Generation and Corruption*, Aristotle asks "whether alteration has the same nature as coming-to-be, or whether to these different names there correspond two separate processes with distinct natures." The question arises out of a consideration of his monist and pluralist predecessors [314ª1–314ᵇ12]:

Those . . . who construct all things out of a single element, must maintain that coming-to-be and passing-away are alteration. For they must affirm that the substratum always remains identical and one (*aei gar menein to hypokeimenon tauto kai hen*); and change of such a kind we call altering. Those, on the other hand, who make the ultimate kinds of things more than one, must maintain that alteration is distinct from coming-to-be; for coming-to-be and passing-away result from the association and disassociation of the many kinds. [314ᵇ1–8]

It follows, as an obvious corollary, that a single matter must always be assumed as underlying the contraries . . . whether the change is of place, or of growth and diminution, or alteration. Further, the existence of this [single matter] and of

38 For the claim that if Aristotle accepts common elemental matter he must hold that elemental transformation is an alteration, see Charlton (1970), pp. 75, 133–134. For the denial of this, see Robinson (1974), p. 171, and Code (1976), pp. 356–367.
39 Gill (1989), p. 45, n. 9.

alteration must stand and fall together. For if the change is an alteration, then the substratum is a single element, and all things which change into one another have a single matter. And conversely, if the substratum is one, there is alteration. [314ᵇ28–315ᵃ2]

So Aristotle seems to hold that if the substratum remains one and the same through a change, the change is an alteration. Thus the monists, who hold to a single element, must maintain that generation and corruption are special cases of alteration. (To avoid tedium I will say "generation" and allow "and corruption" to be understood where appropriate.)

Aristotle goes on to a brief discussion of the views of Empedocles, Plato, and then the Atomists, who seem able to admit alteration as distinct from generation: "They explain coming-to-be and passing-away by their [the atoms'] disassociation and association, but alteration by their grouping and position" [315ᵇ8]. He then comes to a more general point I mentioned in the previous section: "Since almost all our predecessors think that coming-to-be is distinct from alteration, and that, whereas things alter by change of their affections, it is by association and disassociation that they come to be, we must concentrate our attention on these theses" [315ᵇ16ff.]. The thesis on which he will *not* concentrate attention holds that generation is a species of alteration. There follows a lengthy digression introduced by the claim that the discussion should start with an inquiry into whether things change because the primary things are indivisible magnitudes – atoms – though it is hard to see why Aristotle would think this should be the starting point.[40] The digression concludes with his assertion that association and disassociation do not involve indivisible magnitudes. Aristotle then returns to the general point quoted above: his predecessors thought that generation comes about through association and disassociation, and things alter by changes in their affections. But now he tells us that it is wrong "to suppose . . . that coming-to-be in the unqualified and complete sense is defined by association and disassociation, while the change that takes place in what is continuous is alteration. On the contrary, this is where the whole error lies" [317ᵃ17–20]. His predecessors fall into two groups: (1) those who held that generation is an instance of alteration, and (2) those who held that, rather than being an instance of alteration, generation is, or at least comes about through, association or disassociation. He denies this, rejecting (1), but what is the connection between (2) and (3) – namely, its being wrong to think that alteration is the change that takes place in what is continuous? On the reading C. J. F. Williams gives the passage, the association and disassociation Aristotle has in mind occurs "at points of division or contact," whereas the change that takes place in what is continuous does not occur at a point, but "throughout a body

40 See Williams (1982), p. 64.

which undergoes alteration, say of color or temperature."[41] The continuous, then, is that which is spatially continuous, as opposed to the points of contact at which atomic association takes place, and the distinction is between changes that take place at points of contact and changes that take place in spatially extended zones. Although this might make sense if Aristotle is thinking only of the atomists, he seems to have a broader target in mind. He had, for example, said earlier [314ª12] that Empedocles, Anaxagoras, and Leucippus, because they are pluralists, all distinguish generation from alteration, and all take generation and perishing to result from association and disassociation [314b5].

Aristotle's comment will apply to almost all his predecessors if he means they assume that the change which takes place in what is *temporally* continuous is alteration.[42] The point then is that his predecessors assumed that generation and corruption are association and disassociation on the grounds that, in disassociation the association does not continue, and in association a previously nonexistent association commences, whereas they took alteration to be a change in something that persists through the change. In their view, association and disassociation begin and end things; the changes that take place in continuants are alterations.

Aristotle then goes on to introduce his own position: (1) unqualified coming-to-be and passing-away are not effected by association or disassociation; rather, (2) they take place when a thing changes from this to that as a whole, though (3) his predecessors supposed that all such change is alteration. He gives us no reasons in support of (1), but support can be found elsewhere in the corpus – most notably at *Metaphysics* V, 6, 1016b8: "if you put two pieces of wood touching one another, you will not say that these are one piece of wood, or one body, or one continuum of any other sort." To place one board on another board is not to generate a new thing. We shall return to this claim in a later chapter.

Williams' comment on (2) and (3) is that "not all such change is alteration." In other words, he takes Aristotle to be saying that generation and corruption are *subsets* of the changes in which a thing changes from this to that as a whole. Some cases in which a thing as a whole changes from this to that might then be mere alterations: the entire leaf, as opposed to just a portion of it, changes from green to orange. But Williams adds that at 319b14 Aristotle seems to deny that *any* such change is alteration: "When the thing as a whole changes, nothing perceptible persisting as identical substratum (for example, when the seed as a whole is converted into blood, or water into air, or air as a whole into water), such a process is a coming-to-be – and a passing away of the other sub-

41 Ibid., p. 79.
42 "In that which is continuous" is a rendering of *en toi synechei*. See 319ª19 for another instance in which Aristotle uses *synechos* for temporal, rather than spatial, continuity.

stance." In this passage, if a thing changes as a whole, no perceptible substratum persists, so the leaf's change of color is not an instance of a thing's changing as a whole from this to that. "As a whole," then, does not seem to be opposed to "in some of its magnitude," which would exclude a part of a leaf's changing color but not the whole leaf's changing color. Unless subsequent texts give us reason to modify the doctrine, I shall understand Aristotle to be saying that whenever a thing changes from this to that as a whole, the change is a generation or a corruption. (On the alternative reading, only some such changes are generations or corruptions.)

When Aristotle says that "they suppose that *all such change* is alteration," does he mean that they suppose that whenever a thing changes from this to that as a whole the change is an alteration, or does he mean that they suppose that every change that takes place in what is continuous is an alteration? As he is still commenting on the implications of the continuity claim, he means that they hold that when a thing changes from this to that as a whole the change is an alteration *because* it is a change in what is continuous. They allow generation and corruption only in what is not continuous – i.e., in associations – and they hold that any change that takes place in what is continuous is an alteration, even if the thing as a whole changes.

Aristotle's own view, then, is that (1) generation and corruption cannot be attributed to association and disassociation, and (2) not every change that takes place in what is continuous is an alteration. ("On the contrary, this is where the whole error lies.") Some changes that take place in what is continuous are generations and corruptions. And as we saw in the previous section, a change in what is continuous will not be an alteration if the thing changes "from this to that, as a whole":

But they suppose that all such change is alteration; whereas in fact there is a difference. For in that which underlies the change there is a factor corresponding to the definition and there is a material factor. When . . . the change is in these factors, there will be coming-to-be or passing-away; but when it is in the thing's affections and accidental, there will be alteration. [317ᵃ22ff.]

(At 314ᵇ13 Aristotle had said that it is obvious that alteration is distinct from corruption, "for while the substance of the thing remains unchanged, we see it altering just as we see in it the changes of magnitude called growth and diminution.") A change in the affections is an alteration, but when a thing changes from this to that as a whole, the change takes place in the substratum and the factors corresponding to the definition and the matter change. The examples Aristotle gives are a seed's changing into blood or water changing into air.[43] That a change takes

43 The passage is ambiguous, in that Aristotle might mean (1) that only the change

place in what is continuous, then, does not mean that the change is a mere alteration: a change can be the destruction of one thing and the genesis of another, even if something persists through the change.

His predecessors held that all changes in things that are continuous are alterations, and that coming-to-be and perishing are caused by association and disassociation. Aristotle denies both these claims: association and disassociation are not cases of coming-to-be or perishing, and his account thus far is compatible with *all* changes being changes in what is continuous. At 320ᵃ2 he identifies this continuant: matter is the substratum receptive to coming-to-be and passing-away. When air turns into water, there is an unqualified perishing of air and an unqualified generation of water, yet matter persists. The seed changes into blood, and nothing perceptible remains of the seed, yet the seed's matter endures as the matter of the blood. How are we to understand the role of matter?

The First Interpretation. There are two ways to interpret this. In this section I present the first, which has Aristotle holding that in generation and corruption matter is a persisting substratum, though it is not a persisting *perceptible* substratum. I discuss three variations on this interpretation: one that accepts traditional prime matter as this substratum; one that for elemental transformation accepts somewhat qualified matter (e.g., hot matter for air–fire transformations); and one that accepts a persisting substratum for the process itself of generation and corruption, but denies that this substratum is the substratum of either the terminus ad quem or the terminus a quo. In the following section I argue for the second interpretation, according to which there is no persisting substratum for generation and corruption.

The first interpretation has for its proof-text 319ᵇ7–20, where Aristotle states:

Since, then, we must distinguish the substratum and the property whose nature it is to be predicated of the substratum, and since change of each of these occurs, there is alteration when the substratum is perceptible and persists, but changes in its own properties. . . . The body, e.g., although persisting as the same body, is now healthy and now ill, and the bronze is now spherical and at another time angular, and yet remains the same bronze. But when nothing perceptible persists in its identity as a substratum, and the thing changes as a whole (when, e.g., the seed as a whole is converted into blood, or water into air, or air as a whole into water), such an occurrence is a coming-to-be of one substance and a passing-away of the other – especially if the change proceeds from an imperceptible something to something perceptible (either to touch or to all the senses), as when water comes to be out of, or passes away into, air, for air is pretty well imperceptible.

involving both matter and form is a change of a thing as a whole, or he might mean (2) that in some alterations a thing as a whole changes, but in generation and corruption the thing as a whole changes and the change involves both the *logos* and the matter. Either way, the doctrine is the same.

The first interpretation takes Aristotle to be saying that both alteration and generation and corruption involve a persisting substratum: in the one case a perceptibly recognizable persisting substratum; in the other, a persisting substratum that is not perceptibly recognizable.

As Joachim pointed out,[44] Aristotle's remarks here follow his repudiation of the inclination of common opinion to identify perishing with passage into imperceptibility: "For they distinguish what is and what is not by their perceiving and not perceiving . . . perception on their view having the force of knowledge." Aristotle does not take generation and corruption to require an imperceptible term – these are simply "the most obvious and generally recognized instances of *genesis* and *phthora*." Generation and corruption require only that there be no persisting perceptible substratum: the seed as a whole is converted into blood, the one replacing the other, and there is nothing corresponding to the bronze of the other example – nothing perceptible of which we can say that it was the seed and now is the blood. Our first interpretation takes Aristotle to be saying that, even so, there is a persisting substratum – matter – when the seed changes into blood, though it is not a persisting *perceptible* substratum. Matter is the enduring substratum throughout the change; but when you look, all you see are first the seed and then the blood.

We have seen passages in which Aristotle says that if a change involves a persisting identical substratum, the change is an alteration, without the qualification that the substratum must perceptibly persist. At 314, for example (quoted above), he says that "Those . . . who construct all things out of a single element, must maintain that coming-to-be and passing-away are alteration. For they must affirm that the substratum always remains identical and one [*aiei gar menein to hypokeimenon tauto kai hen*]; and change of such a kind we call altering." And in another passage quoted above:

It follows, as an obvious corollary, that a single matter must always be assumed as underlying the contraries – whether the change is of place, or of growth and diminution, or alteration. Further, the existence of this [single matter] and of alteration must stand and fall together. For if the change is an alteration, then the substratum is a single element, and all things which change into one another have a single matter. And conversely, *if the substratum is one, there is alteration.* [314b28–315a2]

On the first interpretation, then, Aristotle either ends up holding that generation is a special type of alteration – the type in which the persisting substratum is not perceptibly persistent – or modifies his idea of alteration to require perceptibly persisting substrata. In either case, generation involves a persisting substratum. Among the passages that favor the first interpretation are *Physics* I, 191a31, "my definition of matter is just this –

44 Joachim (1922), p. 108. Joachim cites 318b18–33; see also 319a23ff.

the primary substratum of each thing, from which it comes to be, and which persists in the result, not accidentally," and *Generation and Corruption*, 319ᵇ19, "the substratum is the material cause of the continuous occurrence of coming-to-be."

If water changes into earth, what is the persisting (imperceptible) substratum? Aristotle distinguishes the substratum from the affections. The foul taste of stagnant water is an affection of the water, as musicality is an affection of the educated man. The obvious substrata in these cases are the water and the man, respectively, and these do not survive the perishing of the water or the man. This accords with the *Metaphysics* VII view that the substance of a thing is its substratum: the what-it-is of the stuff in my glass is water, and this is what tastes odd.

So the substratum that survives the change from water to air cannot be the ordinary, everyday substratum. To avoid traditional prime matter, following a lead from Montgomery Furth,[45] we might say that the fluid survives. Water is cold and fluid, air hot and fluid, so the fluid persists through the change from water to air or vice versa.[46] Fluid matter survives, which before the change is in the form of water, and after the change exists as air. This fluid matter might be the persisting substratum for the change.

If air (hot and fluid) changes into water (cold and fluid), fluid matter persists, but if the water then changes into earth (dry and cold), fluid matter does not persist, though cold matter does. Fluid matter persists through the first change, cold matter persists through the second change, but neither persists through both changes. On the first interpretation, Aristotle holds that a persisting substratum survives through every change. Does this mean (*a*) that *the same* persisting substratum survives through every change, or does it mean merely (*b*) that some substratum or other survives every change, so that one substratum might survive the change from *A* to *B*, and a different substratum survive the change from *B* to *C*?

Richard Sorabji does not think (b) would be damaging to Aristotle's account of change.[47] But why should we think that (b) is not in fact Aristotle's account? The case for a persisting matter that we are discussing pertains to a substratum for elemental transformation. Even if we grant a persisting matter for elemental transformation as well as for alteration, growth, and locomotion, we still need not grant it for all changes. In *Generation and Corruption*, 334ᵇ7–13, Aristotle says that when the hot and the cold combine and destroy each other's excesses, "then

---

45 Furth (1988), pp. 223–227. See also Gill (1989), pp. 68–75.
46 Though this itself poses problems: if qualities possess numerical identity, can a numerically identical moistness inhabit first one substance and then another, numerically diverse?
47 Sorabji (1988), p. 13.

there will exist neither their matter, nor either of the contraries in actuality without qualification, but rather an intermediate." Nor is there to my knowledge any place where Aristotle says that the matter of the elements exists in actuality in flesh or bone. One possibility is that he accepts a type (a) persisting substratum for accidental changes and for elemental transformation, but not for the death of Socrates or the burning of a log. In that case, he does not require a type (a) substratum for every change.

The first option, (a), is incompatible with fluid matter as the substratum for the first change and cold matter for the second. But it would seem that fluid matter or cold matter cannot be the substrata even on option (b). For air, following Aristotle's physics, can be transformed either into water or into fire. If it changes into fire, which is hot and dry, the persisting substratum of the hot and fluid air will be hot matter. If instead it changes into water, the persisting substratum will be fluid matter. Thus what the substratum of the air is at a given time will depend on what happens to it subsequently: if it turns into fire, its substratum was hot matter; if it turns into water, its substratum was fluid matter. And air would occur in two varieties, each with its own substratum, one not potentially water, and one not potentially fire. In that case, it is difficult to see why Aristotle would count air as one element rather than two.

Thus, the matter that might be a persisting substratum for change would seem to be neither hot nor cold, neither solid nor liquid, but rather traditional prime matter.

There is, however, another possibility. One might take the matter for generation to be different from the matter of the generated and the perished. The matter of air is hot and liquid, the matter of water cold and liquid, and the matter of fire hot and dry. But the matter for the generation of water out of air might be mere liquid matter, and the matter for the generation of fire out of air mere hot matter. In other words, the substratum that persists through genesis need not be the substratum of the terminus ad quem or a quo. The transition from air to fire might involve three substrata: one for the air, one for the fire, and one for the transition itself. This intermediary substratum is present in both termini, in the sense that, for example, both air and fire are hot, but it is a substratum in its own right only for the generation as such. And it is imperceptible in that in elemental transformation all we see is one element replacing another: we never see mere hot matter – we see hot, fluid matter replaced by hot, dry matter.

This possibility has not been seriously considered in the literature because the assumption that to persist through a change the substratum must be there at the start and end of the change[48] has been combined

48 As an anonymous referee for Cambridge University Press has said, it seems analytic that "to persist through a change the substratum must be there at the start and the end." It is

with the assumption that the change includes the old and the new elements. This precludes our identifying the substrata for the elements as, in each case, involving a pair of Aristotle's basic contraries, as the substratum that involves heat and fluidity does not survive the transformation of air into water (and it precludes our identifying the substratum of the dying Socrates as a man, as the corpse is no longer a man). If we think of the change as the generation as such, however, it can have its own substratum: insofar as we are dealing with air or fire, generation either is not yet taking place or has already occurred. Thus the substratum for wood might be x, for the ashes z, and for the burning itself y.

By way of analogy, consider Aristotle's definition of change as the actualization of the potential as such. If we have all the building materials we have a potential house; when we are finished building we have an actualized house. But the actualization of the potential house insofar as the house is still potential is not the structure in its current state of completion (which is the actualization of the potential house insofar as it has been actualized) but the process of building. We can think of the substratum for generation as the substratum for the *process* of generation, in which case it is not the substratum for the starting and end points.[49]

This substratum can, in the transition from air to fire, be mere hot matter if we accept option (b), according to which some substratum or other survives every change, but there need not be a substratum that survives all changes, because it is now relieved of the burden of being the substratum of the initial substance. On option (a), according to which the same substratum persists through every change, the substratum must be prime matter. On either option, it is receptive of contraries in that it can become either solid or fluid, so it meets one of Aristotle's requirements: "The substratum is the material cause of the continuous occurrence of coming-to-be, because it is such as to change from contrary to contrary and because, in substances, the coming-to-be of one thing is always a passing-away of another" [319a20]. But since, at an elemental level, hot matter never exists except in the form of air or fire – i.e., as solid or fluid – does this substratum really exist as described? Perhaps, and perhaps not: "Whether, therefore, the substratum is or is not something,

---

not analytic if we take "persisting through the change" to mean "persisting while the change is taking place." In that case, before the change began we might have had a different substratum, and the completion of the change might result in a third substratum.

49 One might wonder whether a process, as opposed to a substance, can have a substratum. It can; indeed, for Aristotle it must, for there must be something that is undergoing the process, and that will be the substratum. What is this substratum in the current example? It would seem that it cannot be the house, for the house does not yet exist. Neither can it be the building materials: although they are being relocated, they are not coming into existence. So it must be the house, after all; but the house as a potential house being actualized, not as an actual house. And this is the same thing as the building materials qua having their potentiality to be a house actualized.

what comes to be emerges out of a not-being; so that a thing comes to be out of a not-being just as much as it passes away into what is not" [319a25]. The substratum for genesis will function as that which is potentially (e.g., fire) but not (yet) actually fire. This raises some vexing questions:

If it [unqualified coming-to-be] signifies the primary [category], there will be a coming-to-be of a substance out of a not-substance. But that which is not a substance or a "this" clearly cannot possess predicates drawn from any of the other categories either – e.g., we cannot attribute to it any quality, quantity, or position. Otherwise, properties would admit of existence in separation from substances.

For if a substantial thing comes to be, it is clear that there will be (not actually, but potentially) a substance, out of which its coming-to-be will proceed. . . . Then will any predicate belonging to the remaining categories attach actually to this? In other words, will that which is only potentially a "this" (which only potentially is), while without qualification it is not a "this" (i.e., is not), possess, e.g., any determinate size or quality or position? For if it possesses none, but all of them potentially, the result is that a being, which is not a determinate being, is capable of separate existence; and in addition that coming-to-be proceeds out of nothing preexisting – a thesis which, more than any other, preoccupied and alarmed the earliest philosophers. [317b9; 23]

Aristotle's answer, I take it, is that that which is potentially fire is actually air, and since it is actually air, it can actually have properties. (The house that can be constructed out of the building materials does not exist, so it has no weight. But the building materials weigh sixteen tons, so the house that can be built from them potentially weighs sixteen tons.) The problems mentioned above arise only if we consider the starting point not as actually air but simply as potentially fire. But this is just how we have been considering the substratum for generation as such: as actually hot but not actually fluid; were it considered to be actually fluid, it would be the substratum for air, not for the generation of fire out of air. So whether this substratum is something remains a problem if we hold that only determinate beings can have separate existence.

Another problem can arise from a totally different set of considerations. Bonaventure and Duns Scotus accepted a doctrine known as the plurality of substantial forms. According to this doctrine, an entity with its own substantial form can acquire another substantial form without losing the prior one, and thereby become another entity with two substantial forms (which subsequently might lose the newly acquired form, reverting to its original status).[50] For example, they accepted a substantial form for materiality and another for animacy. Something material might acquire the form of animacy, thereby becoming a living thing, and subsequently

50 Cf. the distinction between "the body" and "the BODY" in S. Marc Cohen (1992).

lose it (i.e., die), reverting to inanimate matter, all the while retaining the substantial form of materiality. Thomas Aquinas (and the Dominicans in general) opposed this (Franciscan) doctrine on the grounds that since substantial form makes something a substance, if the form of materiality were to make something a substance in its own right, any additional form that substance might acquire would be accidental. In other words, we would have entities that were essentially material and only accidentally animate. Animacy would be no more than a phase in the career of more enduring substances, and animals would not be essentially animate, as Aristotle holds.

The problem raised here appears in Aristotle as the problem of the unity of definition. If fluid matter is a substratum persisting through the transition from air to water, why not regard air and water as accidental forms of fluid matter (as we regard snow, ice, steam, and liquid water as forms of H_2O)? The real substance and substratum can simply be fluid matter, hot or cold. Taking this a step further, as water can be transformed into earth, why not say that even matter's fluidity is an accidental characteristic? The real substance and substratum can then be mere terrestrial matter.

The problem with this is that Aristotle gives no evidence of accepting a plurality of substantial forms and yet consistently refers to the elements as paradigmatic substances:

By "substances" I am talking about the simple bodies – fire, earth, and the other terms of the series – and all things composed of them, for example, the heaven as a whole and its parts, and again animals and plants and their parts. [*On the Heavens* III]

Substance is thought to belong most obviously to bodies; and so we say that both animals and plants and their parts are substances, and so are natural bodies such as fire and water and earth and everything of that sort, and all things that are parts of these or composed of these (either of parts or of the whole bodies), e.g., the heaven and its parts, stars and moon and sun. [*Metaphysics* VII, 2, 1028^{b}8–13]

If he had held to a plurality of substantial forms, he would have had maneuvering room in which to say that mere hot matter (or mere prime matter) can be a substratum, and at the same time both-solid-and-hot matter can be a substratum: the one the substratum of air and fire; the other the substratum only of fire. As it is, though, he seems constrained to have to reject one or the other. But he cannot reject both-solid-and-hot matter as the substratum of fire while keeping fire as a paradigmatic substance. So it seems he must reject mere hot matter as a substratum.

The Second Interpretation. But there is something unsettling about the first interpretation (according to which generation, corruption, and alteration all involve a persisting substratum, but only alteration involves a persisting *perceptible* substratum). As Harold Cherniss wrote: "the specific differentia of generation, the imperceptibility of the substrate, seems . . . artificial and arbitrary."[51] So I turn now to the second interpretation, according to which Aristotle holds that in generation and corruption one substratum perishes and another comes to be. This takes him, in saying that there is generation and corruption when "nothing perceptible persists in its identity as a substratum" to mean *not* that in this case something imperceptible persists as substratum, but rather that one substratum replaces another.

In the passage at 319a20 (quoted above) and elsewhere, we see a tendency in *Generation and Corruption* for Aristotle to equate the substratum with matter:

Matter, in the most proper sense of the term, is to be identified with the substratum which is receptive of coming-to-be and passing-away; but the substratum of the remaining kinds of change is also, in a sense, matter, because all these substrata are receptive of contrarieties of some kind. [320a3]

But even in *Physics* I, Aristotle wondered about the status of matter: "Whether the form or what underlies [the substratum, *to hypokeimenon*] is the substance is not clear" [191a19]. Eventually, in *Metaphysics* VII, Aristotle settles on form, rather than matter, as the substance and substratum. At that point, if we assume that the relevant forms do not survive the changes in question (i.e., if we reject a plurality of substantial forms), he was abandoning the claim that there is a persisting substratum for generation (if, indeed, he ever held it; on the second interpretation, even in *Generation and Corruption* he did not). Rather, his view here is that in alteration there is a perceptibly persisting substratum, and in generation and corruption there is no persisting substratum.

Matter can still, on this second view, provide continuity for generation, for as on the first interpretation, matter survives generation and corruption. At *Physics* V, 3, 227a11–13, Aristotle defines the continuous as "a subdivision of the contiguous: things are called continuous when the touching limits of each become one and the same and are, as the word implies, contained in each other; continuity is impossible if these extremes are two." Giving this a temporal interpretation, two things are continuous when the last moment of the first thing is the first moment of the second thing, so that the transition is equally the perishing of the first and the generation of the second. The persistence of matter makes this continuity possible. On the second view, however, this persisting matter does not have the status of persisting substratum.

We saw in Chapter I that Aristotle's "said of" criterion in the *Categories* allows phase sortals to count as said of a subject: both "caterpillar" and "butterfly" meet Aristotle's criteria for being said of a subject. And we saw

51 Cherniss (1935), p. 115.

the introduction of the matter–form distinction in the *Physics*. As to the second of these, as Aristotle wrote *Metaphysics* VII, he wrestled with an implication the form–matter distinction had for the views he expressed in the *Categories:* if Socrates is a composite of form and matter, he is in some sense secondary – a product of form and matter. Either form or matter, then, or perhaps both, would seem to deserve the right to be regarded as primary, not the composite that results from their union. But in Book VII his essentialism leads him to a class of forms that are essences. Since essence is identified, on his view, with form rather than matter, and since form is prior to matter and to the composite, the matter of a composite is shaped by form.[52] The matter of Socrates – i.e., Socrates' body – is living matter because Socrates' form, the soul, is a principle of animacy. Thus a composite's essential form gives determinacy to the composite's matter – the form makes the matter be the kind of matter it is – and Aristotle is willing to say that the form, rather than the matter, is the substratum of the composite. This matter, the living matter that is Socrates' body, does not survive Socrates' death and did not exist before he was conceived. But there is matter that became Socrates' body (menses and food), and there is a material residue, a cadaver, that comes into existence when he dies. The food, the living flesh, and the decaying flesh are essentially different sorts of stuff. In this sense, matter does not survive generation and corruption: when a material substance perishes its matter perishes with it. Yet, in another sense, matter survives the transition from food to flesh to cadaver – *res extensa* continues to exist. The perishing of one substance is the generation of another, and the generation of a substance is the perishing of another, but substance neither comes to be from nothing nor perishes into nothing: material substance comes to be from material substance and perishes into material substance.

So even though Aristotle's considered view is that form, rather than matter, is most entitled to be called "substratum," the persistence of matter through change gives us a sense in which the change is in something continuous (matter), though the substratum (form) does not persist.

Because the second interpretation is compatible with *Metaphysics* VII, I take it to be the view that Aristotle ultimately adopted, regardless of whether it was his view when he wrote *Physics* or *Generation and Corruption*. I take Aristotle to be saying in *Metaphysics* VII that though matter is continuous through generation and destruction, in generation and destruction there is nonetheless no persisting substratum – nothing that before the change was the substratum and after the change is still the substratum. Yet matter persists through every change, including genera-

---

52 Gill (1989), pp. 17–18, argues that the composite is not secondary.

tion and corruption, and so provides continuity for changes involving generation and destruction.

There is, however, always a substratum. As William Charlton has argued, the fact that Aristotle holds there is always a substratum does not mean that he holds that there is always a persisting substratum. To say that there is always a substratum means that if X has turned into Y, there must be something that was the substratum of X – say w – and something that is the substratum of Y – say z. There is always a substratum. But this does not entail that $w = z$. If air is transformed into water, something is preserved, for the matter of air does not perish: it becomes the matter for water. In *every* change, matter is preserved. But the change is not an alteration, for though matter persists through the change – every change – in generation and corruption there is no persisting substratum.

Our choice of examples at this point is important. If a sword is beaten into a ploughshare, the matter is the iron, and it persists through the change. Were we to allow artifacts to count as substances, contrary to the direction I indicated I would take in Chapter 1, we would then have the perishing of the sword, the generation of the ploughshare, and a persisting perceptible material substratum: the iron. *Hence on both interpretations of Aristotle's account of generation and corruption, this change must be a mere alteration.* I take this to vindicate the suspicions I voiced in Chapter 1 about the status of artifacts in Aristotle's ontology; in Chapter 4 we shall find further vindication.

On *any* interpretation, fluid matter or hot matter respectively persist through the change from air to water or fire. But on the second interpretation, fluid or hot matter either are not substrata at all, or they are the substrata only of generation as such. In either case, in elemental transformation there is persisting matter but no persisting substratum. The four elements themselves are the ultimate substrata; what persists is a subsubstantial nonsubstratum. At the start of a change we have water, and at the end of the change we have air. The stuff as a whole has changed from water to air, and we can point to nothing that at the start was water, at the end is air, and yet has persisted. We can point to the water and we can point to the air, but in doing so we do not identify a persisting substance. Yet the matter of the water has not utterly perished; it has become the matter of the air.

On either interpretation Aristotle rejects the Association Thesis we examined in I (B) ("The Persistence of Matter"), holding instead that generation occurs when one thing turns into something else, and that this can take place in what is continuous. The first interpretation takes the continuity to be provided by a persisting material substrate; the second takes it to be provided by a persisting matter that is not a persisting substrate. And on either interpretation Aristotle distinguishes generation from alteration. On the Persisting Substratum interpretation, the

difference is that in generation the persisting substratum does not perceptibly persist: there appears to be a completely different substratum
before us, although according to the thesis, the same substratum is still
there. On the Persisting Matter interpretation, in generation the old
substratum is replaced by a new substratum.

II. Compounds

A. The Doctrine and the Problem

Aristotle holds that there are several levels of physical complexity (*Parts of
Animals* I, 640^{b}17–29; *Meteorology* IV, 12, e.g.):

> Now there are three levels of composition; and of these the first in order, as all will
> allow, is composition out of what some call the elements, such as earth, air, water,
> fire. . . . For fluid and solid, hot and cold, form the material of all composite
> bodies; and all other differences are secondary to these, such differences, that is,
> as heaviness or lightness, density or rarity, roughness or smoothness, and any
> other such properties of bodies as there may be. The second degree of composi-
> tion is that by which the homogeneous parts of animals, such as bone, flesh, and
> the like, are constituted out of the primary substances. The third and last stage is
> the composition which forms the heterogeneous parts, such as the face, hand,
> and the rest. [*Parts of Animals* II, 1, 646^{a}13–24]

The list, as with most lists Aristotle gives, varies slightly from citation to
citation, but the basic model consists of: (1) *the elements;* (2) *the homogeneous bodies made from the elements;* (3) *and the heterogeneous bodies,* this last
class usually including living things and their parts or organs. Homogeneous and heterogeneous bodies are distinguished in that portions of
homogeneous bodies have the nature of the whole:

> Of the parts of animals some are simple: to wit, all such as divide into parts
> uniform with themselves, as flesh into flesh; others are composite, such as divide
> into parts not uniform with themselves, as, for instance, the hand does not divide
> into hands nor the face into faces. [*History of Animals* I, 1, 486^{a}5–9]

In the biological works Aristotle generally lists only animate homogeneous bodies, such as flesh and bone; elsewhere, however, he includes
inanimate homogeneous bodies – the metals, milk, etc.

Materials can be combined two ways. In a mixture (unfortunately, in
Greek a *synthesis*) the materials being combined are merely juxtaposed.
We have a mixture, for example, if we have a jar filled with black marbles
and white marbles. In a compound (unfortunately, in Greek a *mixis*) the
combined materials blend together. Aristotle asks about the status of a
mixture whose parts are not discriminable:

> When the combining constituents have been divided into parts so small, and have
> been juxtaposed in such a manner, that perception fails to discriminate the one

from another, have they been combined? Or is it rather when any and every part of one constituent is juxtaposed to a part of the other? The term, no doubt, is applied in the latter sense: we speak, e.g., of wheat having been combined with barley when each grain of the one is juxtaposed to a grain of the other. . . .

[But] composition [*synthesis*] and mixture [*mixis*] are not the same, but different.[53] Thus it is clear that so long as the constituents are preserved in small particles, we must not speak of them as combined. (For this will be a composition [*synthesis*] instead of a blending [*krasis*] or combination [*mixis*], nor will the part have the same *logos* between its constituents as the whole.) But we maintain that, if combination has taken place [*mimiktai*], the compound [*michthen*] must be uniform – any part of such a compound being the same as the whole, just as any part of water is water; whereas, if combination is composition of the small parti-cles, nothing of the kind will happen. On the contrary, the constituents will only be combined relatively to perception; and the same thing will be combined to one percipient, if his sight is not sharp – while to the eye of Lynceus nothing will be combined. [327ᵇ33–328ᵃ15]

He comes back to the point at 334ᵃ27–334ᵇ2. How can those who hold a view like that held by Empedocles explain how flesh comes to be out of the elements?

They must conceive it as composition – just as a wall comes to be out of bricks and stones, and this mixture will be composed of the elements, these being preserved in it unaltered but with their small particles juxtaposed each to each. That will be the manner, presumably, in which flesh and every other compound results from the elements. Consequently, it follows that fire and water do not come to be out of every bit of flesh. For example, though a sphere might come to be out of this part of a lump of wax and a pyramid out of some other part, it was nevertheless possible for either figure to have come to be out of either part indifferently: that is the manner of coming to be when both come to be out of any and every part of flesh. Those, however, who maintain the theory in question, are not at liberty to conceive things in that manner, but only as a stone or brick both come to be out of a wall.

In holding that there are homogeneous substances in addition to the elements (though composed out of the elements), Aristotle is opposing what he sees as a different tradition. He addresses the topic in *Generation and Corruption*, I, 10. The issue is whether the elements can form a true, homogeneous compound, or only a mixture:

According to some thinkers, it is impossible for one thing to be combined with another. They argue that if the combined constituents continue to exist and are unaltered, they are no more combined now than they were before, but are in the same condition, while if one has been destroyed, the constituents have not been combined – on the contrary, one constituent is and the other is not, whereas combination demands uniformity of condition in them both; and on the same principle even if both the combining constituents have been destroyed as the

53 Barnes here has "composition" and "combination."

result of their coalescence, they cannot be combined since they have no being at all. [327ª35–327ᵇ6]

Commenting on this passage, Aristotle says, "What we have in this argument is, it would seem, a demand for the precise distinction of combination from coming-to-be and passing-away (for it is obvious that combination, if it exists, must differ from these processes)." When wood burns, he says, we do not say that the wood has combined with the fire; the wood simply ceases to exist. With combination, on the other hand, three conditions must be met: (1) "Both of the constituents that are combined must originally have existed in separation"' (2) both "can again be separated out [chôrizesthai] from the compound"; and (3) "while they are combined, the constituents persist potentially, but not actually."

This last condition raises some thorny problems, which Aristotle attempts to handle with the following passage:

Since, however, some things are potentially while others are actually, the constituents can be in a sense and yet not be. *The compound may be actually other than the constituents from which it has resulted; nevertheless each of them may still be potentially what it was before they were combined, and both of them may survive undestroyed.* (For this was the difficulty that emerged in the previous argument, and it is evident that the combining constituents not only coalesce, having formerly existed in separation, but also can again be separated out from the compound.) The constituents, therefore, neither persist actually . . . nor are they destroyed . . . for their potentiality is preserved. [327ᵇ23–31]

The problem is, in what way does the persistence of a constituent as "potentially what it was before" the combination differ from its perishing? If the constituent does not persist actually, has it not perished? Richard Sorabji has said:

We cannot allow, and Aristotle does not want to allow, that the ingredients exist potentially merely in the sense that they can be reconstituted. For that would be tantamount to temporary, or revocable, destruction, and the ingredients could not then be said to persist through the formation of flesh. [54]

One answer was given by Thomas Aquinas[55] and, somewhat later, by Mary Louise Gill: the potential existence of the constituents "means that the preexisting matter contributes certain properties to the higher-level object and that those properties can identify a simpler matter once the composite has been destroyed."[56]

Her interpretation is probably the most plausible one, but it is not clear how it avoids the perishing of the constituents in a compound: the

54 Sorabji (1988), p. 69; idem (1989), p. 44.
55 See note 69 below.
56 Gill (1989), p. 160. But see Sorabji (1989), p. 42, for a reply: when fire and water combine, the compound does not retain their heat and cold, it is lukewarm. Note the passage at *Physics* I, 1, 192ª27: "As potentiality it [matter] does not cease to be in its own nature, but is necessarily outside the sphere of becoming and ceasing to be."

preexisting matter contributes properties to the compound, and these properties can reconstitute the elemental matter when the compound perishes, but don't the elements cease to exist while the compound exists? Perhaps they do, and their potential existence amounts to nothing more than their recoverability.[57]

B. Ontological Sabbatical

There is another interpretation worth considering as an alternative: the simplest and most direct way to deal with the problem is to take Aristotle as holding that the elements *are* capable of intermittent persistence: their persistence can be temporally discontinuous. They are capable, in Sorabji's words, of temporary, revocable destruction, but revocable destruction is not really destruction; it is more like going on sabbatical: the reconstituted elemental matter of a compound is numerically identical with the original matter.[58]

In support of this interpretation, we can cite Aristotle's claim (discussed in Chapter 4) that the unity of a batch of an element is akin to the unity of a heap, for it is not obviously false that heaps can exist intermittently: I can rebuild the woodpile a tornado has scattered, and after I have done so the very woodpile I had before arguably exists once more, though in the interval I had no woodpile. I can strain the noodles out of the chicken broth, and then reintroduce them, and have the same bowl of chicken noodle soup I started with, though in the interval I had no chicken noodle soup but merely the components. And automobile engines and houses can be completely disassembled and then reassembled, and at the end of these processes one has the very house or engine that existed prior to the disassembly. For these sorts of cases Aristotle might claim a special status of potential existence for the substance on ontological leave – a potential existence that differs from perishing in that the potential existent can return *with numerical identity.* That the possibility of intermittent existence was considered by Aristotle is suggested by a passage in the *Physics,* VIII, 6: "Let us suppose, if you will, that in the case of certain things it is possible for them at different times to be and not to be, without coming-to-be and perishing [*aneu geneseôs kai phthoras*]" [258ᵇ15–17]. He goes on to say that if a thing has no parts, this must be the case, but his description of the problem with combination ("if both the combining constituents have been destroyed as the result of

57 Cf. Charlton (1993), p. 211: "What she [Gill] presents as Aristotle's final view on the generation of organisms – that the preexistent material remains only potentially – differs only in emphasis, I think, from the view I have wanted to attribute to him – that it does not remain at all. To say that a material *a* persists in *b* potentially is to say that, like a statue in uncarved wood, it could be got out." A nice reply to these objections can be found in Lennox (1989).
58 Perhaps Gill's interpretation allows this.

their coalescence, they cannot be combined since they have no being at all") also lends itself to this rubric: in a compound the elements pass from actual existence to potential existence, but do not perish.

The closing two paragraphs of *Generation and Corruption* might seem to rule this out for the elements:

We must begin by inquiring whether all things return upon themselves in a uniform manner, or whether, on the contrary, though in some sequences what recurs is numerically the same, in other sequences it is the same only in species. Now it is evident that those things whose substance – that which is undergoing the process – is imperishable, will be numerically the same. . . . Those things, on the other hand, whose substance is perishable . . . must return upon themselves specifically, not numerically. That is why, when water comes to be from air and air from water, the air is the same specifically, not numerically, and if these too recur numerically the same, at any rate this does not happen with things whose substance comes to be – whose substance is such that it is capable of not-being.

But the transformation of water into air, and of the air back into water again, is not a case of Aristotelian combination, which requires two or more ingredients, conditions (1) and (2) above. Elemental transformation, Aristotle repeatedly asserts, is the coming-into-existence of one substance and the perishing of another:

We do not speak of the wood as combined with the fire, nor of its burning as a combining either of its particles with one another or of itself with fire: what we say is that the fire is coming to be, but the wood is passing away. (*Generation and Corruption*, 327ᵇ12–14)

This is just the sort of case he feels challenged to distinguish from combination. In elemental transformation one substance changes as a whole from this to that. Elemental combination, as Aristotle sees it, is more akin to association. It is not mere association, which results in a mixture rather than a compound, but neither is it the perishing of the ingredients. Its modern kin is chemical combination as opposed to mere physical association.

If we run a current through water we can transform the water into two gases, hydrogen and oxygen. These gases were, in some sense, there in the water, but not actually – water is a liquid. This is not a perfectly felicitous analogy, but the status Aristotle wants for the elements in a homogeneous substance is similar to the status we grant to hydrogen and oxygen gas in water. (I say "gas" because the hydrogen and oxygen without this qualifier are *actually* present in the water.) I am not sure that this can all be consistently worked out: Aristotle is working with a concept of material substance as lacking internal structure, as truly homogeneous, while at the same time trying to give his material substances the structured powers that we attribute to atomic and molecular composition. Within those confines, though, we can see what he is trying to do: his compounds, as Gill points out, retain characteristics and powers that can be explained in terms of their ingredients. With elemental transformation, on the other hand, there are no ingredients: there is just the substance *eks hou*.

There is another line of thought that may have led Aristotle in this direction. In the penultimate quotation before this paragraph, Aristotle says, "That is why, when water comes to be from air and air from water, the air is the same specifically, not numerically, and if these too recur numerically the same, at any rate this does not happen with things whose substance comes to be – whose substance is such that it is capable of not-being." In saying, "and if these too recur numerically the same, at any rate this does not happen with things whose substance comes to be – whose substance is such that it is capable of not-being," he is probably alluding to Empedocles, who held that the elements are imperishable. Aristotle denies that the elements are imperishable: when one element is transformed into another the original element perishes. But he also denies that the elements perish when they enter into combinations, and, as in our last passage, he distinguishes combination from generation and corruption.

The elements do not perish when they combine and are not generated when the combination disintegrates; they remained hidden in the combination and merely emerge back into the light. But the combination *is* generated and perishes, otherwise there would be no metals with properties such as malleability and ductility, which do not exist at the elemental level. This is not a perishing for the water that Aristotle takes to be a component of metals, he may have thought, because water cannot change as a whole from this to that in this case – i.e., from water to metal – which his formula for corruption requires. Water can change as a whole from water to air or earth, and these are perishings, but water cannot change as a whole into copper: it can only, along with earth, be an ingredient in metals. And how can it be an ingredient in metals if it perishes when it is poured into the pot?

C. Quantized Dispositional Essentialism

Ontological sabbatical is an interesting idea, and I am not sure anything in the texts rules it out, but it is at best tolerated by the texts. One of the considerations that led us to it, though, is promising: it is important to Aristotle's approach to distinguish cases in which *one* thing changes as a whole from cases in which a *plurality* of things go to form something new, so we should not be surprised to see him handling elemental combination quite differently from elemental transformation.

I want now to propose a way of interpreting Aristotle's account of compounds (without claiming that this interpretation is incompatible with the previous ones) which stresses this consideration.[59] I call it (only slightly tongue-in-cheek) Quantized Dispositional Essentialism (QDE). QDE is supported by the texts, for in at least one place Aristotle puts an important component of it forward as a possible solution to the problem of compounds. It was, I think, the best solution he had, though I doubt that he was absolutely confident in it. QDE gives a sense to the claim that the elements exist only potentially in compounds yet have not utterly perished, without requiring that they reemerge with numerical identity (though it is compatible with that's being the case), and therefore is an easier burden to bear than ontological sabbatical. Furthermore, it allows the potential existence of elements in a compound to consist in some-thing more than a contribution they make to the compound: they are not benefactors who named the compounds in their wills, but more like trustee-benefactors who administer their own bequeathed estates. (The status of a compound formed of water and fire is less akin to that of an American citizen whose father was Irish and mother was French than to that of someone holding dual Franco-Irish citizenship.)

I am borrowing the notion of a quantized phenomenon from physics. The feature I have in mind is illustrated by the energy states of electrons in atoms. The electron in a hydrogen atom, for example, is normally at an energy level called its "rest" or "ground state," but if the atom is bombarded with high-energy photons, the electron can be bounced to a higher energy state. It will, however, quickly divest itself of that excess energy by throwing out a photon equal in energy to the energy it ab-sorbed, reverting to its ground state. The phenomenon is quantized because the electron can only be bumped to a few discrete energy levels. Although we might think that there is a continuum from the ground state to the next-higher energy level and on to the next, and so on, the electron acts as though this continuum is a bus route where it is allowed to get on or off only at designated stops.

Aristotle's elements are *weakly quantized* in being internally disposed to return to their ground states (e.g., water to be cold and liquid), though they can wander from those ground states. They can be found away from their ground states because of external forces (think of the bombarding photon), or because of the circumstances in which they were generated: frost is water formed from air, but it comes into existence away from its (liquid) ground state because it was generated in extreme cold. (This is *weak* quantization because there is a continuum along which water can be hot or cold, and water can take any value along that continuum. It is

---

59 There is yet another interpretation offered in Lewis (1994), pp. 274–275: the elements exist in the compound as its nonproximate (Lewis says "concurrent") matter. On this view, "the concurrent *actual* matter of the mixture is *potential* earth, air, fire, and water." Whether this is compatible with the interpretation I am about to present depends on how we unpack the notion of concurrent matter.

quantization because even if what is generated is ice, which for water is cold, it still has a liquid ground state.)

Aristotle's elements are *strongly quantized* in that there are only four of them, each with its own ground state.[60] Thus, no matter what compound we are dealing with, its perishing can generate only two to four elements.[61] There are only four elements that can be generated out of the perishing of a compound, though such perishing need not yield up the elements in their ground states: it might, in Aristotle's phrase, give us a fire that, for fire, is cold.

Aristotle's *compounds* are quantized in a third way. If an Aristotelian compound has formed out of earth and water, it will eventually decay into earth and water.[62] Suppose we treat elemental earth as having a weight of four, water of three, and so on. Then we can symbolize their "elemental weights" as E_4, W_3, A_2, and F_1. Now suppose we form a compound out of one unit of water (W_3) and one unit of fire (F_1). We get two units of the compound, with a total weight of 4. One might think, then, that when the compound decays, we might get two units of W_2 (total weight = 4; total units = 2). But Aristotle seems to believe that there is only one possible consequence: one unit of air and one of earth. You get out exactly what you put in – no substitutions allowed. The destruction of a compound can only be achieved through the reversal of the process that formed it, which reversal recalls the original constituents: things "which solidify by refrigeration and the evaporation of all their heat, like iron and horn, cannot be dissolved except by excessive heat" [*Meteorology* IV, 6 383ª30–31], whereas pottery, solidified by fire, cannot be dissolved by fire [384ᵇ20–22]. (Air, on the other hand, generated from water by heat, can be destroyed by heat, generating fire, or by cold, generating water.) Moreover, not only *can* the compound break down only into the elements that formed it, but sooner or later it *must*.[63]

This by itself gives some sense to the claim that in a compound the elements do not perish but exist potentially. When water changes into air the water perishes, even though the air it becomes is in a sense potentially water. But that air need not become water; under the right conditions it might instead become fire. The destruction of an Aristotelian compound of earth and air, however, will never generate fire. Yet, had the elements perished in the compound – reverting, for example, to a common, neutral elemental matter – something besides air and earth ought to be able

---

60 It is not clear that Aristotle's compounds are quantized in this way: perhaps there are only a few kinds of metals because of accidental uniformities in the conditions under which they are generated.

61 The destruction of a compound cannot yield up only one element; if it did, the compound would not have been a compound.

62 *Meteorology* IV, 1, 379ª5–6: "All compound natural bodies rot in the end" (tr. H. D. P. Lee). Perhaps not the best translation, but certainly the most poetic.

63 See note 62 above.

to arise out of the compound's dissolution. Assuming that Aristotle's elements are quantized in this way, and that his substances can lack essential properties, let us consider his suggestion.

As we saw above, Aristotle says that air can come to be out of fire, and fire out of air, because these have a common substratum, and then asks how flesh and marrow can come to be out of fire and water [*Generation and Corruption* II, 7]. And we also saw that he lays out the problem by distinguishing those who deny that one element can be generated out of another (i.e., that the elements can be reciprocally transformed) from those who affirm it, saying that the latter are committed to there being something common to the elements. The former group has a problem explaining compounds (their compounds are not really compounds but mixtures), but those "who postulate a single matter for the elements [334^{b}2]"[64] also have a problem:

For if flesh consists of both [fire and earth] and is neither of them, nor again is a composition of them in which they are preserved unaltered, what alternative is left except to identify the resultant of the two elements with their matter? For the passing-away of either element produces *either* the other *or* the matter. [334^{b}4–8]

When an animal passes away, what was the animal reverts to matter; in elemental transformation one element perishes, producing the other. Aristotle wonders how the elements can enter into a compound without perishing in one of these two ways.[65] He then proposes a solution:

Now since there are differences in degree in hot and cold, then although when either is actual without qualification, the other will exist potentially, yet when neither exists in the full completeness of its being [*mê pantelôs*], but both by combining destroy one another's excesses so that there exist instead a hot which (for a hot) is cold and a cold which (for a cold) is hot, then there will exist neither their matter [neither the matter of the hot element, e.g., fire, nor the matter of the cold element, e.g., water], nor either of the contraries in actuality without qualification, but rather an intermediate, and this intermediate, according as it is potentiality more hot than cold or vice versa, will in accordance with that proportion be potentially twice as hot or cold – or three times or whatever. Thus all the other bodies will result from the contraries, or from the elements, insofar as these have been combined, while the elements will result from the contraries, insofar as these exist potentially in a special sense – not as matter exists potentially, but in the sense explained above. And when a thing comes to be in *this* manner, the process is combination, whereas what comes to be in the other manner is matter.

The compound of water and fire, like warm water or cool fire, is incompletely warm and cold, and so does not possess these contraries in actuality without qualification. But unlike warm water, it is not disposed

---

64 Note how he slides from "something common to all the elements" to "a single matter" of the elements.

65 I agree with Lewis (1994), p. 275, n. 55: in a compound the preexisting (elemental) matter is not destroyed.

toward being cold, and unlike cool fire, it is not disposed toward being hot. Rather, it is disposed to an intermediate state.[66] In this condition the contraries do not exist without qualification, yet neither have the elements reverted to matter, which would require their being disposed to nonintermediate states. Rather, they have "destroyed one another's excesses," creating the intermediate compound, "the hot becoming cold and the cold becoming hot when they are brought to the mean" [334b26–27]. This lukewarm compound, as an intermediate, is potentially cold in a way different from the way in which water is potentially cold. Yet, since the water has not perished, it is still there in the compound (or the compound would not be a compound of water), though it is no longer cold. It is in the compound, but not "in the full completeness of its being."

Aristotle has a profound distaste for genetic properties – e.g., the property of having been made in Taiwan, though, of course, he would not doubt that some things have been made in Taiwan. In the case of compounds, one of the sources of the *aporia* was that "if both the combining constituents have been destroyed as a result of their coalescence, they cannot be combined since they have no being at all" [327b4–6, quoted above]. This suggests that to say that something is a compound is not merely to make a remark about its origins and ancestry but to characterize its current status: a compound not only arises from its ingredients, it *is* those ingredients, combined (unlike a mixture). But unlike a mixture, in which the elements retain their dispositions, elemental dispositions in a compound are blended, canceling each other out and producing new intermediate dispositions. Now it will take an external heat or cold to free the elemental natures.[67]

Unlike the case of warm water, which is also not in the full completion of its being, the compound's water-based disposition to be cold is countered by fire's disposition to be hot. The status of the water in the compound is somewhat like the status of water in an oven, in that in both cases the water's disposition to be cold is countered by the disposition of fire to be hot. But unlike the water in the oven, in the compound the water no longer has a distinct existence: the water and the fire have joined to form a compound, disposed to be lukewarm. This compound is, at its material level, the sum of the natures of its elemental constituents, though at its formal level it possesses novel characteristics.[68]

How does Aristotle know that the elements in a compound have not lost their natures? Because of the quantum phenomenon: the decay of a compound of water and fire invariably (or so he believes) yields up the water and fire out of which the compound arose. Had the water and fire

---

66 Cf. Lennox (1989), p. 73.
67 See, e.g., *Meteorology* IV, 1, 379a16–22.
68 For these novel characteristics see *Meteorology* IV.

in the compound reverted to matter and utterly lost their natures, the compound would decay from a clean elemental slate, and might yield up water and fire under some circumstances, and earth and fire under others. But they do not: the compound irrevocably bears the imprint of its elemental constituents, which are in that way still present in it.

This last point – that the compound bears the imprint of its elemental constituents – is true on the interpretations of Gill and Lennox as well.[69] What QDE allows us to add is that the compound can retain the *natures* of its constitutive elements, though not actually and unqualifiedly possessing any of the essential properties of those elements. It retains these natures because its own nature is the counterbalanced sum of the natures of its elemental constituents. We can explain how hydrogen and oxygen somehow persist and retain their natures in water because we accept molecules made of atoms, with the molecule being something more than its constitutive atoms.[70] Aristotle's explanation of compounds is, I suggest, the analogue of this for someone who conceives of compounds as blendings of stuffs.[71]

Thus, the short answer to Sorabji's question is that the potential existence of the contributing elements in a compound amounts to more than the fact that they can be reconstituted from the compound; it turns on their being the *only* elements that can be reconstituted from the compound. Were this not the case, both water and fire would be present in air in just the same way the constitutive elements of a compound are present in the compound. But if they were, then the generation of air from water or fire would not be a perishing of air or fire. Because, however, fire can be transformed into air, and that air subsequently transformed into water, fire is not present in air in the way in which the constitutive elements of a compound are present in the compound.

The same explanation is suggested at *Parts of Animals*, 649ᵇ13–18:

Earth and ashes and the like, when mixed [*michthenta*] with water, are actually and accidentally moist, but potentially and essentially are dry. Now separate

---

69 And on Thomas Aquinas' interpretation in *De mixtione elementorum:* "The substances of the elements . . . are present in the compound, but virtually – through their powers – not actually." The view I am suggesting was rejected by Aquinas: "Some people . . . to avoid saying the compound was apparent and not real, . . . suggested that the elements didn't remain totally distinct in the compound but were averaged out in some way; for they said that the elements could be more or less themselves." Aquinas rejects this view on the grounds that (*a*) substances "don't more or less exist," to which I would reply that the water in warm water doesn't exist less than it does in cold water, and that (*b*) substances don't have contrary substances, to which I would reply that (as Aquinas notes) Aristotle's elements are defined by contrary powers. On Aquinas's view, the compound is a substance with intermediate powers vis-à-vis the elements; on my view, the compound (as opposed to a mixture) consists of elements bereft of their natural dispositions. See Aquinas (1993), pp. 117–121.
70 You can have H_2 and O without having H_2O.
71 See Kerford (1993), p. 499.

[*diakrithenta*] the constituents [in such a mixture] and you have on the one hand the watery components, which take their shape from their container, and these are both actually and potentially moist, and on the other hand the earthy components, and these are all dry; and it is to bodies of this sort that the term "dry" is most properly and absolutely applicable.

This is the same formulation he used a sentence earlier to explain ice. But the constituents in a compound exist only potentially in the compound; otherwise the compound is not a compound but a mixture.[72] And if ice were only potentially water, as flesh is only potentially ashes and smoke, or as air is potentially water, ice would not be a form of water. Ice would stand to water as air stands to water: air is potentially water, but ice is actually water – essentially cold and fluid, though actually solid. So the way in which ice is potentially cold and liquid and the way in which air is potentially cold and liquid differ from the way in which the water in the compound is potentially cold and liquid.

QDE gives us a sense in which the elements can survive in compounds without requiring that they reemerge with numerical identity. But we can, if we wish, hold to both QDE and to the reemergence of the elements from compounds with numerical identity.

If we form water out of hydrogen and oxygen, and then turn the water back into hydrogen and oxygen, it is plausible to say that we have the very same (numerically identical) hydrogen and oxygen again, for the original atomic nuclei are intact. If we now turn these gases back into water, it is not as plausible to say that we have the same (numerically identical) water again if each oxygen atom is allowed to ally itself with a different hydrogen atom than it allied with initially. Intuitively, the numerical identity of a molecule would seem parasitical off that of its constitutive atoms, and the numerical identity of a batch of water parasitical off that of its molecules.

These questions arise because our chemistry is atomic, and, much as Aristotle's biology was not cellular, his chemistry was not atomic, so he did not attempt to trace identity in this way. Nor is it clear that he would want to trace identity in these cases by dyeing bits of matter and tracking them: it is not clear, in other words, that he wants the second-generation water to be numerically identical with the first-generation water only if the matter that was the matter of the first is the matter of the second. What we have to envision is that two elements combine, resulting in a homogeneous mass whose matter cannot be divided into two neat parcels, one of which was the matter of the one element and another of the other, but rather that the matter of the compound is a uniform blend of the matter of the two elements – a blend in which the genealogical claims of each

---

72 I agree with Gill (1989), Lewis (1994), and Scaltsas (1994a) that the elements only exist potentially in a compound; we disagree on how to explain that.

parcel of matter dissolve. And Aristotle may be prepared to do this, and to claim that, nonetheless, numerical identity can be reconstituted from the blend on the ground that form, rather than matter, is the bestower of numerical identity.

This would be no easy task, and the attempt to pull it off would have to be made with one eye fixed on how to avoid entailing that a father and his son are numerically identical. But this is not to say that it is an impossible task (though it certainly is daunting). Suppose we mix five cubic centimeters of lemon juice with one hundred cubic centimeters of water, obtaining one hundred and five cubic centimeters of a mildly lemon-flavored water; then through some sort of distillation process we reconstitute the five cubic centimeters of lemon juice, though in this five cubic centimeters the aromatic lemon oils, citric acid, etc. are no longer suspended in the very same water as originally. Have we really reconstituted the original five cubic centimeters of lemon juice, or have we produced another batch of lemon juice? To opt for ontological sabbatical, Aristotle needs to argue that you now have the original lemon juice, even if the aromatic oils, citric acid, etc. are now suspended in different water. And although this is disputable, it is not implausible: think of the aromatic oils, citric acid, etc. as bearing the form of lemon juice,[73] while the water is the matter. Because the oils, etc. are what turn water into lemon juice, their imparting their form on one batch of water versus another might effect numerical identity, much as on the standard interpretation of Aristotle an organism can survive though its matter may change over time, as long as its form persists.

So there is a way of shouldering the burden, and those with particularly strong shoulders can try adopting both QDE and one component of ontological sabbatical: QDE plus the claim that the elements reemerge from compounds with numerical identity.

73 Much as in his embryology the semen bears the form.

4

Unity

I. The Unity of Definition

A. Nominal Essences

We saw in Chapter 1 that, in *On Interpretation* and in the *Posterior Analytics*, Aristotle wonders how the differentia and the genus make up a unity and questions Plato's method of division. When one is asked whether man is a terrestrial or nonterrestrial animal, the method of division leads one to answer that man is a terrestrial animal. But, asks Aristotle, "what prevents all this from being true of man yet not making clear what a man is or what it is to be a man?" Man is a terrestrial animal, but the method of division gives us no reason to think that being a terrestrial animal is part of man's essential nature. Mere truth is a necessary but not a sufficient condition for a formula's expressing an essential nature; there must be something more, but what? Some interpreters have thought that the missing element must be meaning-equivalence: that if "man" means "terrestrial animal," then "man is a terrestrial animal" states the essence of man. But Aristotle has something else in mind.[1] In a previous article I called his answer to this problem "the doctrine of proper differentiae."[2]

In the *Metaphysics* VII, 4, Aristotle says that "the essence of each thing is what it is said to be in virtue of itself [*kath' hauto*]. For being you is not being musical; for you are not musical in virtue of yourself. What, then, you are in virtue of yourself is your essence."

There are several ways of reading this passage. First, we might take Aristotle to be holding merely that your essence does not consist solely in musicality, though being musical is part of your essence (assuming you are musical). But this interpretation is incompatible with "for you are not musical in virtue of yourself." If my essence is what I am in virtue of

---

1 See Bolton (1976).
2 Cohen (1981); this section is a revised version of this article.

myself, and if my essence includes musicality, I am musical in virtue of myself.

Second, we might take the passage to be in accord with the Quinian claim that whether a thing possesses a property essentially or accidentally depends upon our choice of referring expression. Then Aristotle is saying that if we refer to you by your proper name or by a pronoun, your being musical is accidental, but he is not denying that, referred to as a musician, you are essentially musical. But there does not seem to be any textual justification for this distinction: where one might expect to find it, it is absent, and at the 1015^{b}17–24 example, Aristotle says that Coriscus and the musical and the musical Coriscus (or "the musician, Coriscus") are each accidentally one – i.e., *the musical Coriscus is only accidentally musical:* "Instances of the accidentally one are Coriscus and musical, and musical Coriscus (for it is the same thing to say "Coriscus" and "musical," and "musical Coriscus"). . . . For all these are called one by accident . . . and similarly in a sense musical Coriscus is one with Coriscus." If the musical Coriscus and plain Coriscus are *both* accidentally one, then whether plain Coriscus or the musical Coriscus is *kath' hauto* musical cannot depend on whether we refer to them as "Coriscus" or as "the musical Coriscus."[3] There seems, then, to be no good reason for rejecting the natural reading of our VII, 4, passage: musicians are not essentially musical. And if musicians are not essentially musical, an explication of the meaning of "musician" will not tell us what the musician's essential nature is. "The musical is musical" is an analytic truth, but it does not express the musician's essential nature.

Another passage in VII, 4, 1029^{b}22–1030^{a}18, leads to the same conclusion. Aristotle asks whether compounds such as pale man have essences.[4]

But since there are compounds of substance with the other categories (for there is a substrate for each category, e.g., for quality, quantity, time, place, and motion), we must inquire whether there is a formula of the essence of each of them, i.e., whether to these compounds also there belongs an essence, e.g., to pale man. Let the compound be denoted by "cloak." What is being a cloak? But, it may be said, this also is not said of something in its own right. We reply that there are two ways in which a predicate may fail to be true of a subject in its own right, and one of these results from addition, and the other not.

The explication of the two ways is, as *Notes on Book Zeta of Aristotle's Metaphysics* notes, "so obscure as to offer little help."[5] But the case in hand is dealt with in the second of the two cited ways:

Another [kind of predicate is not said of a thing in its own right] because something else is added to it, e.g. if "cloak" meant pale man, and one were to

3 We rejected a similar interpretation of Aristotle in Chapter 3, pp. 66–67.
4 I translate "pale" rather than "white" in view of 1058^{b}33–35.
5 P. 21.

define cloak as pale; pale man is pale indeed, but its essence is not to be pale [*to dê leukos anthrôpos esti men leukon, ou mentoi ti ên [einai] leukôi einai*]. But is being a cloak an essence at all? Probably not. For the essence is what something is; but when one thing is said of another, that is not what a "this" is, e.g. pale man is not what a "this" is, since being a "this" belongs only to substances.

Aristotle does not explicitly say that *cloaks* are not essentially pale; he says that pale men are not essentially pale. But he does not seem to distinguish between these two questions: whether cloaks are essentially pale and whether pale men are essentially pale. The sentence I have quoted in Greek occurs in the context of a discussion about whether "cloak" expresses an essence, and in the next breath Aristotle answers that it does not. Because in "the pale man" one thing is said of another, "cloak" expresses no essence (or expresses only a nominal essence, as he later allows). The point is explicit at 1058ᵇ3, where Aristotle says, "Paleness in a man, or darkness, do not make one [i.e., do not make a difference in species], nor is there a difference in species between the pale man and the dark man, not even if each of them be denoted by one word." On Aristotle's, view if the pale man and the dark man are of the same species they are essentially the same, and if they are essentially the same "even if each of them be denoted by one word," then cloaks are not essentially pale, and to be told that "cloak" means "pale man" is not to be told the essential nature of the cloak.[6]

Aristotle does not specify what he means by one thing's being said of another, but several interpretations come to mind.[7] One is that here paleness, an item from one category, is being said of another, man, and only the man is a substance. The topic is, after all, as Aristotle explains it, whether there is a formula for the essence of a compound consisting of a substance plus an item from some other category. (We shall examine this interpretation in the following section under the name "Accidental Compound Theory") If this is what Aristotle means, then differentia–genus definitions of substances can work only if the differentia is in the category of substance.

A second interpretation is simply that paleness is accidental to men. At 1058ᵇ33–35 he says that "the same man can be, though not at the same time, pale and dark." This seems to be the point of "pale man is pale indeed, but his essence is not to be pale." "The pale man is pale" and "the cloak is pale," to use the medieval terminology, express only *de dicto*

6 See, e.g., Bostock (1994), pp. 89–90: "Now Aristotle is prepared to distinguish the pale man from the man, since the one underlies the other . . . and on this approach it will be reasonable to say that, whereas the man has an essence, the pale man does not. We would prefer to say rather that the essence of the pale man is just the same as the essence of a man, namely to be a man. In either case we can agree that there is no essence which is peculiar to pale men" (although Bostock goes on to point out a problem).
7 These are discussed in Burnyeat (1979), pp. 22–23, and elsewhere in the literature under the title of "accidental unities" and "accidental compounds."

necessity. On the first interpretation, one thing's being said of another requires two things – a subject thing and the thing said of it; on this second interpretation, it merely expresses a contingent predication, which does not necessarily commit us to a predicated entity.

A third explanation is that there are pale things that are not men. There is no hint of this consideration in the passage before us, but we shall see that Aristotle holds that for any valid differentia d of genus G, being d entails being a G: if pale men constituted a species, only men could be pale. The idea would be that if one thing is not being said of another, there are not two things in the works, and therefore the first thing could not occur without the other.

In any case, if musicians are not essentially musical, and if cloaks are not essentially pale, expressions such as "the essential nature of a cloak" or "the essence of a musician" are misleading, for there is no such thing as the essence of a musician as such – the musician's essence is the same as anyone else's essence. Consequently, VII, 4 continues:

But is being a cloak an essence at all? Probably not. For the essence is what something is; but when one thing is said of another, that is not what a "this" is, e.g., pale man is not what a "this" is since being a "this" belongs only to substances. Therefore there is an essence only of those things whose formula is a definition. But we have a definition not where we have a word and a formula identical in meaning (for in that case all formulae would be definitions; for there will be some name for any formula whatever, so that even the *Iliad* would be a definition), but where there is a formula of something primary; and primary things are those which do not involve one thing's being said of another. Nothing, then, which is not a species of a genus will have an *essence* – only species will have it, for in these the subject is not thought to participate in the attribute and to have it as an affection, nor to have it by accident; but for everything else as well, if it has a name, there will be a formula of its meaning . . . but there will be no definition nor essence.

In the remainder of VII, 4, Aristotle qualifies this, saying that perhaps, in a sense, there are definitions of such things, and they have essences (he speaks of whether cloaks have essences and whether there is a definition of the cloak as equivalent), but not in the primary sense. But by this point he is treating the question as a matter of linguistic convenience. We can certainly explain what the word "cloak" means, and we can explain the what-it-is-to-be of a cloak (to be a cloak is to be a pale man), but in the primary sense definition and essence belong only to substance, and, as the last sentence of VII, 4, shows, Aristotle does not think of pale man as a substance: "And so there can be a formula or definition of pale man, but not in the sense in which there is a definition either of pale or of a substance."

According to Aristotle, synonymy of definiendum and definiens is not a sufficient condition for the definiens to express the essential nature of the things denoted by the definiendum. (Nor do I think he regards it as a necessary condition, but I will not argue that here.) The crucial tie for Aristotle lies not between the definiendum and the definiens, but between the differentia and the genus.

B. Differentiae and Kath' Hauto Entities

No reader can fail to notice how frequently the question of *kath' hauto* predication arises when Aristotle is discussing essence. In the lengthy VII, 4, passage quoted above, for example, he attributes essences only to primary things, and equates primary things with "those which do not imply the predication of one element in them of another." These are the things that are said to be in virtue of themselves (*kath' hauto*). On the other hand, there are the things that are said to be in virtue of another (*kat' allou*). Things said to be *kat' allou* are things that are – or are one – because one thing, e.g., paleness, inheres in another thing, e.g., a man, but this is not the case with things said to be *kath' hauto*. If this is the case, then assuming that man's essential nature is to be a rational animal, the relation between the rationality and the animal in the rational animal must be different from the relation between paleness and the man in the pale man: in the latter case, but not in the former, one thing is said of another. This is explicit at VII, 12, 1037ᵇ14–21.

That there is such a difference was recognized by Aristotle as early as the *Categories* [3ᵃ20–24], though misleading parallels can lead us to miss the point: There, as we saw in Chapter 1, Aristotle says: "No substance, therefore, is in a subject. This is not, however, peculiar to substance, since the differentia also is not in a subject. For footed and two-footed are said of a man as subject but are not in a subject; neither two-footed nor footed is *in* man." On a standard interpretation of the *Categories,* the species man is not in Socrates because the species can exist apart from Socrates, and we might take Aristotle to be making the same point about the relation between the differentia and the species: rationality is not in the species man because rationality can exist apart from man. But a principle invoked at 1ᵇ16–20 rules this out:

The differentiae of genera which are different and not subordinate one to the other are themselves different in kind. For example, animal and knowledge: footed, winged, aquatic, two-footed are differentiae of animal, but none of these is a differentia of knowledge; one sort of knowledge does not differ from another by being two-footed.

In the sense in which rationality is the differentia of an animal species, it cannot be the differentia of anything but a species of animal. But any animal whose differentia is rationality will, *ex hypothesi,* be essentially the same as a man. So in the sense in which rationality is the differentia of man – though not necessarily in whatever other senses of "rationality" there might be – it is false that rationality can exist apart from things essentially the same as men.

Well, this is almost true. Two caveats are in order. First, note that this holds only for what we might term "infima differentia": the differentia that establishes the genus, animal, can exist apart from man. Second, that any animal species whose differentia is the same as man's will be essentially the same as a man presupposes that man has only one infima differentia. But we can imagine that man has two or more infimae differentiae (Aristotle's later biology countenances this) – say, rationality and two-footedness – and that another species might have the two infimae differentiae, rationality and four-footedness, in which case rationality can exist apart from man. Admitting a plurality of infima differentiae, it need not be the case that any animal with rationality as a differentia will be essentially the same as a man. But the doctrine of a plurality of differentiae seems to have been a late development in Aristotle – it is enunciated in *Parts of Animals* I, 2–3 – and therefore of doubtful value for explaining a principle advanced in the *Categories*.[8]

Now according to Aristotle something is present in something else if it meets two conditions: first, if it is in that thing in the undefined sense of "in" by which characteristics are in the things that have them; and second, if it cannot exist apart from the thing that it is in. The principle of 1ᵇ16–20 entails that differentiae cannot exist apart from the species of which they are differentiae: the same differentia cannot differentiate two different (and non-subordinate) genera, and two species of the same genus will be one species, not two, if they possess the same differentia. So, if the differentia is not present in the species, the reason cannot be that the differentia fails the second condition – i.e., that it cannot be found apart from the species. The reason differentiae are not present in their species must be, then, that they fail the *first* condition: they are not in their species in the sense in which properties are in things. They are not properties at all. For if man were an animal possessing the property of rationality, a man would be one *kat' allou*, because one thing, rationality, is present in another thing, an animal. But then "rational animal" would not be a thing said *kath' hauto*, and man would have no essence.

I mentioned above that in the *Metaphysics* VII, 4, discussion Aristotle does not explain what he means by one thing's being said of another: is one thing said of another in "the musical Coriscus" because musicality is accidental to Coriscus or because musicality belongs to a different category than Coriscus? The thrust of the 1ᵇ16–20 principle seems to favor the second interpretation. We can distinguish the two interpretations along the following lines. Let us say that something is *accidental* to

8 For the doctrine, see Balme (1975), pp. 184–185.

something else if that other thing can exist without it, and let us say that if something belongs to a category other than the category of substance it is an *accident*. Aristotle gives the capacity for learning grammar as an essential property of man: it does not indicate man's essence, yet if something is capable of learning grammar that thing is a man, and if that thing is a man, he is capable of learning grammar [*Topics* I, 5, 102ª17–21]. So being capable of learning grammar is essential to man, not accidental. But at the same time it seems to be an accident; it does not belong in the category of substance and Aristotle talks about its belonging to things. Note, this is a special sense of accident, not the one given at 102ᵇ4–9, which specifies what I mean by *accidental*: "An accident is something which . . . may either belong or not belong to any one and the self-same thing, as (e.g.) being seated may belong or not belong to some self-same thing. Likewise also whiteness; for there is nothing to prevent the same thing being at one time white and at another not white." Essential properties are nonaccidental (i.e., essential) accidents. In other words, just because something belongs to one of the nonsubstance categories, collectively termed the categories of accident, does not mean that the things that have it do not have it essentially.

The *Categories* notion of a thing's being present in something is directed toward accidents: if the capacity for learning grammar cannot exist apart from man, and if it is in man in the sense in which characteristics are in the things that have them, then it is present in man. And if it is present in man, then it is different from man, even if it is essential to man. This is one of the features that distinguishes Aristotle's essentialism from other versions: it treats something's being essential to something else as only a necessary condition of its being included in the essence of the thing. Whereas the current central essentialist tendency is to ask whether x can exist without F, Aristotle's central tendency is to ask whether x's are said to be F in virtue of themselves or in virtue of another. That an x is essentially F in the sense that it cannot exist unless it is F, he sees to be a secondary consideration, which he normally tries to explain by an appeal to what x is *kath' hauto*.

In saying this I mean to attribute to Aristotle a doctrine Frank Lewis calls "Accidental Compound Theory (ACT)."[9] We might take Aristotle (as we saw in section A, "Nominal Essences," above) to think of "the musical Coriscus" as merely picking out Coriscus by means of a (contingent) description, but ACT takes Aristotle to hold that we are not here referring to Coriscus under a certain description, but referring to a compound entity consisting of the union of Coriscus and musicality. The musical Coriscus is, in Matthew's phrase, a "kooky entity" that comes into existence after Coriscus has taken trumpet lessons and will perish if he

9 See Matthews (1982); Lewis (1991), pp. 85–114; Lewis (1994), pp. 247–248.

stops practicing. A kooky entity consisting of Socrates plus his being seated is not identical with Socrates simpliciter: the former, but not the latter, ceases to exist when Socrates stands up.

Now one might attribute ACT to Aristotle, and hold that for nonkooky entities – Coriscus, for example – Aristotle accepts what we might call ECT (Essential Compound Theory). Musical Coriscus would then be an accidental compound, and mere Coriscus an essential compound. There is a good deal to be said for this, and some truth to it: in Chapter 5 we shall confront the fact that Aristotle holds that mere Coriscus seems to be a compound (of matter and form). But Aristotle is also pulled in a different direction. He wants to maintain that, although musical Coriscus is a compound of two entities, one from the category of substance and one from a category of accidents (remembering that something's being an accident need not mean it is accidental to its subject), mere Coriscus is one thing, not two. Musical Coriscus is a group of entities; mere Coriscus, a single thing (albeit composed in some sense of form and matter). An accidental unity is one entity inhering in another as a subject; an essential unity is one entity, period.

The origin of this seems to be in a criticism Aristotle has of Plato's Theory of Forms. The criticism is the topic of VII, 6, where the question Aristotle is dealing with is "whether each thing and its essence are the same or different." In the case of things said accidentally (*epi men de ton legomenon kata sumbebekos*), the two are thought to be different: pale man and the essence of pale man. "For if they are the same, the essence of man and that of pale man are also the same; for a man and a pale man are the same, as people say, so that the essence of pale man and that of a man would also be the same." The argument seems to be, following Ross (1961) and *Notes on Zeta*, pp. 33–34: a pale man is a man, so if a pale man is the same as the essence of pale man (and a man is the same as the essence of man), the essence of man is the same as the essence of pale man, which is absurd. "But probably it is not necessary that things with accidental attributes should be the same." (See *Notes* for a detailed account.)

But with things said *kath' hauto* is this so? To the Platonists there is no substance prior to the Ideas. Is the good itself (i.e., the Platonic Form) different from the essence of good? If so, this essence will be prior to the Form if the essence is substance. And if they are severed from one another, (1) there will be no knowledge of the Forms and (2) the essences will have no being,

for there is knowledge of each thing only when we know its essence. And the case is the same for other things as for the good; so that if the essence of the good is not good, neither will the essence of being be. . . . And all essences alike exist or none of them does; so that if the essence of being is not, neither will any of the others be. Again, that which has not the property of being good is not good.

The argument for (1) is that if the essence of F is something different from F, then F will be unknowable. The assumption is that the essence is something ("if the essence is substance"). Aristotle means that if the essence of a thing, a, is, say, b, which is different from a, then to know b will not be to know a but to know some other thing. The a's in the world, then, will be unknowable.

The argument for (2) assumes that the separation entails that the essence of good will not be good: "By 'severed' I mean that if the Idea of good has not the essence of good, then the latter has not the property of being good." Why should that be so? Perhaps Aristotle is thinking that if the essence of the animal is different from the animal, then it will not be an animal, for the essence of the animal cannot be *some other* animal. Perhaps he is thinking that if the essence of the good is different from the good, it cannot participate in the good, since the good, if it is different from its essence, is not good.

Whatever we make of this one thing seems reasonably clear: Aristotle is determined that with primary, *kath' hauto* things, the thing's essence cannot be some other thing. The absurdity of the separation would also appear," he says at 1031^{b}28, "if one were to assign a name to each of the essences; for there would be another essence beside the original one, e.g., to the essence of horse there will belong a second essence. Yet why should not some things be their essences from the start, since essence is substance?" Suppose the essence of horse to be distinct from horse. Then it will be a second entity, requiring its own essence: if the essence of a horse is an entity in its own right, there will be something which is what it is for it to be, and this will be its essence.

The essence, b, of a primary thing, a, cannot be some other thing a is related to in some way, for then either we could ask of the a that enters into the relationship aRb, what sort of thing it is apart from its relation to b, or, if that question is somehow not valid, a is not a primary thing. For if the question is invalid, then a is not what it is in virtue of itself (*kath' hauto*), but in virtue of its relation to another – b. So primary things, those things said *kath' hauto*, must somehow be the same things as their essences.[10]

And so differentiae cannot be accidents, not even nonaccidental accidents: "the differentiae must be the elements of the substance, and not merely essential attributes [*Parts of Animals*, 643^{a}27]."[11] If they were essential attributes, they would, though dependent on the things they in-

10 This point should be distinguished from the one made, e.g., in Frede (1992), p. 402: "Socrates, on Plato's view, is not a human being in himself, but only by participating in something else, namely the form of a man." For it is possible that this is so only because, on Plato's view, Socrates is not essentially human, but, say, an immaterial soul. We have our point if, for any f, Socrates is f only by participating in a form distinct from Socrates, and some values of f express Socrates' essence.

11 "Essential attributes": *tois sumbebêkosi kath' hauto*.

here in, be distinct entities from the things they inhere in, and so could not be the essences (in whole or part) of those things. Rather, the differentia plus the subject would be an accidental unity – i.e., a composite being consisting of the differentia and its subject. Therefore the differentia is not in a subject.

C. The Unity of Definition

In *Metaphysics* VII, 12 (and in *Posterior Analytics* II, v, where he is discussing "terrestrial animal"), Aristotle casts the problem in a different light:

> Wherein consists the unity of that, the formula of which we call a definition, as for instance in the case of man, two-footed animal; for let this be the formula of man. Why, then, is this one, and not many, viz., animal and two-footed? For in the case of "man" and "pale" there is a plurality when one term does not belong to the other, but a unity when it does belong and the subject, man, has a certain attribute; for then a unity is produced and we have the pale man. In the present case, on the other hand, one does not share in the other; the genus is not thought to share in its differentiae; for then the same thing would share in contraries; for the differentiae by which the genus is divided are contrary. And even if the genus does share in them, the same argument applies, since the differentiae present in man are many, e.g., endowed with feet, two-footed, featherless. Why are these one and not many? Not because they are present in one thing; for on this principle a unity can be made out of any set of attributes. But surely all the attributes in the definition must be one; for the definition is a single formula and a formula of substance, so that it must be a formula of some one thing; for substance means a "one" and a "this," as we maintain.

Here Aristotle gives two reasons for holding that the relation between a genus and its differentiae is different from the relation between a subject and its attributes.[12] (In the *Categories* passage, he had said that differentiae are not present in *any* subject but discussed only their presence in species.) First, the genus does not possess differentiae as attributes. To possess paleness as an attribute is to be pale, but the genus, animal, is not two-footed. If it were, it would be both biped and not biped, since there are quadruped animals. The second argument is difficult to decipher, and I do not know what the referent of "the same argument" is. At least part of his case, however, is that the various differentiae of a species must possess a unity that is not obtained merely by being present in the same thing. This same claim seems to be lurking behind the distinction between "terrestrial animal" as opposed to "terrestrial and animal," here in the relation between differentia and genus rather than that among the various differentiae of a species. Where the unity of a thing is *kat' allou*

---

12 A statement he makes a few lines later suggests a third reason: if the genus has no existence apart from its existence in species, it is not a complete substance and hence cannot take on attributes.

(assume terrestrial animal to be such a thing), its unity is due to the fact that the same thing is both an animal and terrestrial.[13] Conjunction is adequate to express this unity: a unity in which two things, though conjoined, retain their own natures, so that we have one thing (e.g., paleness), with its nature, inhering in another thing, with *its* nature. The unity of things that are one in virtue of themselves, on the other hand, cannot be merely conjunctive. Their essences must possess a logical indissolubility mentioned in V, 6: "In general those things, the thought of whose essence is indivisible and cannot separate them either in time or in place or in formula, are most of all one, and of these especially those which are substances. For in general those things that do not admit of division are one insofar as they do not admit of it" [1016b1–5].

The connection between the claim that the unity of things with essences must be *kath' hauto,* and the logical indissolubility claim is provided by the doctrine of proper differentiae.

D. Proper Differentiae

In the *Parts of Animals* I, 2–3, Aristotle offers a solution to the problem of the unity of definition:

If . . . they do not take a differentia of the differentia, they are bound to make their division continuous only in the sense in which a sentence is one by conjunction. For instance, suppose we have the bifurcation Feathered and Featherless, and then divide Feathered into Wild and Tame, or into White and Black. Tame and White are not a differentiation of Feathered, but are the commencement of an independent bifurcation, and are here by accident. [643a18–23]

The correct way of taking differentiae is presented in the *Metaphysics* VII, 12:

But it is also necessary in division to take the differentia of the differentia; e.g., endowed with feet is a differentia of animal; again we must know the differentia of animal endowed with feet qua endowed with feet. Therefore we must not say, if we are to speak rightly, that of that which is endowed with feet one part has feathers and one is featherless; if we say that, we say it through incapacity; we must divide it into cloven-footed or not-cloven; for these are the differentiae in the foot; cloven-footedness is a form of footedness. And we always want to go on so till we come to the species that contain no differences. And then there will be as many kinds of foot as there are differentiae, and the kinds of animal endowed with feet will be equal in number to the differentiae. If, then, this is so, clearly the last differentia will be the substance of the thing and its definition, as it is not right to state the same things more than once in our definitions, for it is superfluous. And this does happen, for when we say "animal" which is endowed with feet, and "two-footed" we have said nothing other than "animal having feet,

13 This is not to suggest that a terrestrial animal stands in the same relation to terrestriality and animality; see 1015b32–34.

having two feet," and if we divide this by the proper division, we shall be saying the same thing many times – as many times as there are differentiae.

If, then, a differentia of a differentia be taken at each step, one differentia – the last – will be the form and substance; but if we divide according to accidental qualities, e.g., if we were to divide that which is endowed with feet into the white and the black, there will be as many differentiae as there are cuts [as there are processes of division].

Before discussing this passage in detail, I want to draw your attention to the fear expressed in the last sentence: the doctrine of differentiae must be restrictive – it cannot allow just anything to count as a differentia. Otherwise there will be as many species as there are discriminations, and no classification will be privileged. We find the same warning in VII, 4: "we have a definition not where we have a word and a formula identical in meaning (for in that case all formulae or sets of words would be definitions)." It is the same warning because we could always coin a single word meaning "brown dog," and then say that we are dealing with an essence. Brown animals could be one species, barking animals a second, and small animals a third, and Fido – small, brown, and barking – would belong to all three species. He would then be three different animals: a small animal, of the same species as a shrew; a barking animal, of the same species as a seal; and a brown animal, of the same species as some bears. As Socrates says in the *Phaedrus* [265E], we want to cut things where the natural joints are rather than in the manner of a bad carver.

The doctrine of proper differentiae rules this sort of case out, and manages to be restrictive, by requiring that we take "the differentia of the differentia." A proper differentia will differentiate the species qua the genus's own differentia. Suppose that the genus is animal, and that the genus animal is differentiated from other genera of living things by the ability to initiate motion. Then species of animals must be differentiated qua being able to do this. This "qua" can be spelled out initially as follows: the differentia of a species is taken qua the differentia of the genus if possession of the species differentia entails possession of the genus differentia.[14] Thus, being cloven-hoofed entails being footed, and being footed is one way to achieve locomotion, but being brown does not entail being a self-mover. So cloven-hoofed animals might constitute a species of animals, but brown animals do not.

I said "might" in the last sentence because if we are arriving at an essence *all* the differentiae must be proper, until we arrive at the ultimate species. And since, in this chain, each differentia will entail the next one, the whole series is implicitly contained in the differentia of the ultimate species, so that the last – i.e., most specific – differentia "will be the form and the substance." This entailment requirement gives us the logical

14 See also Balme (1987) and Deslauriers (1990).

indissolubility that Aristotle mentions. If, as Aristotle holds, something's being sentient entails its being animate, then the unity between sentience and animacy is not merely conjunctive. It is not merely that something happens to be both sentient and animate, for one cannot be sentient without being animate.

The entailment principle also explicates the claim that only things said to be *kath' hauto* have essences. A proper differentia qualifying its genus is not a case of something said to be *kat' allou* because the differentia – the thing that is the candidate for being something said of something else – does not have an intelligible nature independently of that of which it is said: there is no differentia-nature that is specifiable and intelligible independently of the genus.

Does Aristotle try to apply this doctrine? Consider the account given in *On the Soul*. Animals are differentiated from other living things by sentience, desire, and the ability to move themselves about; living things are characterized by growth, reproduction, and nutrition; and in order to be an animal one must be a living thing: one cannot possess the peculiar capacities of an animal unless one possesses the generic capacities of a living thing. Growth, reproduction, and nutrition establish needs, the objects of these needs are objects of desire in animals, and it makes sense to say that having desires entails having needs. There are needs and desires that do not stem directly from the nutritive functions but from the animal's own sentient and desirous nature – e.g., the desire for pleasure itself – but it would not be unreasonable for Aristotle to think that these are parasitical off the primary – i.e., nutritive – desires. It is because the animal must work to get food that it enjoys resting; it is because it needs food that hunger is not enjoyable. The general schema would be that desire enters the world directed toward the nutritive and reproductive needs of animals, but once on the scene also has an agenda of its own, though one that would be incomprehensible without the nutritional and reproductive agenda. Waiting for a bus, you will periodically shift your weight from one foot to the other to reduce discomfort. In this case you are doing what you do in your capacity as a sentient being, not as a nutritive being. But there would be no feet and no waiting for buses without the nutritive part of the soul.

Aristotle takes the abilities to move about in the way animals do[15] and to perceive as presupposing the nutritive soul, at least to the extent that these abilities would be pointless if the animal did not have needs; and there are other ways in which the entailment could be pressed. In line with his principle that nonsubaltern differentiae must be equivocal, if being legged is a differentia of some animals, it cannot in the same sense

15 I add the qualification "in the way animals do" to distinguish the sporadic motions of animals from the motions of the celestial spheres, which do not bring them closer to anything or enable them to avoid anything.

be a differentia of furniture: presumably, the living organs by means of which animals propel themselves along – legs, wings, and fins – are only analogous to the boards that hold up tables, the wings of a plane, or the trunk decorations on a 1960 Cadillac. A wooden leg, for Aristotle, is not really a leg, but a substitute for a leg. Legs, in the sense in which being legged could be a differentia of animals participate in the nutrition and growth of the organism; they are in a sense animate substances.[16] Hence, having them presupposes being animate, and understanding what they are requires understanding that they participate in life.[17]

Even the Aristotelian characterization of man as a rational animal can be understood in this way, if we assume that the rationality that differentiates us from other animals is practical reason: the rationality that is directed toward enabling an organism to live the life of an animal well. And just as sentience can be directed toward itself – the animal can seek to satisfy desires that stem from it qua sentient rather than qua nutritive – so rationality can be exercised for its own sake. But this need not mean that the form of rationality that is the differentia of humans is not practical reason. Once a new capacity enters the scene, it can be directed toward itself. The ability to repair automobiles should be understood in terms of machines needing maintenance, but it may become an enjoyable pastime. Our ability to communicate with each other helps us earn our daily bread, but we also enjoy solving crossword puzzles. We shall return to this topic in Chapter 5, section II, where we discuss the development of the human embryo and the arrival of the rational soul.

If we are willing to allow both immaterial and material substances under the genus of substance, we can push this a step further. Animate substances possess the capacities of nourishment, reproduction, and growth, and these are capacities that only material substances can possess, so these capacities presuppose the genus material substance. There is thus a decent case for saying not only that Aristotle propounded the doctrine of proper differentiae, but that he had it in mind when he went to work.

However, our entailment criterion captures only a part of what Aristotle means by "taking the differentia of the differentia," for it allows a vexing type of case of which Aristotle says, in VI, 5, "there is either no essence and definition of any of these things, or if there is, it is in another sense." Snubness, concavity in a nose, is an example. Assume that the definition of the nose is that it is an olfactory sense organ. Since snubness

---

16 The qualification "in a sense" is made because Aristotle thinks that parts of organisms are less substantial than the organisms themselves.

17 An anonymous reader for Cambridge University Press has pointed out another example of a similar sort of equivocality in a non-differentia case: at *Posterior Analytics* II, 17, 99^{b}4–6, the longevity of quadrupeds is explained by their lack of bile, while that of birds might be explained by their being dry.

is defined as concavity in a nose, that something is snub entails that it is olfactory, and hence snubness meets our criterion for a proper differentia. But Aristotle says that "snub nose" does not express an essence.

Commenting on Aristotle's claim, Aquinas says "snubness is merely concavity in a nose":

Nose is not included in the definition of snub as though it were a part of its essence, but as something added to its essence. Hence snub and concave are essentially the same. But snub adds over and above concave a relation to a determinate subject; and thus in this determinate subject, nose, snub differs in no way from concave.[18]

An instance of snubness is just an instance of concavity, but it can be called an instance of snubness only if it occurs in a nose. In some way, I suppose, this shows that the necessity whereby what is snub is a nose is verbal, akin to the necessity by which cloaks are pale. It is worth noting that as early as the *Topics* VI, Aristotle is suspicious of definitions including a qualification different from but related to the one involved in the definition of "snub":

See, too, if he has rendered being in something as the differentia of a thing's substance, for it seems that locality cannot differentiate between one substance and another. Hence . . . people condemn those who divide animals by means of the terms terrestrial and aquatic. . . . Or possibly in this case the censure is undeserved, for aquatic does not mean "in" anything, nor does it denote a locality, but a certain quality; for even if the thing is on dry land, still it is aquatic. [144^{b}32–145^{a}2]

Here Aristotle is talking about definitions that involve a restriction on location, but it does not seem a very long jump from saying that fish are fish even if they are on the beach to saying that concavity is concavity whether it characterizes lenses or noses.

The doctrine of proper differentiae, coming immediately after another discussion of snubness in VII, 11, can plausibly be supposed to be intended to rule out such cases. Intuitively, the idea is that snubness is not a proper differentia of noses because, although something's being snub entails its being olfactory, a nose is not snub qua being olfactory but qua possessing shape. Someone who lost the ability to smell would, on Aristotelian grounds, no longer have a real nose because he would no longer have an olfactory organ, but the thing that replaced his nose would still possess the characteristic shape in virtue of which his nose was snub, and therefore the determination that "snub" added to "nose" did not belong to the nose qua olfactory.

Adding this restriction to our entailment criterion, the differentia of a species must entail the differentia of its genus, and it must be false that the determination the species differentia adds can occur independently

18 Aquinas (1961), pp. 1349, 1354.

of the genus differentia. Essences introduce unities: "an essence is by its very nature a kind of unity" [1045ᵇ3]. Since the differentia is not in the genus as a subject, and can neither exist nor be understood apart from it, the unity of a differentia and its genus is *kath' hauto*. Essential forms can also place restrictions on matter: one cannot make a saw out of wool or wood [1044ᵃ29], and one cannot have practical reason unless one has sense organs.

Aristotle sees the differentia/genus relation as a type of form/matter and actuality/potentiality relation. It is a type of actuality/potentiality relation in that the genus is a determinable made definite by the differentia: there is no such thing as something that is simply an animal – there are cows and wolves and people – and there is nothing that is colored but has no particular color. This in itself is sufficient for Aristotle to identify differentiae with form and genus with matter. He is now equipped to distinguish accidental from essential unities, with only the latter being capable of establishing primary substances. But if essence establishes primary substances, and essence is identified with form, matter cannot be the substratum.

II. Unity

We saw in Chapter 1 that the *Categories* does not rule out "stonecutter" or "Greek" as species or secondary substances: they and their definitions can be said of Socrates as a subject. The doctrine of proper differentiae, however, does rule them out, as an amphora can be Greek without being a man or an animal. It will rule out many other would-be differentiae on the same grounds: the differentia does not entail the genus. With the restrictions we placed on differentiae as a result of the case of "snubness," the Doctrine of Proper Differentiae (DPD) can also rule out "ball-peen hammer" and other similar cases, as well as phase sortals such as "colt" or "fawn."

This places restrictions on the differentiae a genus can have, but it is indifferent to other considerations. It will not, for example, rule out essences for artifacts. It would not allow "kitchen clock," because a kitchen is not a type of clock, but it would allow a chain of subordinate genera along the lines of armchair/chair/furniture/artifact, though it would rule out Louis XIV as a species of armchair. (It will also condone mathematicians as a species if only humans can possess the abilities that make a mathematician.)

The DPD is developed by Aristotle in distinguishing the sort of unity he wants to maintain between a differentia and its genus, on the one hand, and an accident and its subject, on the other. In the latter case a pale man is a single thing because the man happens to be pale; but the man need not be pale, and what is pale need not be a man, and we can/understand what paleness is without understanding what a man is. In the former case the unity is stronger: if something is hoofed it *must* be footed, and we cannot understand hoofedness without understanding footedness.

Nonetheless, though the relation between being hoofed and being footed is stronger than the relation between being pale and being a man, or between being musical and being pale, from the footedness of the hoofed it does not follow that hoofed animals are either essentially hoofed or essentially footed: that something has hooves entails that it has feet, but not that feet are essential to it. (That Sally is a blonde entails that she has hair, but not that hair is essential to her.) Even if we add that what has feet is locomotive, and what is locomotive is an animal, and that animals are essentially animals, without additional premises it would not follow that having feet is essential to a deer. (Perhaps the deer could grow wings while its legs atrophied, and yet remain the same locomotive animal.) And although it follows from the DPD that as nonhumans can be pale, paleness is not a *differentia* of humans, it does not follow that pale men are not essentially pale: one would not want to argue that because dogs are spatially extended, squirrels are not essentially spatially extended, just as Aristotle does not want to argue that squirrels are only accidentally animals because animality occurs apart from them. To show that pale men are not essentially pale, we want to point out that if the pale man is somewhat exposed to the summer sun, he will cease being pale. But then how can we avoid saying that saws are essentially toothed?

Or should we allow artifacts to have essences? In the *Physics* I, 7, Aristotle is uncertain about how to proceed:

Things which come to be without qualification come to be in different ways: by change of shape, as a statue; by addition, as things which grow; by taking away, as the Hermes from the stone; by putting together, as a house; by alteration, as things which turn in respect of their matter. [190^{b}5–9]

This passage does not sit very well alongside crucial passages from *On Generation and Corruption* and *Metaphysics*, where association does not produce generation, where alteration is contrasted with things' changing in respect of their matter, and where change of shape is distinguished from generation and corruption. These discrepancies can be addressed: certain types of objects (e.g., statues), we might argue, are essentially characterized by their shapes, so that what would be an accidental change for a horse is a substantial change for the Discus Thrower. But the passage does not suggest anything like this. It seems, rather, a straightforward assertion of things Aristotle later came to reject – if, that is, we assume that the things which come to be without qualification are substances. And if the house and the statue are substances, they should have essences.

Of course, that might be something Aristotle could accept: there is no particular reason, offhand, why he should deny artifacts essences, even if he wants artifacts to have a lesser metaphysical status than things that exist by nature. He could prevent that in some other way. He could have essences both for things that exist by nature and for artifacts, but restrict the metaphysical heights to a subset of the things that have essences – those which pass some additional test. In fact, however, he eventually claims that artifacts possess a low grade of unity, and since the extent to which something is *a* thing is the extent to which it is *one* thing, the artifact's claim to be counted as a thing is diminished. With that loss the artifact suffers a corresponding diminution of its claim to have an essence.

The peculiar form of Aristotle's ultimate essentialism derives from this. The logical or quasi-logical devices of the earlier works, though helpful, are insufficient. Solving the problem of the unity of definition, which I take Aristotle to have believed he did with the doctrine of proper differentiae, turns out to be insufficient. The question of substance and essence must be independently approached from a different direction,[19] and Aristotle in fact approaches it from two directions. One, which we address in Chapter 5, is an inquiry into the sort of unity living things possess, and how that differs from the unity of inanimate things.

The other, which we turn to now, is the the account of unity itself – that is, of the various ways in which something can manage to be one thing. This account, given primarily in *Metaphysics* V, 6, and X, 1, has as a consequence that the armchair, even if it passes the PD test, possesses such a low degree of unity that it fails to qualify as a single substance. The question, then, of whether or not it has an essence can be bypassed, for if it is not a single substance there is no "it" here: there is an association of putative substances, and we can ask whether the members of this association have essences; but as we saw in Chapter 3, association does not generate a new entity. When the chair's parts are assembled into a chair, no new substance comes into existence. As no new substance comes into existence but the chair does come into existence, the chair no more has an essence than does the pale man as such.

In V, 6, Aristotle distinguishes things called one accidentally – e.g., the musical Coriscus – from things called one in virtue of themselves. The latter he divides into (*a*) things that are one because they are *continuous,* (b) because the *substratum* does not differ in kind, (c) because their *genus* is one, and (d), because "the *formula* which states the essence of one is

19 Here is another way of looking at this: the logical connection between a differentia and its genus that the DPD establishes does not by itself show that the differentia, though semantically rooted in its genus, cannot count as a distinct entity – i.e., does not show that ACT (see sec. I[B], "Differentiae and *Kath' Hauto* Entities") is false.

indivisible from another formula which shows the essence of the other
(though in itself every formula is divisible)."[20] Apparently summing up in
(d), he says that the things whose substance is one are one "either in
continuity or in form or in formula," drawing (b) and (c) under the
rubric "one in form":

In general those things, the thought of whose essence is indivisible and cannot
separate them either in *time* or *place* or in *formula*, are most of all one, and of these
especially those which are substances. For in general those things that do not
admit of division are one insofar as they do not admit of it, e.g., if something qua
man does not admit of division, it is one man. . . . Now most things are called one
because they do or have or suffer or are related to something else that is one, but
the things that are primarily called one are those whose substance is one, and one
either in *continuity* or in *form* or in *formula*, for we count as more than one either
things that are not continuous, or those whose form is not one, or those whose
formula is not one. [1016ᵇ1–11]

A somewhat different list appears at the start of Book X, where Aristotle
mentions a previous discussion (presumably the discussion in V) and
divides the things said to be one into two main groups: things that are
one because their *movement* is one and indivisible in time and place, and
things that are one because their *formulae* are one, in which case the
thought of the thing is one and indivisible. Each of these groups is in turn
subdivided: the first into the continuous and that which is a whole; the
second into things indivisible in number or in kind.

Things that are one because the substratum is one in kind do not
appear in the second list; presumably Aristotle thinks they can be assimi-
lated into some elaboration of things one in genus. The example he had
mentioned in *Metaphysics* V of things one in substratum were olive oil and
wine, on the grounds that their ultimate substratum is water or air (the
fluid elements). These are not one by continuity: there are portions of
olive oil and wine that are not in contact with others. Nor are they one in
formula: the formulae for oil and wine would presumably be different.
He introduced oil and wine by saying that although wine and water are
each said to be one qua indivisible in kind, all liquid extracts – e.g., olive
oil and wine – are said to be one because the substratum is the same. This
would seem to amount to some sort of generic sameness.

A. One in Movement

The things that are called one because they are continuous are treated
somewhat differently in the two texts. In V, Aristotle says:

Of things that are called one in virtue of their own nature, some are so-called
because they are continuous, e.g., a bundle is made one by a band, and pieces of

20 Barnes lists a fifth, (*e*), at 1016ᵇ11, but I take that passage to introduce a general
   observation.

wood are made one by glue. . . . Of these themselves the continuous by nature are more one than the continuous by art. A thing is called continuous which has by its own nature one movement and cannot have any other; and the movement is one when it is indivisible, and indivisible in time. Those things are continuous by their own nature which are not one merely by contact; *for if you put pieces of wood touching one another, you will not say that these are one piece of wood or one body or one continuum of any sort.* [1015ᵇ36–1016ᵃ9]

The passage seems to have been written in haste, for in it Aristotle put himself in a bit of a quandary.[21] In the first sentence a tied bundle is continuous and one in virtue of its nature. It is difficult to see how this can be reconciled with the definition at *Physics* V, 3, 227ᵃ11–12: "The continuous is a subdivision of the contiguous: things are called continuous when the touching limits of each become one and the same and are, as the word implies, contained in each other; continuity is impossible if these extremes are two."[22] In a bundle of sticks the contiguous surfaces of the sticks remain distinct. The *Physics* definition would apply to the Atlantic Ocean and the Mediterranean Sea, which fuse in the Straits of Gibraltar, but not to two sticks, whose extremes remain distinct whether the sticks are tied together or not. The *Physics* definition is also in line with the Greek word translated as continuous, *syneche*, which suggests fusion.

The third sentence gives us a different account of the continuous: a thing is continuous if it has by its own nature one movement. Presumably the bundle of sticks meets this condition even though the extremities of each stick are distinct from those of the other sticks, whereas a stack of blocks does not. The idea would be that though the stack can be moved as a unit, the bundle's being moved as a unit is due to its nature as a bundle, whereas the stack's is due to the accidental circumstance that it is on a pallet or that your arms can encompass it.

Things continuous by their own nature have one motion and are not one merely by contact, "for if you put pieces of wood touching one another, you will not say that these are one piece of wood or one body or one continuum of any sort." This implies that the touching sticks are not even one by art (as opposed to by their own nature), for they are not one at all. If mere contact does not make the sticks one by art, what sorts of things are one by art? The answer ought to be the bundle and the glued or nailed blocks, but these are given in the first sentence as examples of things one by nature. Aristotle also says in the *Physics* passage that "things that are in contact are not all naturally united," and surely if anything fits that bill it is a bundle of sticks.

Aristotle adds that a thigh and a shin each are more unified than the

21 See Kirwan (1993), p. 136.
22 See also *Categories*, 4ᵇ23–5ᵃ15.

leg as a whole, "because the movement of the leg need not be one." You can lift your thigh while swinging your shin up, or swing your shin while keeping your thigh still, but your shin is a thing "no part of . . . which [that] has magnitude rests while another moves." So something composed of articulated parts capable of independent motion is to that extent less unified.

In the *Metaphysics* V passage, the furniture maker creates things that are one by nature by nailing and gluing things together; but when, preliminary to nailing or gluing, he tests whether the joints have a good fit, he does not create one anything. In fact, through clever joinery one can make furniture and houses the parts of which lock together without any fasteners; pull or lift a part of such a chair and the whole chair will slide across the floor or rise with one movement. I take it that Aristotle would allow that chair to count as one thing. The problem is that he is then classifying it as one by nature. What he might have had in mind is that a chair is one by nature as possessing the nature of a chair, rather than as meeting, say, the *Physics* account of things that exist by nature. But if the parts of the chair are merely in contact and not joined together, so that if you pull on one leg, that leg will come off while the other parts collapse to the ground in a jumble, you do not really have a chair. You did not have one *anything*.

The need for generosity arises because in the previous paragraph Aristotle had been talking about things that are one by accident – e.g., the musical Coriscus. Now, rather than talk about subject/accident composites, he means to be talking about subjects alone. And since the previous paragraph appropriated the phrase "one by accident," he now speaks of the bundle as one in virtue of its own nature, since it is a subject, when he should be speaking of it as one by art or accident. Yet he believes that mere contact does not create a unity (though there are sortals covering things united only by contact), and that things naturally unified are more unified than things unified by art. He should have said that one of the weakest senses in which we can call something one obtains if its components are united only by contact, and that these things, heaps and stacks, are one in a Pickwickian sense weaker than the one in which the cloak (i.e., pale man) is one: in the latter case we have one thing in that we have one substance with a property inhering in it; in the former case we have one thing only in that we have something in contact with something else, and one thing in contact with another amounts to two adjacent things, even if we have a single word for the pair. "Pair," in fact, is another such term: if I have a left shoe and a right shoe, I do not thereby have a third thing – a pair of shoes. Otherwise, to adapt his formulaic objection, any selection of things could be made one thing by coining a term for it.

The same difficulty arises in the *Metaphysics* X, 1, account of unity, where one species of things that are one "primarily and of their own nature and not accidentally" is the continuous, "and especially that which is continuous by nature and not by contact nor by bonds, and another is "that which is a whole and has a certain shape and form . . . and especially if a thing is of this sort by nature, and not by force like the things that are unified by glue or nails or by being tied together, i.e., if it has in itself something which is the cause of its continuity" [1052ª15–25].

Thomas Aquinas puts Humpty Dumpty back together again by taking the first sentence of our V, 6 quote to refer to things that are essentially one because they are continuous in virtue of something other than themselves: the bundle of sticks is continuous in virtue of the band; the blocks of wood are one in virtue of the glue.[23] And this, he says, can come about by nature or by art – i.e., sometimes nature provides the bands or the glue. He then glosses our last sentence as introducing things that are one because they are continuous in virtue of themselves rather than by contact, so Aristotle's point is that contiguous blocks of wood do not have any unity of themselves: if they have one motion that is due to the glue, not to the blocks. The bundle is the sticks/thong composite, and its unity is not due to the sticks; the woodpile, on the other hand, has no unity. This is, it seems to me, what Aristotle ought to have said, though the required interpretation of the glued or tied objects of the first sentence is an act of generosity.

These are, I think, slips. More problematic is the maxim that "a thing is called continuous which has by its own nature one movement and cannot have any other." Does the bundle fit this bill? Perhaps, so long as the thong holding it together is secure, but the force of the "cannot" is puzzling. So long as the tie is secure, the bundle can only have one movement: one is tempted to say that the *bundle* can only have one movement; when the sticks can have more than one movement, the tie has come undone, and it is not clear that the bundle still exists at that point. It would seem to be more like a shoe with the glue and nails stripped away, which is actually no longer a shoe, though it might look like one. But where we might be tempted to say that described as a bundle the sticks can have only one movement, whereas untied the sticks are free to go their separate ways, Aristotle's inclination is to say that the bundle has a single motion and its sticks cannot go their separate ways. An Aristotelian bundle is not the sticks described in a certain way, but the sticks physically secured to each other. The stack, on the other hand, evokes a different response in him. (He is still not inclined to say that the stack is the blocks described in a certain way: the stack is the blocks resting on top of one another.) Things are continuous, he stated in *Physics* V, if the limits of each become one and the same. In that case, the

23 Aquinas (1961), V, L.7: C 850–851, 856.

blocks are fused, like Siamese twins, and the joint is not the exclusive possession of either block. Consequently, where the one block goes, the other must follow: they possess one movement. If the fusion of the limits was meant to entail a single motion, neither the stack nor the bundle fits the bill.[24]

Commenting on these passages, Christopher Kirwan begins by observing that "it is analytic that everything is one something: a plank is one plank, a bundle of planks is one bundle, a consignment of unbundled planks one consignment."[25] Aristotle does not think this is quite right: the flowers in my yard are not one *anything;* they are incorrigibly plural. We may *treat* them as one thing – e.g., the Cohenian flower collection – as we can treat my left shoe plus my right shoe as one thing if we wish. But this does not mean that they *are* one thing.[26]

One way of handling this is by reviving the doctrine of ontological sabbaticals that we flirted with in Chapter 3 (sec. III). There we rejected ontological sabbatical as a way of providing a sense in which the elements are present potentially in compounds, preferring Quantized Dispositional Essentialism. But ontological sabbatical might still be plausible for heaps and other sorts of aggregates. I have a woodpile by the back door of my house. A tornado scatters the logs all over the yard, and I no longer have a woodpile, though I still have the logs. After an hour's work my woodpile exists again. A woodpile, like a lap, can duck in and out of existence – it can seek refuge from life's cares in the realm of nonbeing. Anything this playful either is not a thing at all, or is the most minimal, ephemeral sort of thing there can be. The same thing can happen to my house: if a tornado knocks my house down, I might be able to reassemble it, and then *it* would exist again. (Aristotle would still be free, though, to say that the house has a stronger degree of unity than the woodpile, inasmuch as it has a certain form and function [1052ª22–25].)

But this is not how Aristotle approaches the question. He takes the woodpile not to be one thing at all. To be one, its constituents must be glued, nailed, or tied together, so that the woodpile has a single movement. Aristotle's concern here is to describe the conditions under which a number of things constitute a larger thing, and his basic answer is that this occurs when those things are bound together, so that to move a part

---

24 That the fusion of the limits is so intended is suggested by David Bostock (1991), p. 181.
25 P. 135.
26 Burnyeat (1990), pp. 194–197, has a nice example, which, with some twists and apologies, I set out as follows. Suppose a wagon to be composed of a yoke, a body, an axle, and wheels. Now consider my "wagonsum," Rosebud, which consists of the yoke of one friend's wagon, the body of another's, the axle of a third's, and the wheels of a fourth's. (We were a poor family and could not afford a normal wagon.) Owing to the selfishness of human nature, the parts of my friends' wagons stayed on their wagons, so the parts of my wagonsum were never brought into contact. Was Rosebud, nonetheless, something?

of the large thing will be to move the whole large thing.[27] He is claiming, in other words, that mere association is not generation: bringing things closer together does not create a new thing; even bringing them into contact does not create a new thing. Leibniz, in his correspondence with Arnauld, argues as follows:

Let us assume that there are two stones, for instance the diamonds of the Grand Duke and of the Grand Mogul: one and the same collective name may be given to account for both, and it may be said that they are a pair of diamonds, although they are to be found a long way away from each other; but it will not be said that these two diamonds compose one substance. Matters of degree have no place here. If therefore they are brought closer to one another, even to the point of contact, they will not be more substantially united on that account; and *even if after contact one were to add some other body calculated to prevent their separating, for example if one were to set them in a single ring, all that will make only what is called "one by accident."*

He goes on to say that the two diamonds are not a "single complete substance":

no more than would be the water in a pool with all the fish included, even if all the water with all these fish were frozen; or a flock of sheep, even though these sheep should be bound together to such an extent that they could walk only at the same pace and that one could not be touched without all the others crying out. There is as much difference between a substance and such an entity as there is between a man and a community, such as a people, army, society or college, which are moral entities, where something imaginary exists, dependent on the fabrication of our minds.[28]

Aristotle does not mention things that are not even in contact – e.g., the two diamonds before they are brought together, the solar system, or an army or herd. He does not even consider crowds or armies or the group of people who were shopping in the central marketplace at noon yesterday, which are not even one by contact but will become so if the people in them join hands.[29] I take it that he would say that the unity of a crowd is accidental.

There is another place in the corpus where the issues involved here can help us to understand an otherwise obscure passage. At *Physics* IV, 3, 210^{a}25–210^{b}22, Aristotle, wrestling with the notion of place, asks

27 Kirwan (1993), p. 137.
28 Leibniz to Arnauld, letter of Nov. 28/Dec. 8, 1686, in Mason (1967), p. 94. In a subsequent letter to Arnauld, dated April 30, 1687, Leibnitz claimed that the two diamonds are only an entity of reason, and that brought together they are only an "entity of perception": "what constitutes the essence of an entity through aggregation is only a state of being of its constituent entities. . . . If a machine is a substance, a circle of men holding hands will be too, and then an army, and finally every multiplicity of substances" (ibid., pp. 121–122).
29 One of Leibniz's examples is a group of people joining hands in a circle; he thinks nothing new thereby comes into existence.

whether something can be in itself. He answers that it can qua something else, but not qua itself:

When there are parts of a whole – the one that in which a thing is, the other the thing which is in it – the whole will be described as being in itself. For a thing is described in terms of its parts, as well as in terms of the thing as a whole, e.g., a man is said to be pale because the visible surface of him is pale, or to be scientific because his thinking faculty is. The jar, then, will not be in itself and the wine will not be in itself. But the jar of wine will; for the contents and the container are both parts of the same whole. . . .

And it can be seen by argument that it is impossible. For each of two things will have to be both, e.g. the jar will have to be both vessel and wine, and the wine both vessel and jar . . . so that however true it might be that they were in each other, the jar would receive the wine in virtue not of *its* being wine but of the wine's being wine, and the wine will be in the jar not in virtue of *its* being a jar, but of the jar's being a jar.

Something can be said to be in something else because it is in a part of that thing: because paleness is in the surface of Socrates' body, and therefore in his body, Socrates is pale. The wine-part is in the jar-of-wine-whole because it is in the jar-part, and the jar-part is in the jar-of-wine-whole, so both the jar and the wine are in the jar-of-wine. But the jar-part plus the wine-part *is* the jar-of-wine, so the jar-of-wine is in the jar-of-wine (i.e., in itself). But the wine is in the jar-of-wine only in respect to being in the jar-part, not in respect to being in the jar-of-wine-whole, for if the wine were in the jar-of-wine-whole, the jar it is in would be both the jar and the wine: this "would require that either of two things should be present as both – e.g., that the jar should be both the vessel and the wine, and the wine both the wine and the jar – if it is possible for a thing to be in itself [210^{b}10–13]." The jar-of-wine, then, is only a quasientity. What we really have here is wine in a jar: two things, not one.

Leibniz's example of the water in a pond frozen with all the fish in it is interesting, for the frozen pond would seem to meet Aristotle's criterion of unity of motion, as would a ring with a sapphire securely set in it. Again, Aristotle's problem seems to be that he has set up his scheme so that the bundle is one in virtue of its nature. That he was aware he had a problem is shown by his saying, a sentence after the introductory sentence in which he gives the bundle as an example of things called one in virtue of their own natures, that "of these themselves the continuous by nature are more one than the continuous by art." The continuous by nature (e.g., the thighbone) is a proper subspecies of things one in virtue of their own nature (e.g., the fasces).

On the other hand, Aristotle's choice of examples leaves the status of a chunk of ice in doubt. Its substratum (water) does not differ in kind, and it is continuous and indivisible in movement. Yet the chunk of ice as such does not seem to exist by nature according to the IPP, any more than the jacket as such does: their internal sources of change are due to their matter. And the chunk of ice fails a more stringent test: "In general those things the thought of whose essence is indivisible and cannot separate them either in time or place or in formula are most of all one" [*Metaphysics* V, 6, 1016ᵇ1–2; cf. X, 1, 1052ᵃ30–1052ᵇ1]. The thought of the essence of a chunk of ice is divisible, for chunk is not a proper differentia of ice.

B. One in Formula

In Chapter 1 we saw that in the *Metaphysics* VI, 1, Aristotle sometimes characterizes physics as dealing with things that can be moved. It might seem appropriate, then, that when he wants to enumerate these things he does it in terms of motions: that which is capable only of a single motion to that extent counts as a single thing; that whose parts are fused together, and which therefore cannot go off in separate directions, counts to that extent as a single thing. But the bed and the bundle, though they possess a single motion, do not possess an IP: thus, the unity that stems from having a single motion corresponds to the broad characterization of nature.

One way in which Aristotle could have developed his thought would have been to conclude that single-motion unity is the only sort of unity that exists in the subject domain of physics. He could still have distinguished things with an IP and things without an IP; these would simply be subclasses of things capable only of single motions. However, he says repeatedly that to be *one* thing is to be *a* thing, so if the only way in which things can be one is through possessing a single motion, they will all be things in the same sense or to the same extent.

The narrow characterization of nature must then somehow be captured by the other sort of unity he talks about: the unity of things whose formula is one. But it is difficult to see what he had in mind by this. On the nicest reading, a formula will be one if it consists of a proper differentia and genus, since this gives sense to the claim that in this case the thought of the essence "is indivisible and cannot separate them either in time or in place or in formula" [1016ᵇ1–2]. But, as we have seen, there is no reason to think that this will restrict the domain to things that have an IP.

And some of Aristotle's attempts to help us fail: he says, for example, that "those things that do not admit of division are one insofar as they do not admit of it, e.g., if something qua man does not admit of division, it is one man" [1016ᵇ3–5]. But this does not give us enough, because the shoe qua shoe does not admit of division either – its parts are not shoes. It excludes the heap, whose parts may themselves be heaps, but it does not exclude any of the substances Aristotle terms "nonhomogeneous."

A more promising line of inquiry occurs in *Metaphysics* VII, 17:

As regards that which is compounded out of something so that the whole is one –
not like a heap, however, but like a syllable – the syllable is not its elements, *ba* is
not the same as *b* and *a*, nor is flesh fire and earth, for when they are dissolved, the
wholes, i.e., the flesh and the syllable, no longer exist, but the elements of the
syllable exist, and so do fire and earth. The syllable, then, is something – not only
its elements (the vowel and the consonant) but also something else [*estin ara ti hê
sullabê, ou monon ta stoicheia to phônêen kai aphônon alla kai heteron ti*]; and the flesh
is not only fire and earth or the hot and the cold, but also something else. . . .
[And] it would seem that this is something, and not an element, and that it is the
cause which makes this thing flesh and that a syllable. And similarly in all other
cases. And this is the substance of each thing, for this is the primary cause of its
being, and since, while some things are not substances, as many as are substances
are formed naturally and by nature, their substance would seem to be this nature,
which is not an element but a principle. (An element is that into which a thing is
divided and which is present in it as matter, e.g., *a* and *b* are the elements of the
syllable.) [1041^{b}11–33]

What makes the syllable itself something, so that it is not just the letters, is
form, and as many things are substances as are formed by nature. So it is a
thing's possessing its form by nature that must be added to the Doctrine
of Proper Differentiae, and this will exclude artifacts.
    In VII, 4, Aristotle adds another restriction:

Definition and essence in the primary and simple sense belong to substances.
Still, they belong to other things as well in a similar way, but not primarily. For if
we suppose this it does not follow that there is a definition of every word which
means the same as any formula; it must mean the same as a particular kind of
formula; and this condition is satisfied if it is a formula of something which is one,
not by continuity like the *Iliad* or the things that are one by being bound together,
but in one of the main senses of "one," which answer to the senses of "is"; now
"that which is one" in one sense denotes an individual [*tode ti*], in another a
quantity, in another a quality. And so there can be a formula or definition of a
pale man, but not in the sense in which there is a definition of pale or of a
substance. [1030^{b}5–13]

The senses of unity that answer to the main senses of being do not
include things' being one by continuity or by being bound together. As
the sense of "one" Aristotle gives as denoting an individual seems to be
that of substance, he appears to be saying that things that are one
(merely) by continuity or by being fastened together are not really substances, or not substances in the strongest sense. Things that are bound
together are meant to be, at best, I take it, collections of substances rather
than substances. The status of things that are one by continuity, on the
other hand, is unclear. In particular, it is unclear how Aristotle would like
to treat things like the *Iliad:* is it one by continuity, or an aggregate with
no real unity at all? And it is also unclear how Aristotle wishes to handle

the pond whose water is one by continuity and formula but is capable of running downhill from northern and southern creeks.

C. Parts and Wholes

Aristotle has another recourse. One of his most frequently cited dicta is that a putative organ that cannot fulfill the functions of that organ is such an organ in name only. An eye that cannot see is not really an eye, and a severed hand, incapable of grasping anything, is not really a hand.[30] So, for living things, the functioning of whose parts depends on the part's being functionally united with the rest of the organism, "a part apart is not a part." The part in these cases cannot survive its separation from the organism. (We shall examine this principle more closely in Chapter 5.) Let us call this the *Severed-Hand Principle.*

Aristotle says that such parts are only potentialities [1040^{b}5]: "Yet all the parts [of living things] must exist only potentially, when they are one and continuous by nature, – not by force or even by growing together" [1040^{b}14–15]. They cannot exist separately while retaining their natures as parts; when separated they exist as mere matter, like the lintel which, tossed into the woods by a tornado, is merely a 2 x 6" board.

The Severed-Hand Principle can be understood as flowing from two restrictions: (*a*) the parts in question are organs, and (*b*) organs are understood to be defined in terms of functions. Because the organ is defined functionally, and because it has the definitional functional capacity only if it is united with the body's other organs, it ceases to meet its definition once that unity is broken, and hence ceases to be an organ of the appropriate type.

Perhaps biological organs are the only things that come directly under the Severed-Hand Principle. Nonetheless, Aristotle in effect gives the principle a much broader range. He does not restrict it to living things, but treats it as a universal test for substantiality. He does this because he believes that for inanimate objects as well as for living things, if a part *can* survive its separation from the whole, the whole was not a substance. If I take a shoe apart, the heel remains a heel, the sole remains a sole, and the nails remain nails. The shoe is a collection of parts, each of which has at least as much claim to being a substance in its own right as the whole assembly does, and perhaps more. In this case, Aristotle claims, the whole is not a substance.[31]

Call this the *Indivisibility Principle.* Its clearest expression is at 1041^{a}5:

---

30 See, e.g., 1036^{b}30–33.
31 I take the lintel and the lunch to be special cases: the 2 x 6 is a lintel only in the doorway, and the lunch a lunch only if served at midday, but the things that are lintels or lunches do not perish when they are displaced or eaten later, just as the dinner guest does not perish if the stove won't light.

"No substance is composed of substances."[32] There is no glue in the ontological zoo – not, at least, as a constituent of other things. Aristotle, we have seen, is not inclined to think that we can create new things by juxtaposing old things. The Indivisibility Principle says that even if we nail, glue, or tie things together, they will not thereby constitute a new thing. The result is a downgrading of the unity of a thing that is one in virtue of its movement's being indivisible in time and place, as the movement's indivisibility may be due to nails, glue, or rope. If something is a full-fledged entity in its own right, lashing it to another such entity will neither diminish its claim to be a full-fledged entity nor allow it to transfer its substantiality to the resulting composite. Ontology is a zero-sum game: an entity can contribute to another's substantiality only by giving up its own.

At this crucial juncture in Aristotle's thought, he is following a line developed by Plato. At 156B in the *Parmenides* we read: "Also, since it is one and many, and a thing that comes to be and ceases to be, when it comes to be one, its being many ceases to be, and when it comes to be many, its being one ceases to be. And as coming to be one it must be combined, as coming to be many, separated."[33] As being one and being many are incompatible, what comes to be one ceases to be many, and what comes to be many ceases to be one. When it becomes many, the one it was perishes; when it becomes one, the many it was perish. (So if an animal is one substance, it cannot be many substances.)

We find variations on this elsewhere in the *Parmenides*. At 137C, for example, if there is a one, and it is a whole having parts, the one will "be many and not one." In the *Theaetetus* at 204A–205E, if a syllable is the sum of its parts, then since its parts are many, it is many. If a syllable, then, is a single thing, it is not the sum of its parts but rather something else, indivisible.[34]

---

32 Cf. letter of Arnauld to Leibniz, Aug. 28, 1687, in Mason (1967), p. 134: "If a particle of matter is not one entity, but many entities, I do not conceive how a substantial form . . . is capable of causing it to cease to be many entities and to become one entity."

33 Cornford translation.

34 Some will say, following Wiggins (1967 and 1980), that "thing" and "substance" are dummy sortals, and that identity is sortal-relative, and sortal-relative only to non-dummy sortals: *a* and *b* might be the same letters but different syllables, still, we cannot give any real sense to "*a* and *b* are the same *things*" or "*a* and *b* are the same *substances*." Aristotle does not, on my reading, agree. Undaunted by the task of deciding whether my chair is one thing or many, he says that it is many: machine bolts, pieces of plywood, etc. See Matthews (1982), pp. 229–230, and White (1971), p. 178 (though they are dealing with a different set of problems).

There is something comforting in the thought that there is a number that is the number of things in the universe, or, more humbly, in my office. Moreover, on Aristotle's view, we are wiser shoppers, as often we pay for one thing (e.g., a radio) but in fact get dozens of things. This is much better than paying for a radio and getting a (i.e., one) radio: one pays for a radio, which is not one thing but a collection of things, and so gets many things for the price of one.

To this line of thought Aristotle adds his own twist: he does not hold that if a thing is composed of many parts it is therefore many things and not one thing, but rather that if a thing is composed of parts *that are themselves substances,* then it is not a (single) substance itself.[35] If a thing is one substance, it cannot also be several substances; and if it is several substances, it is not one substance. Thus the parts of living things, though widely regarded to be substances and frequently listed by Aristotle as examples of substances, fail the most stringent test. If the whole animal is one substance, its parts cannot themselves be substances. (The musical Coriscus, on the other hand, passes this test, for though it has two parts – Coriscus and musicality – one of these parts is not a substance, and so the whole is not composed of a plurality of substances. The substance that it is, is Coriscus, though it is not only that substance. Its being not only that substance is its being a substance *kat' allou.*)

I am not sure this has been noted before, but in denying that the parts of substances can themselves be substances Aristotle is departing from the view he took in the *Categories.* There he has an aside (3ª30–33) in which he points out that since one of his criteria for something's being present in something else is that it *not* be in that thing as a part, "we need not be disturbed by any fear that we may be forced to say that the parts of a substance, being in a subject (the whole substance), are not substances." I take it, then, that his initial view was that the parts of substances *are* substances, but that upon reflecting on the nature of associations, aggregates, and unity he abandoned this position. Thomas Aquinas has an interesting gloss on this in his *Disputed Questions on the Soul:*

35 I am trying here to avoid committing Aristotle to holding that a substance cannot be composed of parts, but only to the weaker thesis that if a substance is composed of parts, those parts cannot themselves be substances. Charlton (1991), pp. 131–135, argues that if an Aristotelian whole consists of actual parts, the whole is merely possible, and if the whole is actual, the parts are merely possible: the five cubes into which a beam might be sawed are mere possibilities when the beam is actual. If Aristotle holds this for all substances, no whole is composed of parts. But Charlton is dealing primarily with the (potential) parts of an undivided whole: a beam, say, or a length of string.

    The case seems to me different if we deal with organic parts: as anyone who has dismembered a chicken knows, socket joints are *natural* dividing points, and the eye, heart, or hand have a greater claim to be called "actual parts" than does the Hermes statue hidden in the log. (The possible Hermes statue cohabits the log with a possible Madonna statue and a possible equestrian statue, but the eye socket contains an actual eye, whereas the log, a comparative underachiever, actually contains only wood.)

    True, Aristotle holds that the parts of a thing that is one and continuous by nature exist *dunamei.* But as I read him there is room for play here. A living animal is one and continuous by nature, but its organic parts, e.g., tibia and femur, also have some claim to this status, and each has a quasi-substantial form. This form, functionally or teleologically defined, is responsible for the material unity and continuity of the part, and to that extent makes the part an actual part. The "organ-form," however, is parasitical off the "whole-animal-form" (and hence so is the shape of a bone), in a way in which the whole-animal-form is not parasitical off anything. The eye, conjured up by the animal, has a status intermediate between the animal and the Hermes, a mere want-to-be.

An individual substance not only subsists – i.e. exists in its own right – but does so as a whole instance of some species and genus of substance. Aristotle adds that hands, feet, and suchlike don't so much name substances, primary or secondary, as parts of substances: for though they don't need something else as a subject to exist in (thus possessing one characteristic of substances), they aren't complete instances of any specific nature of thing, and so belong to a species and genus only indirectly.[36]

In other words – if I understand Thomas correctly – an organic part is an incomplete substance because its full definition must refer to the organisms of which it is a part, those organisms being the real substances in the scenario. In this way organs are akin to accidents.

The elements, which Aristotle also frequently lists as examples of substance, are in just as much trouble:

Evidently even of the things that are thought to be substances, most are only potentialities – e.g., the parts of animals (for none of them exists separately; and when they are separated, then they too exist, all of them, merely as matter) and earth and fire and air; for none of them is one, but they are like a heap before it is fused by heat and some one thing is made out of the bits. [1040^{b}5–9]

The elements do not even possess indivisible motions: some of the water from an alpine lake might head down the south slope of the mountain, and some down the north slope. Yet through the agency of heat, water can become an element in a composite material (e.g., bronze) that does have an indivisible motion. The unity of the newly formed composite substance does not derive from its material elements, but from the action of heat on the mixture of material elements.

I can see no reason the doctrine of proper differentiae would exclude the four elements, assuming their differentiae to be his four contraries; it seems reasonable that Aristotle would assume that whatever is hot or cold, fluid or solid, is a terrestrial substance. If so, once more Aristotle appeals to an independent test: the terrestrial elements are not substances, or at least not the purest examples of substances, insofar as they possess the unity of heaps. Thus, a thing's being one because its substratum does not differ in kind [*Metaphysics*, V, 6] is a degraded form of unity, as is the unity by force produced by nails or glue [VII, 16; X, 1].

D. Some Observations

Thus far we have several criteria for substantiality in the *Metaphysics*, in addition to those widely discussed in the literature (a substance must be an individual, a subject, and separate).

1. The differentia of the species must be proper [VII, 4, 12].
2. The thing must be one by nature [X, 1, 1052^{a}20].

36 Aquinas (1993), p. 187.

3. Its parts must be incapable of separate existence [VII, 16].
4. Its movement must be indivisible [V, 6; X, 1].
5. It must be naturally continuous [V, 6; X, 1].
6. Its parts cannot be full-fledged substances in their own right [VII, 16].

Points(3) and (6) amount to the same criterion and can be taken as an elaboration on a claim discussed in the last chapter: coming-to-be and perishing do not come about through association and disassociation, for if things that are substances in their own right, and capable of independent existence, can be the components of a further substance, then coming-to-be and perishing can come about through association and disassociation. In opposition to this, Aristotle claims that the parts of a substance, separated from the substance, exist only as matter. They have lost the form in virtue of which they were what they were, and hence no longer are those things. Disassociation in this case involves a change in the formula or definition of the detached part. And though Aristotle says that the detached part exists as matter, he does not mean that the matter of the part has not changed, even though the form has. The matter of the part will be something like tissue; and tissue, just as much as the organ whose matter it is, is, according to Aristotle, essentially a living substance. So when the part is detached, and the tissue ceases to be animate, the matter, too, has changed. The detached part, like lunch, is only potentially flesh.

To say that the parts of animals exist only potentially is still a strange way of putting the point; for surely, in some sense, and a pretty clear one at that, the parts of animals actually exist. If they existed only potentially in the most direct sense, no animals would (actually) exist. In saying that animal parts exist only potentially I take Aristotle to mean that they are not substances in the fullest sense, because they are not capable of retaining their essential natures apart from the animal. According to the Indivisibility Principle, no substance is composed of other substances. The more or less converse principle, at work here, says that the parts of substances are not substances. (The Indivisibility Principle and its somewhat converse principle can both be understood as an elaboration on the claim that coming-to-be and perishing do not occur through association and disassociation. If an association is a substance, the components that associate cease to be substances when they associate; if the components in an association persist as substances in the association, the association is not a substance.)

Earth, fire, and air are also examples of things that, according to Aristotle, are thought to be substances but are only potentialities. In this case, the reason is that "none of them is one, but they are all like a heap before it is fused [or 'concocted']37 by heat and some one thing is made

37 See Furth (1985), p. 124.

out of the bits [or, 'and something that is one comes to be out of them']."
I have suggested a reason Aristotle might have thought this: the water in a
lake does not possess an indivisible motion: you can draw some of it out
and leave the rest behind. This is one way to understand what Aristotle
means by saying that the elements are like a heap before it is fused by
heat. But there is something unsatisfying about this answer. Heat, Aristotle holds, fuses dissimilar substances (e.g., copper and tin into bronze)
and cold fuses similar substances (e.g., water into ice), so we should be
able to extend his remark: water is like a heap until cold fuses it into a
chunk of ice, which has an indivisible motion. But though the chunk of
ice has an indivisible motion, it fails the Indivisibility Principle: if the
chunk shatters, each resulting part retains its nature as ice, and each
resulting part has as much claim to being a substance as the original
chunk did. So rather than explain his remark by appealing to indivisible
motion, we might do better to treat the elements as akin to heaps by
appealing to the somewhat converse principle to the Indivisibility
Principle – the point being that a chunk of ice or the water in a lake can
shed some of themselves, and the separated portions retain their nature
as water or ice.

These separated parts "must exist only potentially, when they are one
and continuous by nature" [1040^{b}14].[38] Aristotle is talking about the
parts of living things, but the point also seems to hold of ice cubes: the
parts that result when an ice cube shatters existed only potentially in the
ice cube, which could have shattered into different parts. Similarly, the
soup tureen does not contain certain fixed portions: the portions are
created by the ladle. This will happen whenever the whole is "continuous
by nature," for in that case there are no natural lines of division, no
natural fault lines, dividing the whole into actual parts. So although the
parts into which the ice cube shatters, or the soup is doled out, retain
their natures as ice or soup, these so-called substances do not unequivo-
cally fall under the Indivisibility Principle and its somewhat converse.
Water is like a heap, but it is not a heap: it has the unity of things that are
one in substance and continuous.

In the X text, again confining his remarks to things that are one *kath'
hauto*:

There is the continuous, either in general, or especially that which is continuous
by nature and not by contact or by bonds; and of these, those things have more
unity and are prior, whose movement is more indivisible and simpler. That which
is whole and has a certain shape and form is one in a still higher degree; and
especially if a thing is of this sort by nature, and not by force like the things that

---

38 What is the force of the qualification? The femur bone is one and continuous by nature,
separated or not from the organism. Perhaps he means that the femur must exist only
potentially when it is part of an organism that is one and continuous by nature; but see
note 34 above.

are unified by glue or nails, or by being tied together, i.e., if it has in itself something which is the cause of its continuity. A thing is of this sort because its movement is one and indivisible in place and time. [1052ª19–26]

The X text, but not the V, grudgingly allows heaps to be one per se, since it says that the continuous includes, in general, though not especially, the continuous by contact.

The reference to wholes is an echo of a remark in the V discussion: "While in a sense we call anything one if it is a quantity and continuous, in a sense we do not unless it is a whole, i.e., unless it has one form; e.g., if we saw the parts of a shoe put together any which way, we should not call them one all the same (unless because of their continuity); we do this only if they are put together in such a way as to be a shoe and have thereby some one form [1016ᵇ11–16].

Aristotle's primary concern here is to explain how one thing could be made out of a number of other things: the bundle of sticks is made out of several individual sticks and a leather thong. A different set of problems arise if we consider the water in the lake. There is an allusion to this later in X, at 1056ᵇ16: "there is a lot of water, but there are not many waters." What is a lot need not be many or plural. The water in the lake, given his account of the elements, is not made up of a plurality of subunits (except insofar as it is potentially divisible into portions of water). It is continuous by nature. But it is not clear if it is one by nature in any further sense: the dam and the shores of the lake make the water in the lake distinct from other water by preventing the water in the lake from merging with the sea. If the dam breaks, the water in the lake will not cease to exist; it will go to augment the sea. The only sort of unity by nature that water would seem to have on this scheme is unity of formula: every bit of water is the same sort of stuff as every other bit. The same would hold true of air.

Consider again the list that began this section:

1. The differentia of the species must be proper [VII, 4, 12].
2. The thing must be one by nature [X, 1, 1052ª20].
3. Its parts must be incapable of separate existence [VII, 16].
4. Its movement must be indivisible [V, 6; X, 1].
5. It must be naturally continuous [V, 6; X, 1].
6. Its parts cannot be full-fledged substances in their own right [VII, 16].

The water in the lake meets (1) and (5) without qualification. It meets (2), (3), and (6) with various qualifications, but because it can head in two different directions, it fails (4). What makes it fail (4) is not that all of it could be heading in two directions at once, but that some of it could be draining out of one end of the lake, and some draining out of the other. If we capture this capacity by substituting "portions of it" or "some of it" for "its parts" in (3) and (6), so that (6) becomes, e.g., "Some of it cannot be a substance in its own right," it fails (3) and (6).

Could not the same be said about a man? I can lose a limb or a kidney and continue to exist, so it would seem that some of me (i.e., the postpartem remainder) can be a full-fledged substance in its own right. Aristotle must restrict what counts as a part of me or some of me so that all of me, less a limb or a kidney, does not count as a part of me or some of me. Perhaps he has this in mind in saying that I am indivisible in form, and my parts are only potentialities: there is no nonmetaphorical sense in which we can refer to some of me or a part of me. I am indivisible qua man.

5

Living Things

In the *Metaphysics,* Aristotle is an elitist substantialist: he has doubts about whether heaps, the elements, artifacts, and body parts are really substances or are paradigmatic substances. This does not, however, prevent him from using these as stock examples of substances. So we saw H. M. Robinson, in a passage quoted in Chapter 3, giving the transformation of an iron statue into cannonballs as an example of a substantial rather than an accidental change. In fact, Aristotle's most common example of a substance is probably the bronze sphere or statue, though as artifacts these are certainly not paradigmatic substances. Perhaps they are not substances at all, and the transformation of the bronze sphere into a statue is really a case of accidental change – a change of shape in a quantity of bronze. (Robinson's case has to be handled differently, for there several things are generated out of one.)

On the other hand, when Aristotle embarks on a serious examination of living things, he finds they are paradigmatic substances because of the way they exemplify the Indivisibility Principle.

Democritus seems to think there are three kinds of difference [*diaphoras*] between things. . . . But evidently there are many differentiae [*diaphorai*]: for instance, some things are characterized by the mode of composition of their matter, e.g. the things formed by mixture, such as honey-water; and others by being bound together, e.g., a bundle; and others by being glued together, e.g., a book; and others by being nailed together, e.g. a casket; and others in more than one of these ways; and others by position, e.g. the threshold and the lintel (for these differ by being placed in a certain way); and others by time, e.g. dinner and breakfast; and others by place, e.g. the winds; and others by the affections proper to sensible things, e.g. hardness and softness, density and rarity, dryness and wetness; and some things by some of these qualities, others by them all, and in general some by excess and some by defect. Clearly, then, the word 'is' has just as many meanings: a thing is a threshold because it lies in such and such a position, and its being means its lying in that position, while being ice means having been solidified in such and such a way [*Metaphysics* VIII, 2, 1042^{b}11–28]

As the example of ice shows, we are dealing here mainly with nominal essences – with the definition of accidental unities – since the what-it-is of the substance that is ice does not change when the ice melts. Similarly, the threshold and the lintel differ in position, but if we reverse them, their substance – 2 × 4 × 36" oak board – does not change. (At *Topics* VI, 6, 144b33, he says that differentiae should not refer to places, because it does not seem that one essence can differ from another in virtue of location; quoted in Chapter 4, sec. I[D], "Proper Differentiae.") Nor has the lunch served seven hours late perished, "nothing perceptible persisting as identical substratum," and been replaced by something else – dinner. At 7 P.M. it is no longer lunch, but it is the same boring sandwich and salad. A few paragraphs later, Aristotle is still giving examples of definitions of accidental unities: "E.g. what is still weather? Absence of motion in a large expanse of air: air is the matter, and absence of motion is the actuality and substance. What is a calm? Smoothness of sea: the material substratum is the sea, and the actuality or shape is smoothness."

It is clear, then, from these facts that if its substance is the cause of each thing's being, we must seek in these differentiae the cause of the being of each of these things. Now none of these differentiae is substance, even when coupled with matter, yet in each there is something analogous to substance; and as in substances that which is predicated of the matter is the actuality itself, in all other definitions also it is what most resembles full actuality. E.g. if we had to define a threshold, we should say "wood or stone in such and such a position," and a house we should define as "bricks and timbers in such and such a position" (or we may name that for the sake of which as well in some cases), and if we define ice we say "water frozen or solidified in such and such a way" . . . . and similarly in all other cases. [*Metaphysics* VIII, 2, 1043a1–11]

The differentiae here are not substances but are analogous to substances: in substances the actuality itself is predicated of the matter; here, "what most resembles full actuality" is predicated of matter.

Some of the things Aristotle mentions are accidental unities in a sense akin to the one in which the musical man is an accidental unity – they involve only one substance-candidate: this food served at noon is lunch, but served later, dinner; here this wind is Moriah, but there it is Celestine. Others are accidental unities in a different sense: pages that happen to be glued together; boards that happen to be nailed together; faggots that happen to be lashed together; oil that happens to be in emulsion with vinegar. What seems to make these less than substances is that each is a plurality of substances that happen to be joined somehow, with the force of "happen to be" deriving from the fact that the pages, boards, faggots, and the oil and vinegar can exist apart from the things to which they are joined. The parts of the book, the casket, and the vinaigrette are substances in their own right, or at least as much so as the book, and so on, are.

But, as we saw in the last chapter, Aristotle thinks living things hold together differently. So we turn now to his account of life. In Chapter 3, sec. I (A), "Matter and the Substratum," we noted in passing that Aristotle denies that chemical processes can explain the generation of living things and their heterogeneous parts, is inclined to think in his later works that they cannot explain animate homogeneous materials, but does think they can explain the generation of inanimate compounds. As the difference between animate and inanimate things is important to his metaphysics of substance, we now turn in the first section to his reasons for believing that biological organisms cannot be explained chemically. This will give us a detailed account of the difference between the unity of a bed and the unity of the boarder who sleeps in it. In the second section we turn to his account of living organisms as such.

I have tried, in this work, to be conservative about making claims that lack reasonable textual justification. It is only fair for me to admit that the last two parts of the section "The Account of the Soul" are speculative.

I. Chemical Reactions and Biological Organisms[1]

A. The Exegetical Problem

For it is not face without soul, nor flesh, but having perished they are equivocally said to be face in the one case, flesh in the other, just as it would be if they had come to be stone or wooden. . . . And just as we would not say that an axe or some other instrument was made by fire alone, neither [should we say this] of foot or hand, nor by the same token, of flesh, for it, too, has some function. Heat and cold may produce hardness and softness and viscosity and brittleness and the other such affections that inhere in the animate parts, but not the definition [logos] in virtue of which the one is flesh, the other bone. [Generation of Animals, 734b24-34][2]

In this brief passage Aristotle expresses several claims. The first sentence tells us that being alive is an essential property of face and flesh: animate parts are essentially animate. The second sentence adds that things which have functions are not made by fire alone, and an axe, a hand, and flesh have functions. The last sentence is an explanation and gloss on the second: fire may produce hardness and softness, viscosity and brittleness, and other such characteristics, but (by implication) these will not specify the functions that in these cases enter into the definitions of these things.

---

1 This section originally appeared as "Aristotle on Heat, Cold, and Teleological Explanation" in Ancient Philosophy (1989). Portions of the original paper were read in November 1986 at the Trenton State College Conference on Matter and Explanation in Aristotelian Science and Metaphysics. I am indebted to several of the conference participants for their comments, including Allan Gotthelf, Montgomery Furth, James G. Lennox, John M. Cooper, and William Charlton.
2 The translations in this section are my own, from the Bekker edition.

(If I use a rock to drive a nail, the rock is serving a function, but this function will not be embedded in the definition in virtue of which a rock is a rock.)

In this section I examine two of these claims: (1) things that have functions are not made by fire alone, and (2) heat and cold can produce some of the characteristics of flesh and bone, but not their *logoi*. I examine them in order to determine what there is specifically in Aristotle's conception of the action of heat and cold that led him to these claims.[3]

Why does Aristotle think that things with functions cannot be explained by heat and cold? In our passage it is Aristotle's view that heat cannot account for the production of the axe, the hand, or flesh, since all of these have functions that are referred to in their definitions. In *Meteorology* IV, 385ª4–11, on the other hand, he tells us that flesh, bone, and stone *are* differentiated from each other by the sort of characteristics he lists in our *Generation of Animals* passage, and for that reason heat and cold *can* produce flesh and bone [390ᵇ2–10].

The different lines he takes in these two works can be explained by his ambivalence in the *Meteorology* on a related question. There, in chapter xii, he says that although flesh and bone, and even fire and water, have a final cause, and though what they are is determined by their functions (even if their definitions are not apparent [390ª19]), somehow the functions of flesh, bone, bronze, and silver are accounted for by the sort of characteristics listed, and these characteristics can in turn be accounted for by the action of heat and cold. But no one, he adds, would suppose this to be the case for the head or the hand, or for a saw or a box.

The *Meteorology* and the *Generation of Animals*, then, agree that what can be explicated by means of these affections can be accounted for by the action of heat and cold. But whereas the *Meteorology* holds that flesh's having a function is compatible with flesh's being explicable by heat and cold, the *Generation of Animals* offers flesh's having a function as a reason for concluding that flesh cannot be explained by heat and cold.

Even in *Generation of Animals* there are passages in which Aristotle seems to explain the production of flesh and bone through the action of heat and cold:

---

3 The justification of this approach must ultimately lie in the results it yields, but by way of a prima facie defense, I offer the following. Aristotle did not inherit a neat distinction between what we would call "biology" and "chemistry." So it is unlikely that he first decided for theoretical reasons that chemical explanations in principle cannot explain flesh and bone, and then, because his chemistry turns on the action of heat and cold, put the point by saying that heat and cold cannot explain flesh and bone. (As I indicate in the paragraph below, in the *Meteorology* IV he maintained that heat and cold can account for flesh and bone.) His progress is more likely to have followed the opposite course: something about the way in which heat and cold work in his physical system led him to decide that they cannot account for animate things – a claim that, given the nature of his physical theory, amounted to saying that biology is not reducible to chemistry.

The formation of the uniform parts is by cooling and heating, for some things are solidified and congealed by cold and others by heat. . . . The nourishment oozing through the blood-vessels and the passages in the several parts, just as water does when it stands in unbaked earthenware, flesh or its analogue is formed: it is by cold that flesh is solidified, and that is why it is dissolved by fire. The excessively earthy portions of the [nourishment that is] rising up, having little moisture and heat, becomes cooled as the moisture evaporates with the heat, becoming hard and earthy in form, as nails, horns, hoofs and beaks; hence they can be softened by fire, but none of them can be melted by it. . . .

The sinews and bones are formed by the internal heat as the fluid congeals; hence bones, just like earthenware, cannot be dissolved by fire; it is as though they had been baked in an oven by the heat present at their formation. [743a3–21]

A bit further on, he offers a similar account of the formation of an embryo and suggests that an account by heat and cold is compatible with a teleological account. "Cooling is a deprivation of heat. Nature uses both, having the power of necessity to make one thing this and another that. But in the embryo their cooling and heating take place for the sake of something" [*Generation of Animals*, 743a36–b6][4]

Two schools of interpretation have formed around these texts. According to the first, which I will call the reductionist thesis, Aristotle means that though heat and cold produce flesh and bone, an account of the production of flesh and bone in terms of heat and cold will not be felicitous. According to the second, he means that heat and cold cannot account for the production of flesh and bone at all.

Martha Nussbaum holds the former view: heat and cold can account for the production of the embryo, but the account would be otiose – perhaps something like a hard-nosed epiphenomenalist's account of my decision to go to the movies. From many practical points of view, the teleological explanation is preferable, but if we knew enough of the details, and had the time and interest, the chemical account could explain everything.[5] And according to Richard Sorabji, "Aristotle thought teleological explanations were compatible with the existence of such [necessitating] causes, but . . . he wavered on . . . whether they were compatible with their having *explanatory value*."[6]

On the majority antireductionist view, Aristotle held that some things cannot be given a chemical account at all – not that they can, but the account would be otiose. On this view, Aristotle's teleology has an on-

4 In *Parts of Animals,* Aristotle says that "though respiration is for the sake of something, this thing comes from those by necessity. . . . The hot of necessity goes out and comes back in again as it offers resistance, and the air flows in. . . . And the hot within, as the cooling takes place, offers resistance, and this causes the inflow of air from without and also its egress" [642a36–642b2].

5 Nussbaum (1978), pp. 69–80.

6 Sorabji (1980), p. 162; Charles (1984), e.g., pp. 57–58, 235–236, may reflect this view.

tological foundation; on the Nussbaum–Sorabji line it has at best only a heuristic foundation.

Thus, Allan Gotthelf poses the reductionist's challenge as finding "a way of specifying the *series* of heatings, coolings, and movings around of material in the developing embryo which . . . heat effects, without referring to the form."[7] John Cooper, in "Aristotle on Natural Teleology" wrote:

One could put Aristotle's view by saying that one kind of causal explanation refers to antecedent material conditions and powers: what makes wood burn when fire is applied to it is that fire is hot and so has the power to act in this way on wood. The given material natures of fire and wood are simply such that this happens. But similarly what makes a particular series of transformations take place in the generation of the dog is that it is a fundamental fact about nature that each kind of living thing reproduces so as to preserve itself.[8]

In "Hypothetical Necessity," he added, "However much certain particular stages in the formation of a living thing may be materially necessitated, the end product, the finished living thing, is never the result of such necessitation."[9] Gotthelf and Cooper take the line that Aristotle held that even if every individual event in the development of an embryo can be explained chemically, the series of events cannot.

On the interpretation I will offer in this chapter, Aristotle's claim was not that, even if these changes can be explained individually without teleology the series of changes cannot, but rather that some aspects of these (individual) changes can be explained chemically but others cannot. Because this does not concede the explanation of individual changes to the reductionists, I understand it to be a stronger form of antireductionism than Cooper and Gotthelf defend.[10] It has the advan-

---

7 Gotthelf (1987), p. 242; italics mine. Lennox (1982) writes: "In a manner unclear from the texts we have, the natural, or life-promoting, heat operates according to an order or pattern . . . that reflects the organization of the parent organism. This power of orderly heating is able to initiate an organized set of changes in the female's material, changes eventuating in and directed toward a child. . . . In parallel with craft production, the male parent, by means of having the form he does, determines the pattern of the heating contributed by the semen. This heat acts in an orderly way. . . . "

   Gotthelf poses the question by asking whether it was Aristotle's view that the development of an organism can be explained by means of the potentialities of the elements that compose its matter, or whether the embryo has an "irreducible potentiality for form." I prefer to avoid talk about element-potentials, in order to leave open the possibility that the potentialities of Aristotelian compounds might not be reducible to the potentialities of Aristotelian elements – i.e., that Aristotle took his chemistry not to be reducible to his physics. (See section I[D], "Active and Passive Potentialities," below). However, that his compounds are formed by the action of heat and cold, and that heat and cold form a primary set of elementary opposite qualities for Aristotle, suggest the contrary.

8 Cooper (1982), p. 215.

9 Cooper (1985), p. 161.

10 Although it should be noted that they only grant that heat and cold *may* account for individual changes in Aristotle.

tage of escaping an obvious objection to their thesis: if each change can be explained nonteleologically, why should the series as a whole require a teleological explanation?

Our interest in Aristotle is not purely antiquarian; it is also philosophical. This makes it tempting to speculate on how his views should be translated to compare them with current views. I yield to this temptation, taking Jonathan Lear to express the current antireductionist view.

According to Lear, "It is [often now] thought that if we understand all the properties of the matter we will see form as emerging from these properties. It is important to realize that Aristotle's world is not like that. In Aristotle's world, forms cannot be understood in terms of matter. Forms must occupy a fundamental ontological position: they are among the basic things that are."[11] Lear explains this as follows:

In the twentieth century much work has been done by philosophers to show that teleological explanations are compatible with mechanical explanations. For example, one can say that the spider builds its web in order to secure nourishment, but one can also explain its orderly activity via its neurological makeup and genetic inheritance. It is important to realize that Aristotle does not believe in any such compatibility. For Aristotle, the reason one has to cite the form in its final, realized state is that only by reference to that form can one understand teleological behavior.[12]

On the interpretation I will offer, Aristotle was not committed to rejecting the modern line. Lacking evidence for the directive structures we now know reside in matter at microscopic levels, he attributed macroscopic structure to form rather than to matter because he and his opponents took matter to be scarcely formed, and Aristotle realized that such unstructured matter could not account for macroscopic structure. His partisanship for form is a product of his conception of matter, not independent of it, and had he known what we know today, had he realized that matter is more highly formed than he thought, he might have taken a different tack.[13] The discovery of microscopic biological structure can thus be viewed as vindicating, rather than refuting, Aristotle's deepest instinct: macroscopic biological structures require prior structures.

At the heart of the problem is an uncertainty over the difference Aristotle saw between the realms studied in chemistry and biology – inanimate nature and animate nature – and between the processes that govern these realms. If we want a reflection of our division of physical science in Aristotle we can start by taking the account, scattered throughout his writings, of the elements – earth, air, fire, and water – to constitute

11 Lear (1988), p. 20.
12 Ibid., p. 36.
13 I believe that this is the view held in Furth (1988).

the center of his physics. The account in *On Generation and Corruption* of the composition of the elements out of the contraries hot/cold and dry/ moist, and of elemental transformation, can then serve as his analogue of subatomic physics. The best statement of his chemistry – his account of the composition of compounds out of the elements – is in *Meteorology* IV, where the effect of heat and cold in forming and breaking down compounds takes the place that electron bonding occupies in today's chemistry. And finally there are the biological treatises.

This gives us an Aristotelian physics, chemistry, and biology. And looking at these three areas we will be struck by an important difference between the first two and the last: his biology is teleological; his physics and chemistry either not teleological or only marginally teleological.[14] So Montgomery Furth, writing about Aristotle's most complex inanimate compounds (e.g., bronze and pitch) can say: "The present level is the upper limit of what, according to Aristotle's view, can come-to-be or can *be* at all by the agencies of *matter* and *force;* to get beyond this point requires the further agencies of *form* and *end*."[15]

Why should this be so?

When Aristotle invokes the distinction between things that can be explained nonteleologically and things that require teleological explanations, he does not typically point to elements and inanimate compounds on the one hand and organisms on the other. He typically invokes the distinction to talk about *matter* as opposed to *things* constituted by that matter: silver and the jewelry box made of silver or iron and the saw made of iron. The action of heat and cold, he says, can account for the production of silver, iron, clay, and bronze, but not for the production of a jewelry box, saw, sword, or jug [see, e.g., *Meteorology*, 390^{b}10–14; *Generation of Animals*, 735^{a}1–5].

This is not a distinction between raw materials we find and artifacts we produce. Some of the materials Aristotle lists (e.g., clay) occur naturally: we just pick chunks of them up or dig them out of the ground. But bronze, an alloy, is produced by industry, and though iron occurs naturally in the earth's core and in meteorites, the iron we are familiar with is, as it was in Aristotle's day, refined from ore. Why should Aristotle think that the action of heat and cold can explain what goes on in the iron refiner's shop, where ore is heated and the slag drained off, but not what goes on in the foundry next door, where molten copper and tin are cooled in a mold? The same sorts of processes seem to go on in both shops.[16]

---

14 In *Meteorology* IV he suggests that the final cause, though difficult to detect, exists even at the elemental level, but *de minimis non curat lex.*

15 Furth (1988), p. 79.

16 It is not enough to say that Aristotle thinks that some things require teleological explanations and others do not. We want to know just how he draws the line. We want to know

If we limited our discussion to the examples we have just been considering, we might hope to explain Aristotle's view by means of the matter/thing distinction. But the quotation from Aristotle with which I began this section casts doubt on this and shows that it is the role of heat and cold, not the matter/thing distinction, which is crucial; the matter/thing distinction is a useful guide only up to a certain point. For in that passage Aristotle holds that flesh is to be treated like axes or feet, and not like silver or clay: the production of flesh cannot be explained by the action of heat and cold. If this claim depends on the matter/thing distinction, there must be something that can play the same role to flesh that iron plays to the sword, something that can be the constitutive matter of flesh. But here we run into a snag – there is nothing that can play this role. For though there is a matter out of which flesh is, in a sense, constituted, flesh is not constituted out of that matter in the right sense.

Flesh, according to Aristotle, is a homogeneous material, and the elements, we saw in Chapter 3, section I ("Change and Continuity"), are present in flesh only potentially, not actually: they can be produced out of it, but they are not actually there in it.[17] Flesh, then, is not composed of the elements in the way in which the statue is composed of bronze or the man of organs. The bronze is actually present in the statue and the parts of the man are organs. The bronze materially constitutes the statue; the organs materially constitute the man. But the elements are the matter of flesh, not as actual material constituents but as that out of which (*eks hou*), in the sense of "source" (see, e.g., *Physics,* 190^{b}1–5; *Metaphysics,* 1032^{a}17; and *Generation of Animals,* 724^{a}20ff.), and, we might say, "that into which." The elements are potential in such compounds, for the conditions opposite to those that formed the compound will destroy it, just as "that which is solidified by deficiency of heat is melted by heat – such as ice, lead, or bronze" [*Meteorology,* 385^{a}33].

Since flesh is a homogeneous material, there is nothing else that materially constitutes it, so the matter/thing distinction cannot cover this case. How then does Aristotle distinguish matter that can be explained through heat and cold from matter that cannot – inanimate and animate homogeneous materials?

---

why he thought that his chemistry could fully explain the production of some things but not of others. What is it about the production of bronze and iron that leads him to think that an account of their production can ignore teleological considerations? Is it something he noted about the kind of material they are? Did he think that certain kinds of substance always merit nonteleological explanations even if they can only be produced in laboratories? Or did he think that the crucial point was how they were produced, not what they were? What would he say about Tang and styrofoam, linen and mayonnaise, stained glass and aviation fuel?

17 See also McMullin (1965), p. 306. For Aristotle's account of homogeneous substances as opposed to mixtures, see, e.g., *Generation and Corruption,* 328^{a}11–16, 334^{a}26–33, and *History of Animals,* 486^{a}5–8.

B. Flesh and Blood

I propose to approach this question through an examination of Aristotle's account of blood. That account is nicely positioned in Aristotle's physical theory to help us gain a purchase on larger questions about his teleology and his explication of life.

The milk an infant takes in is a homogeneous substance, produced in an animal by nature yet not animate. Digested and transformed, it ultimately becomes flesh and bone, which, according to Aristotle, are animate. Somewhere along the line an inanimate homogeneous substance was transformed into animate homogeneous substance. At what point? And what did this change involve?

Aristotle holds that the milk, concocted by the action of heat, is first transformed into blood, which is then transformed into flesh. This intermediate substance, blood, is either animate or inanimate. Ideally, he should have a way of deciding this, and the considerations that enter into this decision should be clues to how he distinguishes the animate from the inanimate, and so to how he distinguishes things that have teleological explanations from things that do not.

It might seem that, as Aristotle lists blood as one of the parts of animals, he must have thought of blood as animate.[18] But not all the parts of animals are "ensouled." Aristotle has a fairly standard list of how to categorize the parts of animals; the basic list occurs in many places with small variations.[19] In some variations, as at Parts of Animals, 647b13, he lists along with blood, as one of the uniform parts of animals, bile, which, like urine and feces, he takes to be a residue [677a13], a waste product that serves no further purpose, a mere "offscouring" [677a30]. It is not likely that he thought these latter substances were animate, and so there is no reason to assume that he considered all the parts of animals animate. Rather, he seems to list as parts of animals any material stuff, animate or inanimate, naturally produced in the organism – a usage that includes as parts material we would call "body fluids" as well as those we would call "parts."[20] In a passage deleted by Ogle and Peck but accepted by Düring [Parts of Animals, 656b19–22], Aristotle, if the passage is authentic, states, "nothing bloodless has sensation, including the blood itself, but the things made out of it [have sensation] . . . for it [blood] is not a part of animals."[21]

---

18 For the listing, see Generation and Corruption, 640b19; for the conclusion, see Furth (1988), p. 45.
19 See, e.g., Parts of Animals, 646a12–24; History of Animals, 486a5–487a9; Generation of Animals, 715a9–11.
20 This generous use was noted by A. L. Peck in his introduction to the Loeb Classical Library edition of Aristotle's Parts of Animals (Harvard University Press, Cambridge, 1983), p. 28.
21 Düring (1980b), pp. 148–149. On p. 149, Düring says that Aristotle nowhere "denotes"

Blood, present from the outset in animals, is their most indispensable and most universal part [*History of Animals,* 520ᵇ11], for blood is the matter out of which the whole body is formed [*Parts of Animals,* 668ᵃ5, 10], "the matter out of which all [the parts] are made [668ᵃ20]." Consequently blood and blood vessels are the most universal of uniform parts in animals [*History of Animals,* 511ᵇ3–6], and in the embryo the heart is the first organ to appear [*Generation of Animals,* 740ᵃ3–6; 741ᵇ15]. Blood alone is potentially body and flesh [668ᵃ27], while flesh, in turn [511ᵇ4–5], is that which *ho malista dê esti to sôma tôn zôiôn* – that which to the greatest degree is the body of animals (in Peck's translation, that which par excellence constitutes the bodies of animals). Blood thus occupies a crucial juncture in Aristotle's physical theory as the matter out of which flesh, and therefore animals, is formed.

On Aristotle's account, plants contain no digestive system and excrete no wastes: the nourishment they take in from the soil is already fully concocted, and they can use it in the form in which they absorb it [*Parts of Animals,* 655ᵇ32–37]. The ground is, as it were, their stomach [650ᵃ22–23]. Animals, on the other hand, must process their food before their bodies can use it to produce new flesh and the other uniform parts. (Aristotle seems to have had no notion of metabolism, and hence of the use of food to generate calories.) Flesh is continually perishing and needs to be replaced; thus starvation produces emaciation. Nourishment is the production of new flesh to replace the flesh that perishes, and hence to maintain the organism. The production of flesh in excess of this requirement is growth.

This production begins in the digestive system. The food animals eat passes into the stomach and then the intestines. The matter that cannot be used continues through the digestive system and is excreted as a waste product. These useless residues, which Aristotle sometimes refers to as a "sediment of the food," are excreted as decayed forms of food. The useful part of the food is turned into blood, the last or final food or nourishment in living things [650ᵃ34].[22] Blood, after being heated in the heart, is turned in the smaller blood vessels into flesh, which "may be compared to the mud a running stream deposits" [647ᵇ3]. In *Parts of Animals* the blood vessels are compared to the branches of a river:

Just as in irrigation systems the biggest channels persist while the smallest ones are first and quickly concealed by the mud, though when it leaves they become

---

blood as a part of animals. In the passage I have just cited [647ᵇ10–14], blood is listed as one of the (uniform) parts *in* animals [*en tois zôiois*], not as one of the uniform parts *of* an animal [*morion tôn zôiôn*]. Lewis (1994), pp. 257–267, treats blood as one of the parts *of* an animal.

22 If he is being careful in this formulation, the qualification "in living things" is made to distinguish the final product in animals from decayed food on the shelf.

visible again, so in the same way the largest blood vessels persist, while the smallest ones become flesh in actuality, though potentially they are no less blood vessels. Accordingly, blood flows from healthy flesh wherever it is broken, for there is no blood without vessels, though the vessels are not visible, just as the channels in the irrigation system are not [visible] before the mud is cleared out. [668a27–668b1]

Blood, then, is the final form food takes before it becomes flesh. This suggests that blood, like milk (the first food), is inanimate. For the ultimate nourishment is still a form of nourishment, and it is what can be nourished, not the nourishment whereby it is nourished, that is a living substance.[23] Blood thus fails to meet one of criteria the *On the Soul* lists for biological life [413a22–33; 413b12].[24]

Further evidence for the inanimacy of blood comes from the account in *Parts of Animals*, 649a16–19, b21–35, where Aristotle equates blood's being defined as hot and liquid with what would be the case if we had a special word for hot water or pale men. In that heat would be included in the definition of blood, blood would be essentially hot, but not "in respect of its substratum," for blood's heat is an affection due to an external cause (the heart), not *kath' hauto* (just as water is not hot *kath' hauto* and the pale man is not pale *kath' hauto*). Outside the organism blood congeals and cools [649b30]. But if Aristotle is true to form and thinks blood is animate, he should have said that the blood which escapes the body, rather than merely undergoing an incidental change that renders it cool and solidified blood, is no longer blood except in name alone.

Why should Aristotle think that blood is a form of nourishment? In part this conclusion is based on observation – he says that the large number of blood vessels surrounding the intestines indicates that blood is a product of digestion. But a more theoretical consideration stands behind his claim.

At every stage in the digestive process there is something that serves to hold the food and the residues that are produced during digestion [*Parts of Animals*, 650a32]: the mouth and esophagus hold the untreated food [a16]; the stomach is a sort of internal bag of earth containing dissolved food [a21–28]; and the blood vessels are the receptacle for the blood. So, Aristotle says, it is clear that blood is the final form of food in living things. The conclusion that blood is a form of food is derived, then, from an argument of this sort:

1. Food and waste products require a receptacle.
2. Blood is not a waste product.
3. The cardiovascular system is the receptacle for the blood.

23 *Per accidens* the nourishment might be alive – e.g., oysters on the half-shell.
24 I qualify life as biological here because Aristotle attributes life to the celestial spheres though they are not capable of nourishment. See Bolton (1978): 258–278.

4. Hence blood is a form of food.[25]

The support for (2) is presumably observation: if blood were a waste product we would regularly excrete it, but in fact, except for menstruation, we lose it only as a consequence of damage or illness. Premise (3), too, is based on observation.

The most interesting premise is (1): food and waste products require a receptacle. Blood requires a receptacle because, like the untreated food and wastes, it "is not continuous [*syneches*] with nor organically united [*sympephukos*] with [flesh]; it just stands in the heart and in the blood vessels as in a jar [*Parts of Animals*, 650b6–7]. Held in the organism by containing tissue, membranes, and vessels, these substances are not joined to these or any other parts of the organism – no more than the wine is joined to the amphora. Flesh is conjoined with flesh; the blood vessels and the bones form systems. But blood, like food and the residues – and unlike the blood vessels – does not form a subsystem of the organism and is not conjoined with any of the organic systems: if one is cut, it simply leaks out. It is a contained substance rather than a connected part. Imprisoned in the organism by the containing tissue, it has no personal loyalties to the organism. Aristotle takes this to explain why we get no sensation when blood is touched: "Indeed, none of the residues yields any sensation either, nor does the nourishment [650b4]. He takes the same line at *History of Animals*, 520b14–16: "In no animal is the blood capable of sensation when touched, just as the residue of the stomach is not." Since blood, untreated food, and wastes are not conjoined with flesh – the organ of touch[26] – touching them produces no sensation in the animal.

Aristotle holds that the brain, too, is insensitive, and for a similar reason: "that the brain has no continuity with the sensory parts is clear through inspection." It is connected with the spinal cord (Aristotle tells us at 652a26 that many people think the brain is marrow, and he thinks it is the source of marrow), and so with the bones rather than flesh. But the brain, if not conjoined with flesh, is at least conjoined with the bones whose function is to support and protect the softer parts. And these do form a system:

A bone does not exist alone by itself [*auto kath' hauto*], but as part of, or as joined and attached to, a continuous whole, so that nature may use them as though they were one and continuous, or two and distinct for bending. And similarly no blood vessel exists alone by itself, but all are parts of one vessel. For a bone, if somehow it were separate, would be unable to perform the function for the sake of which the nature of bones exists, for being not continuous but unconnected, in no way

---

25 For the argument to be valid, the first premise should be that only food and waste products require receptacles. Of course, Aristotle did not think that this revised premise would be true.

26 See, e.g., *Parts of Animals*, 653b22–25.

could it be the cause of bending or straightening; and not only that, but like a thorn or an arrow sticking in the flesh it would cause harm. [654ª33–655ᵇ9]

An isolated bone or a bone fragment no longer conjoined with other parts into a system is in effect a foreign body. Blood, not being conjoined with its vessels, is also in effect a foreign substance – no more a proper part of the animal body than dissolved nutrients in the soil are proper parts of the plant or the dinner is part of the dinner guest. If blood is not a proper part of the animal, then it must be some form of contained foreign matter, either a waste residue of food or food processed for use – that is, for conversion into flesh.

C. Growth, Life, and Shape

Blood's liquidity shows Aristotle that blood is not organically conjoined with flesh. Liquids have no intrinsic shapes – they take on the shape of the containing receptacle.[27] All Aristotle's homogeneous substances lack intrinsic shapes in one sense: flesh, like bronze, can take on various shapes. Liquids are still more devoted to their shapelessness. Bronze, so long as it is not melted, will at least take the shape imposed on it and keep it; liquids assume the shapes of their containers, but will not retain those shapes. They are like pupils who behave only while the teacher is in the room.

As a consequence, the transition from fluid to solid is central to Aristotle's account of growth and of the formation of the embryo. Consider the *Generation of Animals* passage I cited earlier:

The nourishment oozing through the blood vessels and the passages in the several parts, just as water does when it stands in unbaked earthenware, flesh or its analogue is formed: it is by cold that flesh is solidified, and that is why it is dissolved by fire. The excessively earthy portions of the [nourishment that is] rising up, having little moisture and heat, becomes cooled as the moisture evaporates with the heat, becoming hard and earthy in form, as nails, horns, hoofs and beaks; hence they can be softened by fire, but none of them can be melted by it. . . .

The sinews and bones are formed by the internal heat as the fluid congeals; hence bones, just like earthenware, cannot be dissolved by fire; it is as though they had been baked in an oven by the heat present at their formation. [743ª3–21]

27 Wastes are not liquid in English, but they are moist – the Greek term (*to hugron*) straddles these two English words. In *Parts of Animals*, we saw, he divides the uniform parts into two broad groups: fluids and solids [674ᵇ21–29]. The solid ones are matter for the nonuniform parts, "for each of the instrumental parts is composed of them." Nourishment, on the other hand, is moist or fluid, "for all things that grow take [nourishment] from liquid." Finally there are the [moist] residues or waste products that are the sediment of solid food and, in animals with bladders, liquid food.

The solidification of blood in an organism produces flesh and bone. Similarly, the formation of the embryo, a special case of this process, takes place by a solidification out of blood (the menses). The semen, Aristotle holds, provides form, not matter: it is not a material ingredient in the fetation, but [Loeb] "performs its function simply by means of the *dunamis* which it contains" [736ᵃ27]; having done that, the physical part of the semen evaporates [737ᵃ10–15]. Semen acts as a catalyst, coagulating the menses and imparting its "movement" to it, an action Aristotle says is the same as that of rennet in solidifying milk into cheese [729ᵃ11 ff., ᵇ5–9; 739ᵇ21 ff.]. The result is that the menses becomes solid flesh. In the case of the embryo, the resulting substance is then capable of growth – a criterion of life listed in the *On the Soul.* Until this solidification takes place, the embryo exists only potentially in the menses.

Discussing growth in *Generation and Corruption,* Aristotle says that the growth of nonuniform parts occurs by the growth of the uniform parts out of which they are composed. How do the uniform parts grow?

Flesh and bone and each of the other such parts are twofold, like the other things that have form in matter. For both the matter and the form is called flesh or bone. Now, that any part can grow by the addition of something is possible in respect to form, but not of matter [321ᵇ19–24].

Aristotle goes on to say that we must regard what happens in the growth of flesh along the same lines as when someone, using the same measure, measures water out, scoop after scoop: "In this way the matter of flesh grows, without an addition to every part of it (something flows in and something flows out) but to every part of its figure and form (*tou de schêmatos kai tou eidous*) [321ᵇ25–28]." This obscure passage is subject to various interpretations.[28] The key to understanding it, I think, is given in the discussion's introduction: the passage is meant to explain the growth of the homogeneous materials. The nonuniform parts grow (in form) by the *growth* of their matter – the homogeneous parts; but the growth of the homogeneous parts is not by the growth of their constitutive matter – as I argued above, there is no such matter – but by an *addition* of matter that is a growth in respect to form. In his example, the water the man has poured out is increasing, but not because it is growing; it increases by accretion due to the additional measures of water that are added.[29] Through the addition of matter (water) a lake grows larger, but the water in it does not grow larger; there just is more water in the lake.

The growth of a lake is by accession of like to like (water added to water), not contrary, and involves no transformation. In the case of flesh,

---

28 See, e.g., Joachim (1922), pp. 129–132; Verdenius and Waszink (1966), pp. 24–27; and Williams (1982), pp. 109–111.

29 When air is generated out of water, Aristotle says, there is an increase in volume, but nothing is growing [*Generation and Corruption,* 321ᵃ10].

however, unlike the water-measurer, there is not only an increase by the addition of matter. The growth of homogeneous parts is not by mere accretion, but by the accession of contraries that acquire the form of the homogeneous parts to which they accede.

Hence it is as though every part of the flesh has grown, and as though not. For there has been an accession to every part in respect to the form, but not in respect to the matter. The whole, however, has become larger because of the accession of something called food, the contrary, and the change of this food into the same form as that of flesh – as if moist were to accede to dry and, having acceded, were to be transformed and to become dry. [321^{b}32–322^{a}3]

This accession is twofold, since flesh and bone are twofold (matter with form): the food takes on the form of bone (or flesh), and thereby the (whole) bone (or tissue) becomes larger. The growth is proportional, as is obvious in the case of the hand [321^{b}29]; indeed, all things naturally composed have a limit and a *logos* of size and growth, which is why the growth of a fire is not biological growth – the fire will grow without limit as long as there is fuel [*On the Soul*, 416^{a}18]. Thus the nonuniform parts grow in form and structure by means of the growth of the uniform parts: the tissue that constitutes the heart grows by transforming blood into tissue, and by this means the heart grows.

In any case, what is capable of biological growth must be solid. The growth of the lake, by like to like, is mere increase, and the growth of fire, though by contrary, is without the "limit or proportion" due to soul. Limit and proportion are strangers to a liquid, which Aristotle defines as "that which, being readily adaptable in shape, is not determinable by any limit of its own" [*Generation and Corruption*, 329^{b}30–31, Barnes]. Hence the contrast between liquid nourishment[30] and solid parts: only the latter can grow. Because the capacity for growth (not mere increase) is another of Aristotle's criteria for animacy, this is another reason blood cannot be animate.

Aristotelian liquids are inanimate. This way of dividing things can be difficult for us to grasp. We think of substances, liquid or solid, as having internal atomic, molecular, and cellular structures, and we look to those internal microscopic structures to tell us whether things are animate or inanimate. To take such a gross, everyday physical characteristic as liquidity to rule out animacy is, we know, somehow to deal with the question on too large a scale. Aristotle did not know that. Seeking the nature of life, and the material basis it requires, he saw that structure is the key and concluded that fluids are incapable of life because they are incapable of the requisite structure. If we want to be generous, we can say that his instincts were right on the general point: the key to life *is* structure, and

---

30 Nutriment is liquid, and "everything takes growth from liquid" [647^{b}26–28].

the structure is a double helix. Of course, he lacked the means to look for structure on the microscopic level.

D. Active and Passive Potentialities

Passive Potentialities. Still, why cannot heat and cold explain shape? For it is through their agency that Aristotle explains solidification. The elemental composition of *homoiomere* (compounds) explains why they are light or heavy, but their further abilities are not simply a function of their being composed of so much earth and water. Magnetism belongs to the lodestone in virtue of the lodestone's own form,[31] and not just as being made of so much of this element, so much of that. If that were not so, a mere mixture of the right elements in the right proportions would be magnetic. Iron, too, has its own nature, distinct from elemental natures, and its own dispositions, distinct from elemental dispositions. It derives its weight from the composition of elements it is made from, but it has other properties that do not characterize the elemental mixture from which it is formed. Otherwise the untreated mixture of elements would have the same properties as the compound that heat produces by acting on the mixture, and the action of heat would have brought nothing new into existence.

Since *homoiomere* possess their own natures, they, unlike mixtures, cannot be explained solely by elemental potentialities. Yet the production of inanimate *homoiomere* can be explained through the action of heat and cold. The right amount of heat applied to the right mixture will produce the new substance, which will have properties that do not exist in the untreated mixture.

Although Aristotle, in explaining inanimate *homoiomere*, appeals to form and not just to element-potentials, he still says the production of the inanimate *homoiomere* can be explained through the action of heat and cold.[32] So when Aristotle claims that heat and cold cannot explain flesh, he does not mean that because flesh has properties which do not exist at lower levels of material organization it must be explained by form, rather than matter, *and so* not by the action of heat and cold. If that were his view, he would have to make the same claim for iron. His biological antireductionism does not derive from a general claim about emergent properties, but from a specific claim about the types of properties that can emerge through the action of heat and cold.

At *Meteorology* IV 384^{b}24–385^{a}11, he gives his account of these properties. Heat and cold form mixtures of the elements into compounds – the *homoiomere* – that differ from one another in virtue of their active poten-

---

31 The *logos tês mixeôs:* Joachim, (1922), p. 130.
32 See, e.g., *Meteorology*, 390^{b}3.

tialities (or "powers"). The active powers are abilities these substances have to act on the senses: their color, fragrance, sweetness, and so on. But these substances also differ by "more intrinsic" passive potentialities, in virtue of which "bone, flesh, sinew, wood, bark, stone, and all other homogeneous natural bodies" [385^{a}9–11]. These passive potentialities he lists as the ability or inability of substances to solidify, melt, flex, break, give off fumes, take an impression or fragment, be softened by heat or water, be cut, compressed, or split, and their plasticity, malleability, ductility, viscosity, and combustibility.[33] They are more intrinsic than the active powers because substances can retain their external appearance even though they are thoroughly decayed: ancient corpses that seem well preserved sometimes suddenly turn to dust [390^{a}23]. A decayed bone, lacking the structural ability to support tissue, though outwardly looking like an undecayed bone, is a bone in name only.

If we stick to the passive dispositions, which Aristotle says in the *Generation of Animals* are the differentiae of the inanimate *homoiomere*, Aristotle does not seem to have any reluctance to grant that they can be explained through the action of heat and cold, and this is what he tries to do:

Skin is formed by the drying up of flesh, just as scum or mother forms on boiled liquids. Its formation is due not only to its being on the outside, but also because what is glutinous, because it cannot evaporate, remains on the surface. In other animals the glutinous substance is dry (so the outer parts of bloodless animals are testaceous or crustaceous); in blooded animals the glutinous substance is more fatty. And in those of them whose nature is not too earthy, the fat collects under the protection of the skin. [743^{b}6–14]

He also cites heat and cold to explain the locations of some *homoiomere* in the embryo: fatty flesh, being glutinous, cannot evaporate, so as it cools it dries and hardens into skin. Then more fatty tissue collects below the skin, which is hard and dry in comparison, forming a subcutaneous membrane. In bloodless animals the fatty tissue is drier, so it hardens into a rigid exoskeleton. This sort of account explains why the outer layer of flesh is hard and dry – why it turns into skin – and explains the formation of the membrane (which is also for the sake of something) that surrounds the embryo: "For the outer surfaces dry up by necessity when they are heated as well as when they are cooled" [739^{b}28]. But it cannot explain everything. Let us take a look at its limitations.

Active Potentialities. First, to explain the passive potentialities of flesh and bone is not to explain everything. If we look at these explanations we find that Aristotle's paradigmatic case of this type of explanation is the one given above: when a fairly viscous substance is heated, its outer surface becomes thick and dry. This is how he explains the formation of

33 Ibid., 385^{a}12–18, with the discussion following.

skin, and the development of the omentum around the stomach "into such a form as has been described is the result of necessity. For, whenever dry and moist are mixed together and heated, the surface invariably becomes membranous and skin-like" [*Parts of Animals*, 677b21]. The same explanation is repeated at *Generation of Animals*, 739b20–31, where a membrane, the chorion, forms to keep the fetus dry. But flesh has an *ergon*, and though the *pathê* that are found in flesh and in other animate parts may be explained by heat and cold, this principle cannot.

Heat and cold can explain passive potentialities: the softness of flesh, the dryness of skin, and the hardness of bone. These in turn explain how flesh and bone are suited to serve certain functions. But to explain how the outer layer of flesh comes to be (usefully) dry is not to explain why that outer layer is flesh. Aristotle uses heat and cold to explain the *structural* qualities of *homoiomere* – their passive potentialities. For inanimate *homoiomere* this completes the account, so they can be explained by heat and cold. But animate *homoiomere* have additional active potentialities which heat and cold cannot explain.

Flesh, for example, is an organ of touch. And though Aristotle has suggested that an isolated chunk of flesh will not possess the capacity for sensation, nothing in his account suggests that a piece of flesh cut off from the organism instantly loses its passive potentialities. Similarly, a bone fragment will retain its passive potentialities until it decays. Under the right conditions this can take years, and if the bone is frozen, its decay can be completely arrested [*Meteorology*, 379a26–30]. But the bone has lost its ability to grow. Passive potentialities explain why the skin around the embryo is dry just as they explain the skin that forms on pudding; it is, in the quotation above, the very same explanation in both cases. But to explain how a tough skin forms on a heated softer substance is not to explain live tissue. And therefore, since flesh is not flesh without life, and since Aristotle does not envision his chemistry's explaining anything more than passive potentialities, heat and cold cannot explain the production of flesh: they play a role in its formation – in "setting" it – and they can explain why flesh has *some* of the properties it has, but not the ones in virtue of which it is flesh.

What we see in these passages turns out, then, to be consistent.[34] The structural properties of flesh and bone are explicable through heat and cold – which can explain why bone is hard and flesh soft, as they must be to do their jobs – but their animacy and activity are not. The structural properties of flesh and the meat in the butcher's case are the same, but the *logos* is different, for the meat in the butcher's case is insensitive. The structural properties of teeth and artificial teeth might be the same, but

---

34 I do not mean to include *Meteorology* IV in the scope of this statement; there his view really was different.

they are still different substances, the one living and capable of growth to a limit, the other not, and heat and cold cannot account for that difference. Aristotle thinks inanimate *homoiomere* can be exhaustively accounted for by sensible and structural qualities, but it was clear to him, at least most of the time, that this could not be the case with animate *homoiomere*. Bone can retain its structural and sensible qualities for weeks after the animal's death, and hence, on his famous view, for weeks after it has ceased being bone. But it does not retain the ability to heal – a specialized case of replication and growth. The bones lying in the field have the structural characteristics of the bones in a cow, but their fractures are permanent. So the *logos* of bone cannot be found in its structural qualities, and hence cannot be explained by the action of heat and cold.

Conclusion. Second, the characteristics Aristotle explains this way are all, if I can be allowed the term, "material characteristics." These are characteristics that will characterize every bit of any lump of a given homogeneous material. (A striking example of his reliance on material characteristics is his argument in *On the Heavens* [296a25–31] against the earth's rotation: if the earth rotated, he says, and if the rotation were a natural not a violent motion, then any portion of earth – a clump of soil in the palm of your hand – would rotate.) Shape is ruled out, for material does not have a particular shape – material of a given kind can occur in various shapes – and the shape of the whole is not the shape of any sample drawn from the whole. (In the *History of Animals* I, i, shape is brought in as distinguishing the instrumental parts, not homogeneous ones.) So the shape of the embryo cannot yield to this analysis. Aristotle's account by heat and cold can explain why the embryo's outermost layer is dry, but not why the embryo has a humanoid form. In certain cases he can, owing to his mechanics or chemistry, explain why a lump of homogeneous material attains a certain shape: the earth, he says in the *On the Heavens* [297b1–15], if it was generated would have naturally come to be spherical due to the falling in of heavy matter toward a center,[35] and his physics can explain why hills tend to be conical. But those are exceptional cases, and it is hard to see how this sort of account could apply in the case of the embryo. Its form, if it were a consequence only of material necessity, should be the shape of the bottom of the womb, as Aristotle's account begins with a liquid.[36] But though the embryo obviously fits into the womb, its shape is not the womb's shape – the shape described by the

35 Of course he thought the earth is ungenerated.
36 Lennox (1982), p. 223, thinks the embryonic material is not "totally amorphous," but that different sections of it have different potentialities. I see no reason for believing Aristotle thought this was so before the semen acted on the menses, and the passage Lennox cites in support [*Generation of Animals*, 734b11–12], the automaton passage, seems to me to have a different point.

fetal position is not the shape of the fetus. The shape of the embryo is dictated by the sperm, which, in solidifying the primal fluid, also provides the form – in this case, the literal organization of the embryo – and the articulation of the embryo is a consequence of that organization. Material necessity can explain why the coating around the embryo is hard and dry, but not the fact that it wraps around something articulated into fingers and arms, heads and ears.

Aristotle's opponent would have to explain how it happens that the small bones of the fingers grow where they grow, in the relation they have to each other, by appealing to heat and cold and the bloody soup we presume is there before the hand develops. All this would have to be done without the benefit of the organizational plan that is, on Aristotle's view, the sperm's contribution. The development of the fingers would have to be explained as the product of the heat and cold acting on extremely similar target *homoiomere* yet producing extremely diverse and fortuitous effects. Aristotle could, as anyone could, see a small change triggering a large and complex change: one hoplite out of line on the battlefield could lead to the loss of the Athenian Empire. Make the wheels on one side of a cart a little smaller than those on the other side and the cart goes in circles; a slight turn on the rudder and the great ship veers off course. Who could not notice this? But it is a long way from seeing that a little match can cause a major conflagration to seeing the sort of thing we are talking about, which in Aristotle's world would have been akin to throwing a torch into a simmering vat and seeing an elephant take shape. It would have been completely arbitrary of him to assume that this was how things really worked.

We can see this sort of move in *On the Soul* II, iv. Fire, alone among the elements, seems capable of nourishment and growth, and this has led some people to believe that fire is the cause of nourishment and growth in living things. It is a concurrent cause (*synaition*), Aristotle says, but not the principle cause (*ou mên haplôs ge aition*); for in these things there is a limit and *logos* to their growth, and this is due to soul, not fire, and to the *logos*, not the matter [416a10ff.]. Then, at the end of iv, he tells us that "all food must be capable of being digested, and what produces digestion is warmth; that is why everything that has soul in it possesses warmth." But this warmth, in light of the preceding passage, does not account for growth and nourishment, for it does not account for the limit or the *logos*. It is a necessary but not a sufficient condition for nourishment and growth. This claim should hold as much for the parts of living things as for the things themselves. Fingers could not grow without warmth, but warmth does not explain why the fingers grow only to a certain size, nor why their length exceeds their cross-section. The same holds for the making of a sword: heat and cold harden and soften the iron so that it can be shaped, but the sword is produced by the action of the sword-smith's tools [*Generation of Animals*, 734ᵇ37–ᵃ1].

Aristotle's explanations of the structural properties of animate *homoiomere* through the action of heat and cold on mixtures of elements are not intended as explanations of the animate *homoiomere* themselves. He clearly points this out: "hardness and softness, stickiness and brittle-ness (and whatever other passive qualities are found in the parts that have life) may be caused by mere heat and cold, yet when we come to the principle in virtue of which flesh is flesh and bone is bone, that is no longer so."

II. The Account of the Soul

Aristotle's account of the soul is given in *On the Soul* II, 1:

We say that one kind of being is substance [*ousia*], and this in one way as matter, which in itself is not a this [*tode ti*], in another way form and essence [*morphê kai eidos*], which is that precisely in virtue of which something is said to be a this, and thirdly that out of both. Matter is *dunamis*, form (*eidos*) is *entelecheia*, and the latter in two ways: the one as knowledge; the other as contemplating.

Bodies seem to the greatest degree to be substances, and especially natural bodies, for these are the principles of the others. Of natural bodies some have life, others do not: by life we mean self-nourishment, growth and decay. There-fore every natural body that has life must be a substance, and a substance in the manner of a compound.

Since there are bodies of this type – i.e., having life – the soul cannot be a body, for the body is not *of* a substrate, but rather *as* substrate and matter. Necessarily, then, the soul [psychê] is substance as the form [*eidos*] of a natural body having life potentially [dunamei]. The substance is *entelecheia*. The *entelecheia*, then, of the sort of body we have been talking about. This is said in two ways: the one as knowledge; the other as contemplating. It is clear that the soul is *entelecheia* as knowledge is, for both being asleep and being awake presuppose the existence of soul, and being awake is analogous to contemplating, and sleep to having knowl-edge but not using it. In the same individual knowledge is prior in origin. There-fore the soul is the first *entelecheia* of a natural body having life in *dunamis*. Such a body possesses organs. . . . If, then, we have to give a common formula for all souls, it will be the first *entelecheia* of a natural organic body. For which reason it is not necessary to ask whether the soul and the body are one, just as it is not necessary to ask whether the wax and its shape are one, or in general the matter of each thing and that of which it is the matter: unity and being are said in many ways, but the most proper way is that of *entelecheia*.

The two basic claims in this crucial passage are (1) that the soul is the form of the body, the living creature being a composite of these two, and (2) that soul is form as first *entelecheia*. Several different strands come together here, and it will be worthwhile to deal with them individually.

A. One Substance

Even as Aristotle is placing (1), the hylomorphist thesis, out on the table, he refers to the body as a compound of form and matter ["every natural body that has life must be a substance, and a substance in the manner of a compound"], when one might have expected the body to be, not a compound of form and matter, but simply the material component in the compound. This is presumably because we can think of the living body either as that which is distinguished from the soul or as ensouled. In the latter case the body is a living thing; in the former it is being played off against the soul and is only one component of the living creature.[37] Aristotelian matter, we have seen, is always informed: we may distinguish the shape of a saw-blade from its matter, the steel, but the steel is itself a compound of matter and form.

The soul is the form of a body having life in *dunamis*. If we translate the last four words as "having life potentially" there seems to be a difficulty, for Aristotle goes on to say, at 412[b]25, that that which is capable of life (*to dunamei on hôste zên*) is not that which lacks soul but that which possesses soul. But that which possesses soul is actually alive, not potentially alive.[38] We can avoid this seeming paradox if, roughly following Hicks, we read *dunamei zôên echontos* as "having the capacity for life" – i.e., having the ability to engage in respiration, growth, etc., even if not currently engaging in them.[39] This is a capacity only living things have, and Aristotle's point is that the soul is the form of living things – not that the soul is the form of things that are potentially, but not actually, alive (e.g., seeds, 412[b]26–29). Alternatively, we can read "having life potentially" with the understanding that having life potentially does not rule out also having life actually (that something is capable of life does not entail that it is not alive): the living thing's body *kath' hauto* has life potentially, and as the body of a living thing has life actually. In either case, soul is the form of things that have the abilities that life implies: self-nourishment, growth, and decay.

The unity of soul and body is for Aristotle a special case of the unity of form and matter, which is in turn a special case of the unity of actuality and potentiality. This dark doctrine from the *Metaphysics* [e.g., VIII, 6]

37 Cf. Hicks (1907), p. 310, citing Zabarella. Aquinas uses this distinction to deal with the problem I discuss in the next paragraph. In one sense, he says, "body" indicates something having three dimensions and excludes all further perfections, such as the ability to perceive (think of this as the Cartesian sense). In this sense, my body is only one component of me, my soul another. But "body" can also be used so as not to exclude further perfections. In this second sense, animal is a species of body, and I *am* a body, rather than having a body as a component. See, e.g., Aquinas (1993), "Essence and Existence," selection 6.

38 This, pointed out by Hicks, was vexing to Ackrill (1972/73). See also S. Marc Cohen (1992), pp. 68–70); Wilkes (1992), pp. 111–112).

39 See note 37 above.

seems to mean that a bronze sphere is not two things, the bronze and the sphere, but one thing, whose matter is capable of being cast in a spherical shape, and that in fact *is* cast in a spherical shape. The relation between the bronze and the bronze sphere is thus that of the determinable to the determined, with the form being the determination. (In our particular case, though, the soul is the substantial or essential form of the composite, whereas in the case of the bronze sphere the form, sphericity, seems really to be accidental – at least if we take Aristotle to hold that artifacts do not have real essences.)

We have seen that it is a principle of Aristotle's in the *Metaphysics* that no substance can be composed of other substances. It is also his principle that mundane things are composed of matter and form (the hylomorphist thesis). It follows that the matter and form out of which these things are composed cannot both be substances if the composite is a substance: if Socrates is a substance, either his matter or his form must fail to be a substance. The alternative is that both Socrates' matter and his form are substances, and Socrates is not a single substance, and therefore not a substance at all: to be a thing is to be one thing. This is not an attractive option to Aristotle.

If Socrates is a substance, and the substance that he is is a composite of matter and form, and these are, as Aristotle says, prior to the composite, his substantiality must derive from his matter and form. This might come about in three ways. He might be a substance because: (1) his form is a substance but his matter is not; (2) his matter is a substance but his form is not; (3) though neither his form nor his matter are substances, in combination they constitute a substance. If either his form or his matter is a substance, *Metaphysics* VII seems inclined to pick form as his substance, so we should favor (1) over (2). And since on (3) his matter is not a substance, it would seem that in any case Socrates' matter is not a substance: if Socrates is a substance, either his form is a substance or neither his form nor his matter is a substance.

The view under consideration, then, is that Socrates, composed of form and matter, is a substance, though his body is not in itself a substance. This may seem a strange view to attribute to Aristotle, for we have seen him routinely list living things and their parts as substances. But there is no reason to assume that in listing these he means to be listing matter as opposed to form rather than the composite of matter and form or, what amounts to the same thing, matter informed by animacy. If we distinguish matter from form, setting the one against the other, then matter qua matter – uninformed matter – is not a substance. Rather, it is a *dunamis*.

But then neither, it would seem, is unenmattered form a substance: to ask whether the soul can exist without the body is like asking whether the axe's edge can exist without the axe's steel, and at 413a3–5 he explicitly says that the soul does not exist apart from the body. Yet one of Aristotle's requirements for substantiality is separability. So insofar as he holds that Socrates' substantiality derives from his form, to that extent he must downgrade the separability criterion. Perhaps this is why separability is not mentioned in the opening lines of *On the Soul* II. Instead, Aristotle invokes only the individuality criterion: matter *kath' hauto* is not a *tode ti*, while form is that in virtue of which a thing is said to be a *tode ti*. Separability still points to Socrates as the primary substance here, though he is a *tode ti* in virtue of his form or soul. Perhaps Aristotle is thinking that though it is the composite, not the form, that is separable, it is separable because it is a *tode ti*, and it owes that to form, not matter. Hence form is the principle or source of the composite's substantiality. And in fact we do sometimes see Aristotle inclined to say that form is the substance *of* a thing, rather than a substance (e.g., the opening lines of *Metaphysics* VII, 3, VIII, 2, and 1035ᵇ14–21).

On the questions of whether (1) Socrates' form is a substance from which Socrates derives his substantiality, whether (2) though Socrates is a substance, neither his form nor his matter is a substance, or whether (3) Socrates is identical with his body, alternative interpretations proliferate, and perhaps the answer most faithful to the Stagirite is ambivalent.[40] In a sense Socrates' body is a substance, for in a sense Socrates is his body.[41] In a sense his form is a substance: it is in virtue of form that Socrates is in a sense his body; and his soul is in a sense the substrate, as being that in virtue of which he is an individual. But the ways in which Socrates' form and matter might be said to be substances, or the substance of Socrates, ought not threaten Socrates' own substantiality (though perhaps they do).

One can even argue that Socrates, his form, and his body are one and the same thing.[42] The complexity of the discussion on this sort of issue is particularly aggravated – in part because, as we saw in Chapter 4, Aristotle lists a variety of senses in which a thing can be one, and in part because it is not clear what he means by "one and the same." There we saw that Aristotle may allow kooky entities like the sitting Socrates. Gareth Matthews (1982), following up on an important article on Aristotle's concept of identity by Nicholas White (1971), takes Aristotle to hold that though Socrates and the sitting Socrates are "numerically the same (person or thing)," they are only accidentally the same, where "accidental sameness is not identity and . . . does not guarantee that every attribute" of the one is an attribute of the other. Spellman (1990) says that in *Sophistical Refutations* Aristotle holds that numerical sameness is not sufficient for sub-

---

40 Aristotle's perplexity on this issue is recorded in the *Metaphysics* VIII, 2–3, 1043ª12–1043ᵇ4.

41 See, e.g., Kosman (1987); Lewis (1994), pp. 254–256.

42 See, e.g., Lewis (1994), p. 255; countered by Haslanger (1994).

stitutivity,[43] and that he "comes to think that there are two varieties of numerical sameness, essential and accidental sameness . . . such that substitutivity is said to hold in the first case in certain contexts where it fails in the second."[44] As opposed to ACT (Accidental Compound Theory), Spellman argues that "accidental unities are specimens of kinds, although not necessarily of natural kinds." A third approach takes the musical Coriscus to be Coriscus referred to under that description, and hence identical with Coriscus.[45]

So the precise nature of the relationship between Socrates and his soul is unclear. Could it be identity? Aristotle says (e.g., *Metaphysics* VII, 1031ᵇ18–19) that primary things and their essences are one and the same, and not accidentally, so if Socrates' soul is his essence, and if being one and the same is being identical, Socrates *is* his soul, and this thing has his body.

But if Socrates and his soul are numerically identical, how could Aristotle state that we ought not to say the soul weaves, but the woman weaves, or that we ought not to say the soul is angry, but the man is angry? If Socrates is identical with his soul, then it would seem to follow that whatever attributes the one has, the other has as well: if the man is angry, his soul is angry; if the woman weaves, her soul weaves.

One way out of this dilemma is to distinguish form and essence, so that the soul, though the form of the body, is not the essence of the ensouled thing: Socrates can then be identical with his essence, though he is not identical with his form. Thomas Aquinas draws this distinction: the essence is the essence of the form–matter compound, and so involves matter – the definition of man (rational animal) involves flesh and bones – whereas the form (rationality), he holds, does not. Aristotle does not draw a clear distinction between form and essence, and at times uses these terms interchangeably,[46] but we might want to push this distinction onto him. For despite his claim that the essence of a primary substance and the substance are one and the same, and despite his tendency to equate (substantial) form and essence, there are numerous passages that will not allow us to interpret the relation between a material thing and its form as identity. In *Metaphysics* VII, 8, for example, he says that "when we have the whole, such and such a form in this flesh and these bones, this is Callias or Socrates," and he denies that the agent produces the thing in the sense of form or substance or essence[47] – the agent produces the whole, composed of form and matter, that gets its name from the form.

43 He does not cite a passage, but probably has chapter 24 in mind.
44 Spellman (1990), p. 18. On Spellman's view (p. 26), even essential sameness does not guarantee identity, so neither variety of numerical sameness guarantees identity.
45 See, e.g., Miller (1973); Ackrill (1981), p. 38.
46 See, e.g., *Metaphysics* VII, 1033ᵇ5–19. At 1035ᵇ32 this is quite explicit: *eidos de legô to ti ên einai.*
47 "Essence" explicitly at 1033ᵇ7.

So either we need, following Aquinas, to insert a distinction between form and essence, or we need to deny that the sense in which a thing and its essence are one, and not accidentally, requires numerical identity. The latter of these two has extensive support in the secondary literature and will do the least violence to the texts, for Aristotle asserts the unity (oneness) and sameness of primary things and their essences in the course of arguing against the alleged Platonic claim that the essences of things are distinct individuals, separate from the things whose essences they are. To avoid this, the only weight we need give Aristotle's claim is to take him to be insisting that the essence of a material thing is *not separate* from that thing. It might, for example, be an inseparable, proper part of the thing.[48] Socrates, then, a compound of form and matter, derives his substantiality somehow from the form but is not the form: he is that form in this matter.

B. The Primacy of Form

Why should Aristotle think that form, rather than matter, is the substance of Socrates?[49] The answer to this question turns on the interpretation of the notoriously difficult *Metaphysics* VII, on which a host of commentators have broken their teeth. The general outline of the answer seems to be conveyed by Aristotle's claim that matter in itself is not a particular thing [1029a20], while separability and being an individual (*tode ti:* 1029a28] belong mainly to substance, (though he also says, in VII, 8, that form is a such, not a this).

He takes up the issue in chapter 10, where he asks what the parts of substance are:

If then matter is one thing, form another, and the compound of these a third, and both the matter and the form and the compound are substance, even the matter is in a sense called part of a thing, while in a sense it is not, but only the elements of which the formula of the form consists. . . . For each thing must be referred to by naming its form, and as having form, but never by naming its material aspect as such. . . . For even if the line when divided passes away into its halves, or the man into bones and muscles and flesh, it does not follow that they are composed of these as parts of their substance, but rather as matter; and these are parts of the concrete thing, but not of the form, i.e., of that to which the formula refers, and therefore they will not be in the formulae either. [1034b33–1035a22]

In 1035b he says that he can put this more clearly. The formula of the acute angle includes the formula of the right angle, but not vice versa,

---

48 The problem involved here deserves far more attention than I give it, but addressing it would take me too far afield. There is a clear discussion of it, along with a review of the literature, in Spellman (1990) and Kirwan (1993).
49 See, e.g., *Metaphysics* VII, 8, 1033b18, and *On the Soul* II, 1, 412a7–8 for the equation of form and substance.

because the right angle is mentioned in the definition of the acute angle, but not vice versa. Similarly, the semicircle is defined in terms of the circle, not vice versa, and the finger in terms of the whole body, but not vice versa:

for a finger is such and such a part of a man. Therefore the parts which are of the nature of matter and into which as its matter a thing is divided, are posterior; but those which are parts of the formula, and of the substance according to its formula, are prior, either all or some of them. And since the soul of animals (for this is the substance of living beings) is their substance according to the formula, i.e., the form and essence of a body of a certain kind (at least we shall define each part, if we define it well, not without reference to its function, and this cannot belong to it without perception), therefore the parts of soul are prior, either all or some of them, to the concrete animal [*tou sunolou zôiou*], and similarly in each case of a concrete whole, and the body and its parts are posterior to this its substance, and it is not the substance but the concrete thing [*to sunolon*] that is divided into these parts as its matter. To the concrete thing these are in a sense prior, but in a sense they are not. For they cannot even exist if severed from the whole, for it is not a finger in any state that is the finger of a living thing, but the dead finger is a finger only homonymously. [1035ᵇ11–25]

Aristotle here gives two reasons for the priority of form to matter: the parts of animals (1) are defined with reference to capacities (e.g., perception) that require soul, and (2) cannot exist apart from the whole. There are several ways to unpack this second claim. Perhaps he merely means that the severed part is inanimate. But even so, we can ask why it is inanimate, and the reason that suggests itself is that the part's function can only be understood in terms of the organism as a whole: because it has eyes, the animal can see; the severed part is not a part because apart from the organism it cannot perform the function in terms of which it is defined. For Aristotle it is in virtue of soul that the animal is the one thing it is, and, without soul, what once was an animal reverts to the unity of a heap.[50]

The unity of the organism manifests itself in a variety of ways. It manifests itself, for example, in the fact that the parts of animals are naturally contiguous or continuous. But this arrangement, in turn, can be explicated as a device to allow functional unity: if the muscles were not attached to the bones, and if the bones were not linked by ball joints, the animal could not forage. The parts of animals are, Aristotle says, tools of the soul – the means by which the animal manages to carry on a life. And often the animal can get by with less than its full complement of parts, though there is a limit to this.[51]

---

50 See Scaltsas (1994a) for one interpretation of this.

51 "Some parts are neither prior nor posterior to the whole, i.e., those which are most important and in which the formula, i.e., the substance, is immediately present, e.g., perhaps the heart or the brain; for it does not matter which of the two has this quality" [1035ᵇ25–27].

C. Entelecheia

The soul is form as first *entelecheia*.[52] Here Aristotle plays off *entelecheia* against *dunamis*, as he does in the account of change in *Physics* III, 1. A *dunamis* is a power, capacity, or potentiality; an *energeia* or *entelecheia* is the employment or exercise of the power or capacity, or the actualization of a potentiality. In our passage, the *dunamis* of matter is contrasted with the *entelecheia* of form.

I want to suggest that there is an implicit distinction here. Every actualization or realization (*energeia*) of a *dunamis* is the completion (*entelecheia*) of that *dunamis:* water can be hot; its actually being hot is the completion or fulfillment of that capacity. *But though every realization of a* dunamis *is the completion of that* dunamis,[53] *not every realization of a* dunamis *is the completion of the substance that has the* dunamis.[54] The heating of water is the completion of water's ability to be hot but is not the completion of the water itself. A thing is complete, Aristotle says, when all its parts are within it [*Metaphysics* V, 16], but one of the parts of water is coldness (he speaks of parts of form as well as of matter). Since it is part of water's nature to be cold, warm water does not possess all that belongs to water by nature and therefore is incomplete. So though being heated completes water's ability to be hot, it does not complete water's nature, but diminishes it. Similarly, a rock's violent motion away from its natural place is the completion of a potentiality the rock has, but not a completion of the rock or its form or nature.

Entelecheia in general is contrasted with *dunamis*, but *first entelechy*, a capacity or aptitude [*hexis*], is contrasted with its exercise, *second entelechy*, and stands to it as a sort of *dunamis* or power. I say "a sort of" *dunamis* or power because in *Metaphysics* V, 12, Aristotle defines *dunamis* as most basically a source of change, while the exercise of an aptitude need not, according to him, involve a change at all: when you contemplate something you already knew, you do not thereby change. I will call the *dunamis* that marks a thing's ability to become different from what it currently is, or to change something else, a "base *dunamis*." To it corresponds a base *energeia* or *entelecheia*, which is a change or *kinêsis*.[55] But in the same text a *dunamis* can also be a state in virtue of which things are resistant to

---

52 *Entelecheia* derives from a root meaning "full," "complete," or "perfect." Various words involving the same root mean: of a citizen, "possessing full rights"; of a sacrificial animal, "unblemished"; of a laborer, "receiving full wages"; and of a person, "full-grown."

53 I awkwardly say "every realization of a *dunamis* is the completion of that *dunamis*," rather than "every realization is the completion of a *dunamis*" to allow for an actuality that involves no potentiality.

54 This claim, though not entailed by Ide [(1992), pp. 4–14], can be understood as an interpretation of it.

55 See L. A. Kosman (1984).

change, especially destructive change.[56] Paralleling this is the *dunamis* the exercise of which does not, in L. A. Kosman's phrase, consume the corresponding potentiality. The idea is that when water is actually hot it is no longer potentially hot; its potentiality for being hot is exhausted as it is heated.[57] Yet bravery and knowledge are abilities that are preserved or strengthened, rather than lost, through exercise.[58]

A *first* entelecheia, *unlike a base* dunamis, *marks a thing's ability to exhibit or become what it really is, rather than for it to become different.[59]* This is what hot water does when it cools, what ice does when it melts, and what rocks do when they fall.

Complete and Incomplete Actions. In *Metaphysics* IX, Aristotle distinguishes complete [*teleion*] from incomplete actions: an action is complete if the end is present in it. He explicates this by saying that at the same time one sees and has seen, thinks and has thought, and is living and has lived, whereas it is not true that at the same time one learns and has learned, is being cured and has been cured, is building and has built, is coming to be and has come to be, or is walking and has walked. As it stands, the passage is seriously flawed, for at the same time one is walking and has walked, is building and has built. Scholars help the passage out by supplying objects for some of the verbs for incomplete actions: at the same time, it is not true that one is learning calculus and has learned it; is building a house and has built it; or is walking to Thebes and has completed that journey, although at the same time one sees a cat and one has also seen that cat.

Commentators sometimes equate complete actions with second entelechies,[60] and it is indeed striking that the examples Aristotle lists in *Metaphysics* IX as complete actions all reappear in *On the Soul* as the exercises of first entelechies of living things – i.e., as second entelechies. But then, building and walking also appear in *On the Soul* as exercises of first entelechies (i.e., as second entelechies), and all the above examples of incomplete actions except coming-to-be are possible only for living things, while it does not seem true that at the same time one is reproducing one has reproduced: the ability to reproduce is a first entelecheia in *On the Soul,* but its exercise does not seem to be a complete action. So we cannot equate the exercise of a first entelecheia with a complete action: some first entelechies, like the ability to reproduce, seem to be capacities for incomplete actions; others, capacities for complete actions.

56 See, e.g., Gill (1989), pp. 219–227.
57 Kosman (1984), pp. 131–132. There are, however, other ways of reading the text; see, e.g., Gill (1984), pp. 179–181.
58 See Gill's distinction between what she calls the first and second potentiality–actuality models; ibid., pp. 172–183, 214–227.
59 Ibid.
60 This seems to happen in Kosman (1984), pp. 129–132,

There is, however, an important similarity between complete actions and second entelechies. In the *Metaphysics* passage, Aristotle calls an incomplete action a *kinêsis* – a process, change, or movement – whereas a complete action is an *energeia* (in some stricter than usual sense, since in the everyday sense any change is the energeia of a potentiality). This can be glossed as implying that seeing is not a process: it has no beginning, middle, or end, and cannot take place slowly or quickly. In *On the Soul* II, 5, he similarly says that while acquiring a capacity involves alterations, exercising a capacity one already possesses does not: "it would be absurd to speak of the builder as being altered when he is using his skill in building a house":

For what possesses knowledge becomes an actual knower by a transition which is either not an alteration of it at all (being in reality a development of its true self or actuality [*eis auto gar hê epidosis kai eis entelecheian*] – or at least an alteration in a quite different sense. [417ᵇ5–7]

Because building a house is an incomplete action, the distinction between complete and incomplete actions is not at issue here. Aristotle's claim is that exercising a capacity or skill one already has does not in itself involve one's altering, except in that through exercising the capacity one might come to possess it more perfectly or increasingly. This is not quite the same as the claim he makes for complete actions, which he says are not processes. The carpenter, exercising his capacity for building a house, does not thereby change, though house building is an incomplete action and hence a *kinêsis* (so *something* is changing). Growth, as a second entelechy, is merely the exercise of an existing capacity but, like house building, is also a process, though Aristotle does not consider it an alteration: growth is a change [*kinêsis*] in the category of quantity, while he generally limits alteration to change in the category of quality.⁶¹

But if growth is *simply* a change of quantity, the development of an animal from a fetus to an adult involves more than growth. A child does not just become larger as it grows; it changes, acquiring new capacities. As Aristotle says in *On the Soul* II, 5, the sense in which a boy may be a general and the sense in which an adult may be a general are not the same: the boy can only realize his potentiality to be a general "by change of quality, i.e. repeated transitions from one state to its opposite." This is not a question of simply exercising a disposition one already has, but of acquiring new dispositions, and can be a laborious process. How, then, if exercising a first entelechy is not undergoing an alteration, can growth in the sense of maturation be a first entelechy of living things?

Aristotle's answer is that perhaps, after all, there are two senses of alteration: "the change [*metabolês*] to conditions of privation, and the

---

61 Although this is not the only difference between growth and alteration. See *Generation and Corruption* I, 5, 320ᵃ25–27.

change to a thing's dispositions and to its nature [*kai tên epi tas hexeis kai tên phusin*]." Growth (and the cooling of warm water), I suggest, may be alterations, but then, whereas some alterations merely involve the loss of a characteristic (and perhaps its replacement by another characteristic), making a thing different from what it previously was, others cause it to become what it is by nature or to acquire a disposition that belongs to it by nature, the latter two counting as only Pickwickian changes. Aristotle's standard phrase for essence is, after all, literally, "the what it was to be" of a thing.

The falling rock undergoes a change of place, but in descending becomes whole again. The growth of a young animal brings it to completion and is analogous to the rock's descent. On the other hand, the heating or freezing of water, though actualizations of capacities water possesses, are not exercises of dispositions it has: water, though capable of being hot or solid, is disposed toward being cold and liquid, and its becoming hot or solid makes it less complete.

To explicate essential form or nature as a set of first entelechies we need to distinguish between a mere capacity and a disposition, a disposition being, roughly, a capacity along with a predilection to exercise it. A *first entelechy* is a capacity but not necessarily a disposition, as is clear from Aristotle's examples: in the *Metaphysics* IX, 6, he says "that as that which is building is to that which is capable of building, so is the waking to the sleeping, and that which is seeing to that which has its eyes shut but has sight, and that which is shaped out of the matter to the matter." That which is capable of building stands to that which is building as first entelechy to second entelechy. But though the lazy carpenter is capable of building, he is not disposed to build, nor is iron disposed to being wrought into a sword, though it is capable of it.

A first entelechy need not be a disposition, but it can be. And we also need to distinguish natural from acquired dispositions. Bravery is a disposition: the brave man is disposed toward brave acts (though both the brave man and the coward are capable of brave acts, only the brave man is in the habit of performing them); but his bravery did not come to him by nature.

The form of a thing as a first entelechy – its essence or nature – on the other hand, should primarily be a set of *natural dispositions,* capacities the thing is prone to exercise by its nature (including, in the case of growth, a disposition to acquire other dispositions): fire is by nature disposed to heat things and to rise, and this is its form; living things are disposed to grow and reproduce, and that is their form. (Mere capacities could be included in some derivative way: water is disposed to being cold and liquid but is capable of being hot and solid.)

Aristotle would then abandon the claim (if, indeed, he accepts it) that exercising a capacity does not involve alteration, at least *tout court.* If the capacity is for acquiring new abilities, this will not be true. In some way he must have realized this, for as he describes it the exercise of the capacity to learn a language involves many alterations, unlike the exercise of an already acquired capacity to speak a language.

Complete and Incomplete Substances. If it seems unreasonable to hold that water, by nature cold and liquid, can be hot or solid, it will seem even more unreasonable to allow an individual to acquire an essential disposition it does not yet possess. Water, even if hot or solid, is disposed toward being cold and liquid, but the human infant is not even disposed to reason – it is merely disposed to acquire the capacity to reason.[62] To resurrect a passage from the *Topics* we quoted in Chapter 2, this time at greater length:

Every affection [*pathos*], if intensified, subverts the substance of the thing, while the differentia is not of that kind, for the differentia seems rather to preserve that which it differentiates, and it is absolutely impossible for a thing to exist without its appropriate differentia. . . . To speak generally, a thing cannot have as its differentia anything in respect of which it is subject to alteration; for all things of that kind, if intensified, subvert its substance. If, then, a man has rendered any differentia of this kind, he has made a mistake, for we undergo absolutely no alteration in respect of our differentia. [149a3–11]

Is it paradoxical to hold that a human infant is essentially rational if one also holds that an infant is not capable of reasoning, and that it must undergo alterations before it acquires that ability? Perhaps, but if one has already granted that water can be essentially cold yet actually hot, given all the proper caveats it is not too difficult to take the next step, and Aristotle, I believe, did this, though I am not claiming that he was fully aware of doing so. Whether he was aware of it or not, my claim is that his account of embryonic and neonate humans implies this. In the next section we shall see that it is Aristotle's view – if I have understood him correctly – that an infant is an incomplete or imperfect human and stands to an adult the way an imperfect particular, on one reading of Plato, can stand to the form of humanity: the particular is essentially, yet imperfectly, human. Plato (again, on one reading) made that a permanent affliction of particulars; it does not seem to me implausible that Aristotle, a student at the Academy for seventeen years, could make it an affliction of particulars in some situations. Aristotle's infant, if it survives and grows, will attain its full form; the rock, dislodged from the ledge, will return to its natural place. The relation between particular and form that

---

62 Aristotle's distinction between the actual and the potential was perhaps, in his eyes, his most important contribution to the history of thought. That this distinction should end up raising as many questions as does the Platonic divide between particulars and forms seems appropriate.

is an unbridgeable metaphysical chasm in Plato becomes a matter of luck and patience in Aristotle.

Aristotle replaced, as the conventional and rather uninformative wisdom goes, Plato's transcendent forms with immanent forms, but Aristotle's immanent forms, in the case of most living things, can initially be only latent. What living things possess initially is a sturdy foundation in which can be found the blueprints, the tools, and the capacity for finishing the job of constructing themselves. In this sense, to say that the form is immanent can be misleading. The form of a human being is immanent in the fetus or infant as a final cause or end, not as actually present and fully informing the matter. It is in the fetus as the rational soul is in the fetus: potentially, not actually. Yet the human fetus is not a mere animal. As potentially possessing the rational soul, it is an incomplete human being, for it is by nature capable of reasoning. It has an Internal Principle of Change (IPC) for possessing a rational soul, and this is its nature, as the rock on the ledge has an IP for being down below, and that is its nature. Once the IPP has been interpreted as involving a dispositional understanding of essence, there is no particular reason I can see why one of the dispositions established by a thing's IP should not be a disposition to acquire further dispositions. (If we all by nature desire to know, and if learning grammar, music, or Greek consists in acquiring sets of dispositions, then we are naturally disposed to acquire certain types of dispositions.)

Aristotle pays a great deal of attention to the ways in which materials can be worked up into increasingly formed states, whether we are talking about the elements being made into honey, wood being made into a bed, or the matter of an embryo being made into an animal. When Aristotle makes growth to a certain form or limit a characteristic of living things,[63] he announces that inanimate substances can reach their complete states when they are first formed, but living things characteristically do not. Neither the fetus nor the unfinished bed has yet attained its form, but the fetus has by nature a more sophisticated kind of unity and is heading, by that nature, toward a goal. The bed, on the other hand, is in a way always a heap. That it seems to be more is the magic of the carpenter's art.

The complete or perfect is that which has all the parts proper to it or which cannot be excelled in excellence for the kind of thing it is.[64] Thus Aristotle talks about complete and incomplete eggs: incomplete eggs must grow before an animal emerges.[65] Aristotle thinks the eggs fish lay are often like this – unfinished. An egg or a grub, in any case, is incomplete compared with the young of live-bearers.[66] Even live-bearers,

---

63 *On the Soul* II, 416a15–18.
64 *Metaphysics* V, 16.
65 E.g., *Generation of Animals*, 732b1–5, 733a28, 749a25.
66 Ibid., 733a2.

though, in a way produce a grub first: "since the most imperfect embryo is of such a nature; and in all animals, even the viviparous and those that lay a perfect egg, the first embryo grows in size while still undifferentiated into parts; now such is the nature of a grub."[67] Aristotle may be hindered by his tendency to characterize growth as increase in the category of quantity, but what concerns him here is not really the embryo's growing larger, though he notes that this happens, but its maturation – the differentiation of its organs and the consequent increase in its abilities.[68] It is the lack of development of some parts rather than its need to grow larger that makes an animal incomplete: Aristotle gives as examples premature babies whose nostrils have not fully formed and newborn animals that lack eyes.[69]

The perfect animals, all viviparous, give birth to *complete* animals; comparatively imperfect animals give birth to a complete embryo, "which, however, is not yet a complete animal."[70] The complete embryo that is an incomplete animal possesses only the nutritive or generative soul (it is capable of growth), but it is not capable of sensation or locomotion.[71] It is therefore only potentially an animal. The complete animal, on the other hand, has all its organs, though it is not fully grown.

The newborn infant is in an intermediate state. It acquired the sense faculty before it was born but has not fully exercised it.[72] In the weeks after it is born, it is asleep more than it is awake, and in this condition its perceptions are unconscious and akin to those of sleepwalkers: it perceives, but "without knowledge of the waking state."[73] This state, which may be a training ground for full-blown perception, is a continuation of the state the infant was in before birth: "infants . . . live in their sleep owing to former previous habit." Aristotle characterizes the prenatal sleep as an intermediate condition between the life of plants and animals, though the embryo in its early stages is not really engaging in sleep, "but only something resembling sleep," for "at this time animals . . . actually live the life of a plant," and as plants cannot be awake, neither can they be asleep.

---

67 Ibid., 758ª32–36.
68 In at least two places he may be aware of this limitation: at *Physics*, 261ª36, arguing that all changes except locomotion involve opposites, he identifies the opposites for growth as "either greatness or smallness or completion and incompletion of magnitude," and at *Metaphysics* V, 16, he says a substance is complete when it has all its parts and "in respect of its proper kind of excellence it lacks no part of its natural magnitude." In the first case, some sort of growth is being distinguished from mere increase in size; in the second, the development of all the parts of a creature points to maturation, as may "natural magnitude regarding its proper kind of excellence."
69 *Generation of Animals*, 774ᵇ35; *History of Animals*, 491ᵇ27.
70 *Generation of Animals*, 737ᵇ7–17.
71 Ibid., 739ᵇ34–741ª5.
72 Ibid., 778ᵇ20–779ª25.
73 Cf. *On Dreams*, 462ª16–28.

An even more striking example is provided by larvae and tadpoles. Since one of the essential characteristics of animals is their ability to move themselves, Aristotle is inclined, as we saw in Chapter 4, to accept as proper differentiae for animals determinations that specify the means by which they accomplish this – e.g., "winged" or "footed" or "biped." Yet the pedestrian caterpillar is an immature stage of the winged butterfly. The caterpillar, it would seem, is a complete animal but an incomplete butterfly – a butterfly in the works.

A very different sort of example is provided by victims of accident, disease, and embryonic misfortune. A dog born with three legs, or that has lost a leg in an accident, is in a sense a quadruped and in a sense not: by nature dogs are quadrupeds, but they can get by with three legs. Similarly, one of the senses that forms the sensitive soul in humans is sight, but some people are blind. Here again we have creatures disposed by nature to be a certain way but in actuality not that way. And this may not occur only through bad fortune: perhaps Aristotle thinks that, as we grow elderly, there is a decline that mirrors our rise from the embryonic and the infantile to the mature and complete.

D. Intellect

The complete embryo becomes a complete animal when all its parts have developed, at which point it has the perceptual and locomotive faculties even if it has not exercised them, or has done so only imperfectly. The human infant is a complete animal at birth, but it is unlikely that it is a complete human, for it does not possess the ability to reason. This, however, is a unique case for Aristotle, because he seems to hold that reason (nous), in the medieval vernacular, has no bodily organ. If, for example, in old age reason seems to fail, that is because psychophysical faculties, such as memory, decline in old age owing to the deterioration of their organs.[74] If you cannot remember the three premises from which you are supposed to derive the conclusion, you will be unable to do the proof, but not because your intellect has failed you.

Until now the picture he has drawn of the development of living things has turned on observations and empirical beliefs about the development of bodily parts: that a nearly fully developed embryo is capable of wakeful states, Aristotle says, "is clear in dissections and in the ovipara."[75] But given his belief that no bodily part is the seat of intellect, the methodology he has been using can take him no further. Perhaps that is why the Generation of Animals ends with an account of animals' perceptual abilities, coloration, hair and teeth. There are perfect ani-

74 On the Soul I, 408^{b}18–30.
75 Generation of Animals, 779^{a}8–9.

mals: animals that fully possess all the capacities of an animal. But intellect is not a psychophysical capacity, and to that extent not a capacity things possess qua animals. So just as a complete embryo is not a complete animal, so the complete animal that is a human infant is not a complete human. It differs from other complete animals in that it does not have one of its essential parts, intellect, though it does have all its organs as well as a natural tendency to develop intellect, and if allowed to grow normally it will develop that part. (The young of other mammals, reptiles, birds, and fishes must also grow, but their growth is simply an increase in size of various parts.)

In the *Nicomachean Ethics* X, 6–7, Aristotle says that happiness is activity in accordance with excellence, and so in accordance with the highest excellence in us. It is, therefore, the activity of intellect: contemplation. He then [1177^b26–1178^a8] considers an objection. Intellect is only one component of a composite human nature (*tou synthetou*), even if it is somehow higher and more divine than the human, and we ought to seek a human end, and, being men, to think of human things. He immediately dismisses this objection:

We . . . must, so far as we can, make ourselves immortal, and strain every nerve to live in accordance with the best thing in us; for even if it be small in bulk, much more does it in power and worth surpass everything. This would seem, too, to be each man himself, since it is the authoritative and better part of him. It would be strange, then, if he were to choose not the life of himself but that of something else. And what we said before will apply now; that which is proper to each thing is by nature best and most pleasant for each thing; for man, therefore, the life according to intellect is best and pleasantest, since intellect more than anything else is man.

Here he seems to turn the objection on its head. The objection was that, being human, we ought to seek a human end. His reply is that to do this is not to live in accordance with the better part in us, and therefore someone who does this does not choose "the life of himself but that of something else." "Intellect," a divine and immortal proper part of us, "more than anything else is man." Man, however, is mortal.

Earlier in the *Nicomachean Ethics* [1098^a14ff.] he had argued for a different view. There he had said that happiness consists in the active life (*praktikê tis*), which should mean the life of an animal – a creature that becomes hungry and needs to find food – as opposed to the contemplative life of the thinker, even if the thinker is an animal. The active life suggests cultivation of the moral virtues rather than the intellectual ones. I leave it to others to try to work this out: to decide whether one of these views is primary, and whether they are compatible. But the tension between the two is another indication of the difficulties Aristotle encounters with the problem of the unity of definition when he considers human nature.[76]

On the one hand we have seen him holding that the species is implicit in its differentia – a consequence of the Doctrine of Proper Differentiae, and of the doctrine that the differentia is to the genus as actuality is to potentiality. A corollary of this would seem to be that the species is *merely implicit* in the differentia: "biped," "hoofed," and "sentient" are incomplete expressions, requiring a substantive. Being biped, hoofed, or sentient entail, according to Aristotle, being an animal, and cannot stand alone: they can exist only as qualifying animals. In the case of intellect, however, Aristotle claims that this is not so. Intellect is impassive and imperishable.[77] But this would seem to conflict with the Doctrine of Proper Differentiae, according to which the differentia entails the genus: if our differentia is rationality, then according to that doctrine, to be rational entails being an animal; but if what is rational must be an animal, rationality can be imperishable only in the Pickwickian sense that the species persists though members of it perish: my rationality perishes with me, just as my sensibility and bipedness do. Further, if reason is a proper differentia of humans, and hence entails animality, how can the first mover, which is not an animal, think?[78]

Aristotle can resolve this conflict by distinguishing the rationality that is our differentia from intellect or reason itself.[79] The entailment criterion of the Doctrine of Proper Differentiae requires that the rationality that is our differentia be practical reason, for practical reason entails animality. But one could also hold that practical reason in turn requires unqualified reason or theoretical reason, and that unqualified reason does not entail animality. (Thus, the celestial spheres or the unmoved movers might possess intellect, though they are not animals.) This, I believe, is the solution Aristotle envisaged, and it allows him to distinguish between our highest excellence as biological organisms and our highest excellence *simpliciter,* though with some pressure on the force of "our" in the underlined clause. For insofar as we are capable of pursuing this last excellence there is something superhuman in us, since we humans are, after all, animals.

That this should be Aristotle's view is in keeping with other things he has said: earth in some way aspires to be fire, and the infant aspires to be an adult. But at this point in his account of nature Aristotle encounters a seemingly impermeable membrane: the boundary between the terrestrial and celestial realms. The celestial realm is the land of the imperishable

76 For interesting discussions of this issue, see Cooper (1986), pp. 144–180, and Kraut (1989), pp. 184–189.
77 The intellect he terms "active," at any rate.
78 *Metaphysics* XII, 7, 9.
79 See Chapter 4, sec. I (D), "Proper Differentiae."

and impassive, and entry to it is largely barred to us. Still, Aristotle seems to have thought that human beings, insofar as we live the contemplative life, exercising theoretical wisdom, participate in the celestial realm as best we can, just as, in reproducing, plants and animals participate in immortality as best they can.

I am tempted to conclude this line of thought by taking the final step, arguing that for Aristotle complete humans are incomplete gods. Sarah Broadie, wrestling with whether, for Aristotle, theoretical activity can be both divine and *our* highest good (whether "the supreme human good is godlike existence"), says that, "on standard and supposedly Aristotelian assumptions about the unity and uniqueness of a thing's essence or nature, and the relation of 'essence' to 'perfection,' this claim is self-contradictory."[80] She then goes on to say that these assumptions "belong in a metaphysical apparatus designed by Aristotle to support the philosophy of nature and the scientific study of living things in general" and that perhaps we should not expect them to hold in every context. The account I have given here of the relation of essence to perfection (or, as I prefer, "completion"), and of the unity of essence and nature in Aristotle, loosens the bonds that generate the contradiction Broadie has in mind. Yet it does not seem right to say that on my account of Aristotle humans are incomplete gods, any more than it would be to say that dogs are incomplete people. The closest I can come to this is the following speculation.

Aristotle says, in *Meteorology* IV [389ᵃ29], that "cold is in a sense the matter of bodies," since solid/fluid are the passive contraries, and earth and water, both cold, are the primary embodiments of solid/fluid. And in *On the Heavens* IV [310ᵇ14–15] he says that each element is related to the one below it as form to matter. This suggests that the progression from earth to water to air to fire, and from the center of the cosmos outward, is a progression in which form and the celestial increasingly dominate matter. Heat being a characteristic of the higher elements, hot water, in this series, has taken a step toward being more divine, though by nature water is cold. Similarly, I suggest, for Aristotle the theoretical life might be a step toward a more godlike existence, though by nature our completion is in the practical life.

Aristotelian water, of course, has no inherent disposition to be hot; on the contrary, it is disposed toward being cold, though it has the potentiality to be hot. I do not know whether Aristotle thinks we are disposed to the theoretical life, but I suppose that his best answer would be yes and no: as reasoning *animals,* we are disposed to the practical life; as *reasoning* animals, to the contemplative life. In the former case we respond to our nature's excellence; in the latter, to the excellence that is most noble in

80 Broadie (1991), p. 410.

our nature. Plato, as I read him, holds in the *Republic* that reason must rule for the common good – the good of the whole tripartite soul, of which reason is only one member of the troika. Perhaps Aristotle holds that reason must rule both for the common good and for its own good.[81] And if the demands of the two conflict? They cannot: the maximization of the common good requires the maximization of the noblest good; and the maximization of the noblest good would be hollow without the maximization of the common good. For how could the demands of our nature conflict with the demands of the highest part of our nature? Suppose that a dog's ability to enjoy sensual pleasure is the perfection of the noblest part of its nature – its sensitive soul. And suppose that our dog's addiction to caviar were deleterious to its nutritive soul, because the nutrients provided by caviar were inadequate to support its ability to be nourished, grow, and reproduce. Then the dog's addiction to caviar would not be really the perfection of the noblest part of its nature: the perfection of the noblest part of its nature must be compatible with the perfection of its entire nature, lest nature itself be at fault.

I have argued that, to Aristotle, nature is a principle guiding substances toward their essential properties. In the celestial realm, though, there is no generation and corruption, and the only change that takes place – circular motion – expresses the essential nature of celestial substances rather than enabling them fully to acquire that nature.

It is this division between the terrestrial and the celestial that in Aristotle's system corresponds in significance to Plato's division between particulars and forms, or Descartes's division between the physical and the mental. In Aristotle it also corresponds to his analogue of the mind–body problem: the intellect–body problem. For intellect, or at least active intellect, imperishable and impassive, seems a citizen of the celestial realm, albeit with access to the terrestrial realm as a guest. Intellect is a bridge between Aristotle's two realms.

In Aristotle this penetration of the terrestrial realm by the celestial, in virtue of which there is something divine in us, is paralleled by an un-Platonic penetration of the realm of being (as opposed to the realm of becoming) by change in the form of motion. Celestial motion, circular and uniform, is an unchanging form of change in Aristotle and, as it involves no internal change in the moving bodies,[82] is the type of change that entails the least changing; yet it is a form of change. And though I argued in Chapter 3 that the terrestrial elements, whose natural motions are rectilinear, have an internal principle of stasis, the celestial element involves an inherent active principle of circular motion, to which, on a

---

81 I suggest this with some trepidation, for it seems to make Aristotle more of an "intellectualist" than Plato was.

82 Not even the beating of a wing or the bending of a knee.

cosmic scale, all terrestrial change is ultimately due, as the sun, in the course of its annual journey along the ecliptic, heats and cools earth's chemical and biological broth. The activity that must go on in the realm of incomplete substances and of generation and corruption is, in this way, parasitical off the activity that must go on in the realm of divine, eternal, and complete substance. This is Aristotle's analogue to the Platonic doctrine of the dependence of the realm of particulars on the Forms, with everything set in motion. Is it so surprising, then, that the best part of us – the part that makes us what we are and "more than anything else is man" – is ultimately divine?

III. Concluding Speculation

I have been arguing for an Aristotle whose metaphysics is both (1) more driven by the conclusions he draws from natural processes (the behavior of submerged bladders, wine's turning into vinegar, the structure of an embryo in various stages of development) and (2) more Platonic than is generally thought. Because of the way in which I developed my case, (2) appeared late in the story and consequently received less discussion than (1). I would like to conclude, therefore, with some remarks intended to supplement (2), and since some will think (1) and (2) conflicting, to suggest that a nuts-and-bolts interest in how nature operates is compatible with (2).

I have suggested that Aristotle's incomplete substances are, in a general way, analogous to Plato's imperfect particulars. But there are at least two points of detailed similarity.[83]

First, in the *Philebus* [31D], Socrates, trying to give an explanation for pain and pleasure, says: "when we find the harmony in living creatures disrupted, there will at the same time be a disintegration of their nature and a rise of pain. . . . But if the reverse happens, harmony is regained and the former nature restored . . . pleasure arises."[84] The former nature being restored is, I believe, health, which is destroyed by unnatural processes and reestablished by natural ones: "the unnatural coagulation of the fluids in an animal through freezing is pain, while the natural process of their dissolution or redistribution is pleasure" [32a]. But the health that is a sort of harmony is also an expression of the animal's nature, which for each species is a combination of the limited and the unlimited, with the class of the unlimited containing, in the words of Dorothea Frede, "all things that have no definite measure or degree in

---

83 There are many other points of similarity that are overlooked by those who see a very Platonic Plato and a very Aristotelian Aristotle. Compare, for example, Aristotle's account of blood in section I of this chapter with *Timaeus*, 80d–81b and 82c–e, where flesh and muscle are formed out of blood.

84 I use Dorothea Frede's translation: D. Frede (1993), p. 31.

themselves" – e.g., the hot and the cold, the colder and the hotter – while the limited is "what imposes a definite degree or quantity on what is in itself unlimited."[85] The limit might be, for example, a ratio or a proportion.

Socrates then continues, now describing pain and pleasure as a consequence, not simply of the disintegration or restoration of the animal's health, but of the animal's nature itself:

> To cut matters short, see whether the following account seems acceptable to you. When the natural combination of limit and unlimitedness that forms a live organism, as I explained before, is destroyed, this destruction is pain, while the return towards its own nature [*ousia*], this general restoration, is pleasure. [32B]

We are to imagine that the combination of the limit and the unlimited in a creature imposes a proportion between the hot and the cold, but this proportion can be overcome by unnatural forces. When this happens, the animal departs from the combination that forms it, and the combination is destroyed. This departure from its nature is painful to the animal but not fatal, and the animal's "return to its own nature" is pleasant but not the generation of a new animal. Given that Plato is widely taken to believe that things can approximate their forms in various degrees, it is not surprising to see him holding that things can fall away from their own natures without perishing. But it is perhaps surprising that he should do so in the way he does here, with natural processes supporting the restoration of the animal's nature and unnatural processes playing the devil's role.

Second, in the *Sophist* [265C, 266B], the Eleatic Stranger says that we and all mortal animals, plants, and the lifeless "elements of natural things – fire, water, and their kindred" are products of divine craftsmanship, a doctrine reaffirmed in the *Timaeus* [39E–40A, 77A, 58C–61C, 53A–55C). This is essentially Aristotle's list of the substances that exist by nature: the only difference is that Aristotle generally adds the parts of animals and plants to Plato's list, but we have seen that his considered opinion is that these parts are not quite substances after all. And why are these parts, eventually downgraded by Aristotle, not mentioned in Plato's list? Perhaps because Plato has said, in the *Theaeteus, Parmenides,* and *Sophist,* that what is one thing is not composed of parts.[86] This is not Aristotle's Indivisibility Principle: that states that a substance *can* be composed of parts, so long as those parts are not themselves substances. But the two principles are sufficiently similar to make it plausible that Aristotle's principle is a descendant of Plato's.

Finally, Plato's list is a list of things produced by the divine craftsman – the demiurge – and this might not seem to be the same as a list of

85 Ibid., pp. xxxiii–xxxiv.
86 Although there is one passage in which he backs off from this claim: *Sophist* 245a.

substances existing by nature. But it is possible that the things produced by the divine craftsmen are those that belong to natural kinds,[87] in which case the two domains may coincide. It is also possible that final causes are Aristotle's functional analogue of Platonic Forms. Once or twice in this book I have suggested that I do not find the familiar slogan that Plato accepted transcendent forms while Aristotle insisted on immanent forms very helpful. I would like to conclude by suggesting that Aristotle's final causes are, though not in quite the way Plato envisioned, transcendent forms.

Then I remember my wife Jane's idea for a bumper sticker: It's Not That Simple.

87 D. Frede (1993), pp. xxviii–xxix.

Bibliography

Ackrill, J. L. "Aristotle's Definition of *Psuchê*. *Proceedings of the Aristotlean Society* (1972/73): 119–133. Reprinted in Barnes et al., vol. IV. Duckworth, 1979.

Aristotle the Philosopher. Oxford University Press, 1981.

Aquinas, Thomas. *Commentary on the Metaphysics of Aristotle.* Tr. John P. Rowan. Regnery, 1961.

Selected Philosophical Writings. Tr. Timothy McDermott. Oxford University Press, 1993.

Balme, David M. "Aristotle's Use of Differentiae in Zoology," in Barnes et al. (1975), pp. 183–193.

"The Snub." *Ancient Philosophy* IV (1984): 1–8.

"Aristotle's Use of Division and Differentiae," in Gotthelf and Lennox (1987).

Barnes, Jonathan. "Aristotle's Concept of Mind," in Barnes et al. (1979).

M. Schofield, and R. Sorabji, eds. *Articles on Aristotle.* 4 vols. Duckworth, 1975–1979.

Bolton, Robert. "Essentialism and Semantic Theory in Aristotle." *Philosophical Review* LXXXV (1976): 514–544.

"Aristotle's Definitions of the Soul: De Anima II, 1–3." *Phronesis* III (1978): 258–278.

Bostock, David. "Aristotle on the Principles of Change in Physics I," in Schofield and Nussbaum (1982): 179–196.

"Aristotle on Continuity in *Physics VI*," in Judson (1991), pp. 179–212.

tr. and commentary. *Aristotle: Metaphysics Z and H.* Oxford University Press, 1994.

Bradie, Michael, and Fred D. Miller. "Teleology and Natural Necessity in Aristotle." *History of Philosophy Quarterly* I (1984): 133–144.

Broadie, Sarah. *Ethics with Aristotle.* Oxford University Press, 1991. *See also* Waterlow, Sarah.

Burnyeat, M. F. "Idealism and Greek Philosophy: What Descartes Saw and Berkeley Missed." *Philosophical Review* XCI (1982): 3–40.

The Theaetetus of Plato. Hackett Publishing Company, 1990.

et al. *Notes on Book Zeta of Aristotle's Metaphysics.* Oxford Study Aids in Philosophy, 1979.

Charles, David. *Aristotle's Philosophy of Action.* Cornell University Press, 1984.

Charlton, William, tr. and commentary. *Aristotle: Physics I–II*. Oxford University Press, 1970.

"Aristotle's Definition of Soul." *Phronesis* XXV (1980): 170–186.

"Prime Matter – A Rejoinder." *Phronesis* XXVIII (1983): 197–211.

"Aristotelian Powers." *Phronesis* XXXII (1987a): 277–289.

"Aristotle on the Place of Mind in Nature," in Gotthelf and Lennox (1987b), 408–423.

"Aristotle's Potential Infinites," in Judson (1991).

Review of *Aristotle on Substance: The Paradox of Unity. Ancient Philosophy* XIII (1993): 209–212.

Cherniss, Harold. *Aristotle's Criticism of Presocratic Philosophy*. Johns Hopkins University Press, 1935.

Code, Allan. "Aristotle's Response to Quine's Objections to Modal Logic." *Journal of Philosophical Logic* V (1976a): 159–186.

"The Persistence of Aristotelian Matter." *Philosophical Studies* XXIX (1976b): 357–367.

Cohen, Sheldon M. "'Predicable of' in Aristotle's Categories." *Phronesis* XVIII (1973): 69–70.

"Proper Differentiae, the Unity of Definition, and Aristotle's Essentialism." *New Scholasticism* LV (1981): 229–240.

"Aristotle's Doctrine of the Material Substrate." *Philosophical Review* XCIII (1984): 171–194. Reprinted in *Aristotle: Substance, Form, and Matter,* ed. Terence Irwin. Garland Publishing, forthcoming.

"Aristotle on Heat, Cold, and Teleological Explanation," *Ancient Philosophy* IX (1989): 255–270.

"Aristotle on Elemental Motion." *Phronesis* XXXIX (1994): 150–159.

Cohen, S. Marc. "Hylomorphism and Functionalism," in Nussbaum and Rorty (1992), 57–73. *See also* Matthews, Gareth B., and S. Marc Cohen.

Cooper, John. *Reason and Human Good in Aristotle*. Hackett Publishing Company, 1986.

"Hypothetical Necessity and Natural Teleology," in Gotthelf and Lennox (1987), 243–274, a combination of two articles: "Hypothetical Necessity," in Gotthelf (1985); and "Aristotle on Natural Teleology," in Schofield and Nussbaum (1982).

Dancy, Russell. "On Some of Aristotle's First Thoughts about Substances," *Philosophical Review* LXXXIV (1975): 338–373.

"On Some of Aristotle's Second Thoughts about Substances: Matter," *Philosophical Review* LXXXVII (1978): 372–413.

Deslauriers, Marguerite. "Plato and Aristotle on Division and Definition." *Ancient Philosophy* X (Fall 1990): 203–217.

Düring, Ingemar. *Aristotle's Chemical Treatise: Meteorologica, Book IV*. Goteborg, 1944; reprint Garland, 1980a.

Aristotle's De Partibus Animalium. Garland, 1980b. Facsimile of 1943 Goteborg edition by Elanders Boktryckeri Aktiebolag.

Fine, Gail. "Aristotle and the More Accurate Arguments," in Schofield and Nussbaum (1982).

Review of *Logic, Science, and Dialectic: Collected Papers in Greek Philosophy. Philosophical Review* XCVIII (1988): 373–399.

Frede, Dorothea. *Philebus*. Hackett Publishing Company, 1993.

Frede, Michael. "Categories in Aristotle," "Individuals in Aristotle." (50–63), and "Substance in Aristotle's Metaphysics." *Essays in Ancient Philosophy*. University of Minnesota Press, 1987.

"Plato's *Sophist* on False Statements." In *The Cambridge Companion to Plato*, ed. Richard Kraut. Cambridge University Press, 1992.

Freeland, Cynthia. "Aristotle on Bodies, Matter, and Potentiality," in Gotthelf and Lennox (1987): 392–407.

"Accidental Causes and Real Explanations," in Judson (1991): 49–72.

Friedman, Robert. "Matter and Necessity in Physics B 9 200a15–30." *Ancient Philosophy* III (1983): 8–11.

"Necessitarianism and Teleology in Aristotle's Biology, *Biology and Philosophy*. I (1986): 355–365.

Furley, David. Review of *Nature, Change, and Agency in Aristotle's Physics, Ancient Philosophy* IV (1984): 108–110.

"The Rainfall Example in Physics ii 8," in Gotthelf, ed. (1985).

The Greek Cosmologists. Cambridge University Press, 1987.

Furth, Montgomery. *Aristotle's Metaphysics: Books VII–X*. Hackett Publishing Company, 1985.

Substance, Form, and Psyche: An Aristotelian Metaphysics. Cambridge University Press, 1988.

Gill, Mary Louise. "Aristotle on the Individuation of Changes." *Ancient Philosophy* IV (1984): 9–22.

Aristotle on Substance. Princeton University Press, 1989.

"Aristotle on Self-Motion," in Gill and Lennox (1994): 15–34.

and James G. Lennox, eds., *Self Motion: From Aristotle to Newton*. Princeton University Press, 1994.

Gotthelf, Allan. "Aristotle's Conception of Final Causality." *Review of Metaphysics* (1976). Reprinted in Gotthelf and Lennox (1987), pp. 204–242.

ed. *Aristotle on Nature and Living Things: Philosophical and Historical Studies Presented to David M. Balme on His Seventieth Birthday*. Mathesis Publications, 1985.

and James Lennox, eds. *Philosophical Issues in Aristotle's Biology*. Cambridge University Press, 1987.

Graham, Daniel W. *Aristotle's Two Systems*. Oxford University Press, 1987.

Haslanger, Sally. "Parts, Compounds, and Substantial Unity," in Scaltsas, Charles, and Gill (1994a).

Happ, Heinz. *Hyle: Studien zum Aristotelischen Materie-Begriff*. Walter de Gruyter, 1971.

Hardie, W. F. R. "Concepts of Consciousness in Aristotle." *Mind* LXXXV (1976): 388–411.

Hartman, Edwin. *Substance, Body and Soul: Aristotelian Investigations*. Princeton University Press, 1977.

Hicks, R. D., tr., introduction, and commentary. *De Anima*. Cambridge University Press, 1907.

Ide, Harry A. "Dunamis in Metaphysics IX." *Apeiron* XXV (1992): 1–26.

Irwin, T. H. *Aristotle's First Principles*. Oxford University Press, 1988.

Joachim, Harold H., tr., introduction, and commentary. *On Coming-to-be and Passing-Away.* Oxford University Press, 1922.

Jones, Barrington. "Aristotle's Introduction of Matter." *Philosophical Review* LXXIII (1974): 474–500.

Judson, Lindsay, ed. *Aristotle's Physics: A Collection of Essays.* Oxford University Press, 1991.

Kerford, G. B. "Anaxagoras and the Concept of Matter before Aristotle." In *The Pre-Socratics,* ed. Alexander P. D. Mourelatos. Princeton University Press, 1993, pp. 489–503.

King, Hugh R. "Aristotle without *Prima Materia.*" *Journal of the History of Ideas* XVII (1956): 370–389.

Kirwan, Christopher. *Aristotle: Metaphysics* Γ, Δ, *and* H. 2d ed. Oxford University Press, 1993; 1st ed. 1971.

Kosman, L. A. "Substance, Being, and Energeia." *Oxford Studies in Ancient Philosophy* II (1984): 121–149.

"Animals and Other Beings in Aristotle," in Gotthelf and Lennox (1987), pp. 360–391.

Kraut, Richard. *Aristotle on the Human Good.* Princeton University Press, 1989.

Lang, Helen S. "Why Fire Goes Up: An Elementary Problem in Aristotle's *Physics.*" *Review of Metaphysics* XXXVIII (1984): 69–106.

Aristotle's Physics and Its Medieval Varieties. State University of New York Press, 1992.

Lawson-Tancred, Hugh, tr. and introduction. *De Anima.* Penguin, 1986.

Lear, Jonathan. *Aristotle: The Desire to Understand.* Cambridge University Press, 1988.

Lee-Hampshire, Wendy. "Telos and the Unity of Psychology: Aristotle's *de Anima* II, 3–4." *Apeiron* XXV (1992): 27–47.

Lennox, James. "Teleology, Chance, and Aristotle's Theory of Spontaneous Generation." *Journal of Historical Philosophy* XX (1982): 219–235.

"Commentary on Sorabji." *Proceedings of the Boston Area Colloquium in Ancient Philosophy* IV, ed. John J. Cleary and Daniel C. Shartin. University Press of America, 1989, pp. 64–75.

Lewis, Frank A. *Substance and Predication in Aristotle.* Cambridge University Press, 1991.

"Accidental Sameness in Aristotle," *Philosophical Studies* XLII (1982): 1–36.

"Aristotle on the Relation between a Thing and its Matter," in Scaltsas, Charles, and Gill (1994a).

Lloyd, G. E. R. *Early Greek Science: Thales to Aristotle.* Norton, 1970.

Loux, Michael. *Primary Ousia: An Essay on Aristotle's Metaphysics Z and H.* Cornell University Press, 1991.

Malcolm, John. "On the Endangered Species of the *Metaphysics,*" *Ancient Philosophy* XIII (1993): 79–93.

Mansion, Suzanne. "Deux definitions differentes de la vie chez Aristote?" *La Revue philosophique de Louvain* LXXI (1973): 425–450.

Mason, H. T., ed. *The Leibniz–Arnauld Correspondence.* Manchester University Press, 1967.

Matthews, Gareth B. "Consciousness and Life." *Philosophy* LII (1977): 13–26.

"Accidental Unities," in Schofield and Nussbaum (1982), pp. 223–240.

"De Anima 2.2–4 and the Meaning of Life," in Nussbaum and Rorty (1992), 185–193.

and S. Marc Cohen. "The One and the Many." *Review of Metaphysics* XXI (1967–1968): 630–655.

Maudlin, Tim. "De Anima III 1: Is Any Sense Missing?" *Phronesis* XXXI (1986): 51–67.

McMullin, Ernan. "Four Senses of Potency." In *The Concept of Matter in Greek and Medieval Philosophy*, ed. Ernan McMullin. University of Notre Dame Press, 1965.

Miller, Fred. "Did Aristotle Have the Concept of Identity?" *Philosophical Review* LXXXII (1973): 483–490.

Mourelatos, Alexander P. "Aristotle's Rationalist Account of Qualitative Interaction" *Phronesis* XXIX (1984): 1–16.

Moravcsik, J. M. E., ed. *Aristotle: A Collection of Critical Essays.* Doubleday & Co., 1967.

Nussbaum, Martha C. "Aristotelian Dualism: Reply to Howard Robinson." *Oxford Studies in Ancient Philosophy* II (1984): 197–207.

ed. *Aristotle's "De Motu Animalium."* Princeton University Press, 1978.

and Amelie Oksenberg Rorty, eds. *Essays on Aristotle's "De Anima."* Oxford University Press, 1992.

Owen, G. E. L. *Logic, Science, and Dialectic: Collected Papers in Greek Philosophy.* Duckworth, 1986.

Polis, Dennis E. "A New Reading of Aristotle's Hyle." *The Modern Schoolman* LXVIII (1991): 225–243.

Pratt, Vernon. "The Essence of Aristotle's Zoology." *Phronesis* XXIX (1984): 267–277.

Robinson, H. M. "Prime Matter in Aristotle." *Phronesis* IX (1974): 168–188.

Ross, Sir David, Greek text, introduction, and commentary. *De Anima.* Oxford University Press, 1961.

Schofield, Malcolm, and Martha C. Nussbaum. *Language and Logos: Studies in Ancient Greek Philosophy Presented to G. E. L. Owen.* Cambridge University Press, 1982.

Scaltsas, Theodore. "Substratum, Subject, and Substance." *Ancient Philosophy* V (1985): 215–240.

"Substantial Holism," in Scaltsas et al. (1994a), 107–128.

Substances and Universals in Aristotle's Metaphysics. Cornell University Press, 1994b.

D. Charles, and M. L. Gill. *Unity, Identity, and Explanation in Aristotle's Metaphysics.* Oxford University Press, 1994a.

Shields, Christopher. "Soul and Body in Aristotle." *Oxford Studies in Ancient Philosophy,* vol. VI. Oxford University Press, 1988.

Solmsen, Friedrich. "Aristotle and Prime Matter: A Reply to Hugh R. King." *Journal of the History of Ideas* XIX (1958): 243–252.

Aristotle's System of the Physical World. Cornell University Press, 1960.

Sorabji, Richard. "Body and Soul in Aristotle," in Barnes et al. (1975–1979).

Necessity, Cause, and Blame. Cornell University Press, 1980.

Matter, Space, and Motion: Theories in Antiquity and their Sequel. Cornell University Press, 1988.

"The Greek Origins of the Idea of Chemical Combination." *Proceedings of the Boston Area Colloquium in Ancient Philosophy* IV, ed. John J. Cleary and Daniel C. Shartin. University Press of America, 1989, pp. 35–63.

Spellman, Lynne. "Referential Opacity in Aristotle." *History of Philosophy Quarterly* VII (1990): 17–32.

Stahl, Donald, "Stripped Away: Some Contemporary Obscurities Surrounding *Metaphysics* Z 3 (1029ª10–16)." *Phronesis* XXVI (1981): 177–180.

Van Inwagen, Peter. *Material Beings*. Cornell University Press, 1990.

Verdenius, W. J., and J. H. Waszink. *Aristotle's On Coming-to-be and Passing-Away: Some Comments*. E. J. Brill, 1966.

Wardy, Robert. "Aristotelian Rainfall or the Lure of Averages." *Phronesis* XXXVIII (1993): 18–30.

Waterlow, Sarah. *Nature, Change, and Agency in Aristotle's Physics.* Oxford University Press, 1982. *See also* Broadie, Sarah.

Wedin, Michael V. "On the Mind's Self-Motion," in Gill and Lennox (1994): pp. 81–116.

White, Nicholas P. "Origins of Aristotle's Essentialism." *Review of Metaphysics* XXVI (1972): 57–85.

"Aristotle on Sameness and Oneness." *Philosophical Review* LXXX (1971): 177–197.

Whiting, Jennifer. "Living Bodies," in Nussbaum and Rorty (1992), pp. 75–92.

Wiggins, David. *Identity and Spatio-Temporal Continuity*. Oxford University Press, 1967.

Sameness and Substance. Harvard University Press, 1980.

Wilkes, K. V. "*Psuchê versus the Mind,*" in Nussbaum and Rorty (1992), 109–127.

Williams, C. J. F., tr. and commentary. *Aristotle's "De Generatione et Corruptione."* Oxford University Press, 1982.

"Aristotle's Theory of Descriptions." *Philosophical Review* XCIV (1985): 63–80.

"Aristotle on Cambridge Change." *Oxford Studies in Ancient Philosophy*, vol. VII. Oxford University Press, 1989.

Witt, Charlotte. *Substance and Essence in Aristotle: An Interpretation of Metaphysics, VII–IX.* Cornell University Press, 1989.

Woods, Michael. "Problems in Metaphysics Z, Ch. 13," in Moravcsik (1967), pp. 215–238.

Index

Index Locorum

CPSIA information can be obtained
at www.ICGtesting.com
Printed in the USA
LVHW092221090521
686947LV00004B/149